REVELATION

Return of the Warrior King

Dr. John W. Hall

ISBN: 978-1-945774-42-3

Trust House Publishers
P.O.Box 3181
Taos, NM 87571

www.trusthousepublishers.com

Ordering Information: Special discounts are available on quantity purchases by churches, associations, and retailers. For details, contact the publisher at the address above or call toll-free 1-844-321-4202.

1 2 3 4 5 6 7 8 9 10

This book is dedicated to the gracious and generous people of Field Street Baptist Church.

Their love for the Word of God, for my family, and for me has been a steady source of encouragement.

They exemplify what it means to be eager to hear and live the Word of God.

It is a high privilege to be your pastor

Table of Contents

ACKNOWLEDGMENTS

To Beth-thank you for being my faithful, loyal wife and friend.

To MeiLi, KaiLi, and Julie- thank you for the joy of being your dad.

To Suzanne Rains-my long-time ministry assistant; your wisdom and patient listening have strengthened me more than once.

To the staff of Field Street Baptist Church-thank you for serving out of your gifts and talents, which in turn, allow me to serve out of mine. I'm grateful for your partnership in ministry.

To Jack Ridlehoover-thank you for being my enduring mentor; you are a model for pastoral ministry. You are more than a mentor and dear friend to me.

To Vic and JoAnn Barris-thank you for believing in me and welcoming me into your family. Mrs.Barris, thank you for already agreeing to read this book sight unseen! Mr. Barris, thank you for putting in writing that I'm your "favorite preacher"! I'm honored.

To all the Bible commentators who have spent a lifetime studying the book of Revelation-many of you helped me immensely in my preparations. I owe you an enormous debt of gratitude.

To Dr. Randy White and Corey Evans- for their insistence and assistance with this project at Trust House Publishers.

PREFACE: ABOUT THIS BOOK

This book is comprised of a sequential, expositional series of sermons on the book of Revelation preached at Field Street Baptist Church beginning March 2019 and concluding February 2020. It became clear to me, based on the responses of those who heard these messages, that I should pursue getting these sermons published. For any good that may come from this project, I desire to give all glory to God. It has been my sincere hope that the intensive labor of preparation and delivery of these messages served consistently the task of exalting Christ and helping our congregation to have a greater awe of Jesus, the Warrior King. To this end, I believe God used these messages to stimulate in our church a higher view of Christ. I acknowledge that there are a wide variety of viewpoints, perspectives, and interpretive differences among those who seriously study Revelation. I do not claim to have all the keys to unlock every hermeneutical door in the Apocalypse! I recognize that some will take issue with my conclusions and positions. Nonetheless, I trust that many portions of this book will prove profitable for understanding Revelation and other key ideas tucked away in Scripture. Ultimately, this work should serve as a tremendous encouragement to the church that Jesus Christ reigns supremely, and He will soon return as the triumphant warrior King! May the Lord be pleased to find us, His radiant bride, faithful as we watch for the long-awaited day of His coming again!

"THE REVELATION"

Revelation 1:3, ESV

The PURPOSE of the message this morning is to ORIENT us to the book of Revelation. I want to give you a "flyover" of Revelation.

Put simply, Revelation is a book of prophecy. The Greek title of this book is Apokalypsis, which means "revelation, unveiling, a disclosure" of unseen, future realities or events. It's where we get our English word, apocalypse.

Revelation 1:3 states, "Blessed is the one who reads aloud the words of this prophecy, and blessed are those who hear, and who keep what is written in it, for the time is near."

God speaks through His written word, the Bible, and Revelation is a remarkable portion of that Word.

The Bible, you recall, is the inspired Word of God. The Bible is inerrant, infallible, inspired, authoritative, sufficient, understandable, necessary, and timeless. The Bible has almighty God for its author. The compelling message of Holy Scripture is that sinful man is saved by a Holy God when a sinner repents and believes in Jesus Christ for salvation. The Bible is God's revelation of Himself, and He is perfectly unveiled in the person of Jesus Christ.

Revelation is the only book in Holy Scripture that includes a direct blessing for those who read it, hear it, and act on these words of prophecy.

My intent, without apology, will be to EXALT Christ from this extraordinary book of the Bible. This book points us to the darling of heaven, the Rose of Sharon—Jesus Christ.

As Jesus is the focus of the Bible, so He is the focus of Revelation! In fact, if you read the Bible and you don't see Jesus, you desperately need to re-read it.[1]

- Jesus is the Son of God, the 2nd person of the Trinity.
- Jesus is the eternal, incarnate Word.
- Jesus is the image of the invisible God.
- He is the firstborn of all creation.
- He is before all things, and in Him all things hold together.
- He is the head of the body, the church; and He is the beginning, the firstborn from the dead, so that He Himself will come to have first place in everything.
- In Christ, the fullness of deity dwells in bodily form.
- Christ is the head over all rule and authority.
- Jesus is the one qualified mediator between God and man.
- Jesus is prophet, priest, and King.
- Jesus is the Savior and exalted head of the church.
- He is the heir of all things.
- Jesus is the righteous judge of the world.
- He is the God-Man—one person with two natures.
- Jesus is the sinless One who lived a life here on earth of perfect obedience.
- He is the crucified and risen Lord.
- He is the Lamb of God slain from the foundation of the world.

---

1 Adrian Rogers. Unveiling the End Times in Our Times: The Triumph of The Lamb in Revelation, p. 159, Kindle Edition.

Whatever we might say about Revelation and however we may come to understand this unique letter, it is first and foremost a book which exalts the Lord Jesus Christ!

Revelation has puzzled, confused, and frustrated the minds of the finest Bible scholars.

Neither John Calvin nor Martin Luther wrote a commentary on Revelation.

Along the way from Revelation 1:1 to Revelation 22:21 we will encounter numerous images, symbolisms, figures, contrasts, repetitions, parallels, persons, names, creatures, and numbers.

Along the way we will be careful to avoid the extremes in interpretation and application. We will not waste our time dabbling in wild, imaginative, speculative interpretations. We will ask God to guide our study of this magnificent book and to inspire us to greater worship, faithfulness, and obedience.

No other book poses more interpretive challenges than does the Revelation.

In fact, by way of brief summary, there are FOUR basic approaches to interpreting Revelation. It should be noted that each approach has its proponents and opponents, strengths and weaknesses.

1. PRETERIST Approach- This approach teaches that everything recorded in the Apocalypse took place in the first century at the time John wrote Revelation. In other words, the Book of Revelation relates to that which occurred in the past, but has no reference to the present and future. The problem obviously with this approach is first that it fails to consider that Revelation is a prophecy. It is impossible to see all of the events in Revelation as already fulfilled. Case in point: the Second Coming of Christ. Simon Kistemaker writes, "The Apocalypse depicts progress in

the predictive events that eventually culminate in the coming of the Judge with the attendant judgment on all people."[2]

2. IDEALISM Approach- This approach suggests that the book addresses timeless truths and does not deal with historical events.[3] The approach reduces Revelation to a collection of stories designed to teach spiritual truth.[4]

3. HISTORICISM Approach- This approach sets forth that the book is a chronicle of Western church history, or that Revelation provides a panoramic view of church history from apostolic times to the present. This interpretive method robs Revelation of any meaning for those to whom it was written.

4. FUTURISM Approach- The book (chs. 4-22 or 6-22) speaks primarily to future events at the end of history and leading into the eternal state (chs. 21-22). Only this view does justice to Revelation's claim to be prophecy and interprets the book by the same grammatical-historical method as chapters 1-3 and the rest of Scripture.[5]

With all that said, clearly, there are elements of truth in each of these lenses and approaches.

I suppose if you were to pin me down, I would consistently hold to a modified futurist approach.

I will, by God's grace, strive to be balanced and wise in my own interpretive approach to Revelation.

By definition the word "hermeneutics" as it relates to the Bible, refers to the art and science of seeking to investigate, understand, and interpret the Scriptures.

2 Simon Kistemaker, *Revelation: New Testament Commentary*, p. 39.

3 Daniel L. Akin. *Christ-Centered Exposition: Exalting Jesus in Revelation*, location 575, Kindle Edition.

4 John MacArthur, *MacArthur New Testament Commentary*, p. 901.

5 MacArthur, p. 901.

When you set out to study a portion of God's Word carefully and closely, it is helpful to do an analysis or review of the following:

1. Author-Who wrote the book?
2. Recipients-To whom was the book written?
3. Date-When was the book written? It is VERY important to know historical context and background.
4. Background & Setting-What events precipitated or set into motion the writing of the book?
5. Purpose-the intent/objective of this writing
6. Theological Themes-What are the key theological emphases within the book? What does the author stress to his readers pertaining to theological issues/themes?

Regarding the Authorship of Revelation, it is widely accepted that the Apostle John was the author of this book. That's the same John who wrote the Fourth Gospel and three epistles, 1st, 2nd, 3rd John.

Four times John identifies himself as the author of Revelation (1:1, 4, 9; 22:8).

> *1:1-The revelation of Jesus Christ, which God gave him to show to his servants the things that must soon take place. He made it known by sending his angel to his servant John,*
>
> *1:4-John to the seven churches that are in Asia: Grace to you and peace from him who is and who was and who is to come, and from the seven spirits who are before his throne,*
>
> *1:9-I, John, your brother and partner in the tribulation and the kingdom and the patient endurance that are in Jesus, was on the island called Patmos on account of the word of God and the testimony of Jesus.*
>
> *22:8-I, John, am the one who heard and saw these things. And when I heard and saw them, I fell down to worship at the feet of the angel who showed them to me,*

The Recipients of Revelation according to John 1:4 are the seven churches that are in Asia: Ephesus, Smyrna, Pergamum, Thyatira, Sardis, Philadelphia, and Laodicea.

Accordingly, Dr. Paige Patterson in his scholarly commentary writes, "The best conclusion for understanding the nature of the Revelation of John is to see it as a prophetic circular letter which not infrequently makes use of apocalyptic imagery and device."[6]

Regarding the date most evangelical scholars affirm that Revelation was written in A.D. 95 or 96. This estimation is based on accounts of the early church fathers that the Apostle John had been exiled on Patmos Island during the reign of Domitian who died in A.D. 96.

Now, the Background & Setting of the book of Revelation is important.

At this point John is an elderly man. He is the last surviving apostle and he is in exile on the Island of Patmos. The Roman authorities had banished him there because of his faithful preaching of the gospel.

> 1:9-I, John, your brother and partner in the tribulation and the kingdom and the patient endurance that are in Jesus, was on the island called Patmos on account of the word of God and the testimony of Jesus.

While on the Island of Patmos, John received a series of visions which laid out the future of the history of the world.

The church had begun to feel the effects of relentless persecution. And the storm of persecution was about to break in full fury upon the seven churches so dear to John.[7]

---

6 Paige Patterson. *Revelation: The New American Commentary: An Exegetical and Theological Exposition of Holy Scriptures*, p. 25.

7 MacArthur, p. 900.

Revelation supplied a message of hope to the churches and to the church. Revelation reminds God's people that God is sovereign and in control of all the events of human history. The day is coming when righteousness reigns completely over evil and wickedness.

Revelation reminded the church that Christ will return in unprecedented glory to judge and rule!

The Purpose of Revelation is simply to encourage and comfort believers in their struggle against Satan and his cohorts. The book is a reminder that Christ is the Victor and Satan will be vanquished. Therefore this book of consolation points our attention to the judgment of the world and the ultimate victory for the people of God. Revelation is a message of hope, for Christ will vindicate His saints!

Finally, Revelation Has a Few Critical Theological Themes:

- Revelation, first and foremost, is about Jesus Christ. One of the greatest depictions of the Lord Jesus is found in Revelation 1:8-18. I can't wait for us to explore this marvelous passage of the transcendent, triumphant Christ!
- John gives us a vibrant picture of worship in heaven which stirs our hearts and motivates us to faithful obedience.
- Revelation gives us vivid clues and truths as to the unveiling of end times or last things. Revelation's contribution is primarily to eschatology, the doctrine of last things.
- Revelation points us to the second coming of Jesus Christ. He will defeat Satan, settle accounts with those who reject Him, and bring His faithful people into eternal blessedness.
- Revelation declares the sovereignty of God declaring the providential rule over the kingdoms of men and will accomplish His sovereign purposes regardless of whatever is the opposition.

- Revelation teaches about the final judgment. We need to be certain of our commitment to Christ. No one who rejects Jesus will escape God's punishment.
- Revelation is a book about HOPE—oh, the hope we have in Jesus Christ. One day God will create a new heaven and a new earth. All believers will live with Christ forever in perfect peace and security.

As I close, look with me at the 19th verse of chapter 1. Several commentators I consulted seemed to be in agreement regarding this one verse as being the key to the book.

It reads, "Write therefore the things that you have seen, those that are and those that are to take place after this."

In a way, this verse divides the emphasis of the book. Chapters 1-3 focus on the churches as the word church never occurs after chapter 3, there is good reason to believe that chapter 4 initiates the age of the church.

At any rate, 1:19 may be viewed as the general outline for the Apocalypse.[8]

8 Patterson, p. 34.

2

"THE PROLOGUE"

Revelation 1:1-8, ESV

By strict definition, a prologue is "an introduction to a poem, play, story, etc.; any preliminary act, event, etc."

Thus, Revelation 1:1-20 provides the "prologue" to the book of Revelation.

These verses provide us a rich opening to Revelation. Included in this preamble is:

- A Blessing (1:1-3)
- A Greeting (1:4-6)
- A Declaration (1:7-8)

Let's read this text— [REVELATION 1:1-8, ESV]

> *Rev 1:1 The revelation of Jesus Christ, which God gave him to show to his servants the things that must soon take place. He made it known by sending his angel to his servant John,*
>
> *Rev 1:2 who bore witness to the word of God and to the testimony of Jesus Christ, even to all that he saw.*
>
> *Rev 1:3 Blessed is the one who reads aloud the words of this prophecy, and blessed are those who hear, and who keep what is written in it, for the time is near.*

Rev 1:4 John to the seven churches that are in Asia: Grace to you and peace from him who is and who was and who is to come, and from the seven spirits who are before his throne,

Rev 1:5 and from Jesus Christ the faithful witness, the firstborn of the dead, and the ruler of kings on earth. To him who loves us and has freed us from our sins by his blood

Rev 1:6 and made us a kingdom, priests to his God and Father, to him be glory and dominion forever and ever. Amen.

Rev 1:7 Behold, he is coming with the clouds, and every eye will see him, even those who pierced him, and all tribes of the earth will wail on account of him. Even so. Amen.

Rev 1:8 "I am the Alpha and the Omega," says the Lord God, "who is and who was and who is to come, the Almighty."

What a joy it is to own a copy of the Word of God. If you have a Bible, you have a real treasure in your hand.

THE BLESSING (v. 1-3).

Revelation is the only book in Sacred Scripture with a direct beatitude (blessing) for those who read, hear, and obey this apocalyptic book.

This is clearly articulated in verse 3: "Blessed is the one who reads aloud the words of this prophecy, and blessed are those who hear, and who keep what is written in it, for the time is near."

Why such an assurance of blessing for wading through Revelation? The answer to this question is found in verse 1:

"Rev 1:1 The revelation of Jesus Christ, which God gave him to show to his servants the things that must soon take place. He made it known by sending his angel to his servant John…"

God gave this revelation mediated through Jesus Christ. Of course, God is the source of all revelation. Yet, in this unveiling, Jesus Christ is, as Robert Mounce suggests, "the mediator."[9] Furthermore, Paige Patterson writes, "Here the author is claiming that this revelation [from] Jesus Christ is a direct word from God, an unveiling of His plan and purposes."[10]

Verse 1 makes certain that we understand that God gave this revelation to Christ "to show His servants things that must soon take place." There's your well-defined purpose statement of Revelation.

Make no mistake: whether Jesus was being revealed (objective) or the mediator revealing the Father's message (subjective), this book is about heaven's favorite subject—Jesus Christ!

I believe Jesus reveals Himself in this book, but especially and magnificently in the prologue. This is a revelation of, from, and about Jesus Christ. Three times John uses the phrase "Jesus Christ" in 1:1-5, but never again in the rest of the book.[11]

It is clear also that this book is transmitted through three intermediaries: one divine, one angelic, and one human—all identified in verse 1.

Verse 2 is helpful. It reads--Rev 1:2 -who bore witness to the word of God and to the testimony of Jesus Christ, even to all that he saw.

---

9 Robert H. Mounce, *The Book of Revelation*, NICNT, p. 40.

10 Paige Patterson, *Revelation: The New American Commentary*, p. 52.

11 Daniel L. Akin, *Revelation: Christ-Centered Exposition: Exalting in Jesus*, location 313, Kindle Edition.

The apocalypse is identified as the testimony of Jesus, and apparently Jesus is the one giving the testimony.

In fact, the testimony is equated with the "word of God," giving biblical authority to the witness of Jesus and inferring the deity of Jesus.

There is no question that divine authority and origin are stressed in this opening statement of Revelation.

Note again in verse 3 that we are told that there is a blessing for those who read, hear, and obey this prophecy. Not only is Revelation an apocalypse and a letter, but also Revelation is a work of prophecy. This blessedness rises from the fact that those hearing are hearing the Word of God, the testimony of Jesus.

Verse 3 ends with the statement, "for the time is near." Now, Bible scholars set forth at least four different possibilities for what this phrase might mean.

I must tell you that after having waded through the various interpretive options, I stand with Paige Patterson's view, which is that the early church believed in the imminency (pending nature) of Christ's return.[12] It could also refer to a period of time known as "the time of the end." At any rate, there should be a sense of urgency on the part of the people of God to hear and heed this prophecy.

Transition: This is why the blessing is reserved for those who personally respond and obey, and this is why we must heed the words given to us in this unique book.

---

12 Patterson, p. 54.

A GREETING (v. 4-6).

> *Rev 1:4 John to the seven churches that are in Asia: Grace to you and peace from him who is and who was and who is to come, and from the seven spirits who are before his throne,*

> *Rev 1:5 and from Jesus Christ the faithful witness, the firstborn of the dead, and the ruler of kings on earth. To him who loves us and has freed us from our sins by his blood*

> *Rev 1:6 and made us a kingdom, priests to his God and Father, to him be glory and dominion forever and ever. Amen.*

Fascinatingly, these verses compose for us a Trinitarian greeting.

In verse 4, the human author is identified—John, the beloved disciple of the Lord. Furthermore, the recipients of this letter are identified—the seven churches that are in Asia. These seven churches will be specifically identified in verse 11. You also see in verse 4 a conferral of grace and peace, which may only truly come from God through Christ.

John is unique here in that he extends a greeting from all three persons of the Trinity. First, he describes God as "who is and who was and who is to come."

God is timeless. He has always been. The Bible says nothing about God's origins; Scripture presupposes that God (and for that matter, Christ) has always been. He is eternal. He is infinite with respect to present, past, and future.

Next up is the Holy Spirit- "and from the seven spirits who are before his throne." This is an odd means to allude to the Holy Spirit. Admittedly, this is where I really learned something in studying verse 4.

Normally, we think of the order of the Trinity as what—Father, Son, and Holy Spirit. Not here in verse 4. The Father is mentioned, and now the Holy Spirit. Simon Kistemaker points out, "The Apocalypse speaks of the Spirit but never uses the name Holy Spirit."[13]

Furthermore, Kistemaker and other commentators suggest that John employs the symbolism of the number seven (signifying completeness) and thus describes the Spirit. Thus, the number seven signifies the fullness of the Holy Spirit in His person and work as exemplified in the prophecy of Zechariah 4:2, 6. Paige Patterson writes, "Zechariah has provided the author of the Apocalypse with the perfect picture of the ministry of the Holy Spirit to the seven congregations to whom the prophecy is addressed."[14]

Jesus Christ is mentioned last, yet unmistakably in verse 5: "and from Jesus Christ the faithful witness, the firstborn of the dead, and the ruler of kings on earth. To him who loves us and has freed us from our sins by his blood…"

There are three designations for Jesus:

1. The faithful witness
2. The firstborn of the dead
3. The ruler of kings on earth

Christ is the faithful, true, totally dependable witness. His witness concerning Himself is true. His witness concerning future events is true, and His assessment of the spiritual condition of the seven churches is precise, accurate, and reliable.

Jesus has stared death in the face and rendered death helpless by becoming the firstborn from the dead. He has a high and privileged

13 Simon Kistemaker, *Revelation: New Testament Commentary*, p. 82.

14 Patterson, p. 59.

position as a result of His resurrection, furthermore implying that many others will be resurrected as a result. Jesus died, rose again, and stayed alive. He is the first of a new order, the pledge and promise of our resurrection.[15]

Jesus is the sovereign over all things—earthly and spiritual—all are under His dominion and reign.

Additionally, we are told Jesus is He "who loves us and has freed us from our sins by His blood…"

Oh, how Jesus loves us. How do we know? The cross. Jesus lived the life we should have lived but did not. He died the death we should have died but do not now have to. He paid the penalty we should pay but cannot.

And, He provides for us a salvation we do not deserve, but can freely receive by repentance and faith.

Look at verse 6 with me, please: Rev 1:6 "and made us a kingdom, priests to his God and Father, to him be glory and dominion forever and ever. Amen."

We are now a kings and priests—we reign with Christ and we serve. This is a glorious doxology.

Think about it: to be fully forgiven, cleansed, justified, and reconciled to God is overwhelming and more than enough. Christ, by who He is and what He did, by the cross and the resurrection has made this certain.

Yet, Jesus did more—He made us a kingdom and priests to His God and Father.

What can we say but agree? "To Him be glory and dominion forever and ever. Amen."

---

15 Akin, location 417.

Transition: By way of review, we have the blessing declared in verses 1-3, and the greeting in verses 4-6. In verses 7-8, we have one more aspect.

A DECLARATION (v. 7-8).

> *Rev 1:7 Behold, he is coming with the clouds, and every eye will see him, even those who pierced him, and all tribes of the earth will wail on account of him. Even so. Amen.*

> *Rev 1:8 "I am the Alpha and the Omega," says the Lord God, "who is and who was and who is to come, the Almighty."*

The blessed declaration is that HE IS COMING AGAIN!

Behold…look…pay attention…this is Christ's second coming. Oh, what a glorious, triumphant, victorious day that will be when Christ returns.

John notes specifically that Christ is coming "with" the clouds, not on the clouds. The cloud, I discovered, in Hebrew thought is commonly associated with the divine presence (Ex. 13:21; 16:10; Matt. 17:5; Acts 1:9).[16]

And, when He comes, His sovereignty, His supremacy, His imminence will be visible to all… "every eye will see Him." Even those who pierced Him, even those who flagrantly disregard Him, those who have rejected Him, those who have scoffed at Him, those who have been casually indifferent toward Him… "every eye will see Him."

Moreover, all the tribes of the earth will "wail" on account of Him. Oh, my! This is remarkable. Mounce points out that the mourning of Zechariah 12:10-12 was that of repentance, but the

---

16 Mounce, p. 51.

mourning of Revelation is the remorse accompanying the disclosure of divine judgment at the coming of Christ.[17]

Dear friends, at the looming return of Christ unbelievers will wail, will mourn the judgment that results from their having rejected Him.

"Even so. Amen." John vigorously affirms this thought and reality.

Finally, there is the declaration of verse 8. There are three titles for God here in verse 8: The Alpha and the Omega, The One Who is and Who was and Who is to Come, and the Almighty.

God Himself now speaks. Rev 1:8 "I am the Alpha and the Omega," says the Lord God, "who is and who was and who is to come, the Almighty."

Only here and in 21:5 does God speak. God's sovereignty is timeless. Let this encourage us. He is supreme over all things. He is prior to all creation and He is the one who will bring consummation to His divine purpose for the cosmos.

Dear Church: our God is victorious. The God of this text is a God you can trust.

This is a God who will do what He promises.

He is the Alpha and the Omega. He is the Almighty.

He sent His Son, the faithful witness, the firstborn of the dead, the ruler of kings on earth, who loves us and freed us from our sins by His blood.

Will you now consider giving your heart, your life to Christ? Will you repent of your sins? Will you call out to Christ for the salvation of your soul?

Will you come to the one who will forgive your sins and extend His grace to you and whereby you may know His peace?

Let's pray.

---

17 Mounce, p. 51.

3

"A TRANSCENDENT VIEW OF THE TRIUMPHANT CHRIST"

Revelation 1:4-20, NIV

The New Testament, apocalyptic, masterful literary piece we know as REVELATION, is a compelling, graphic, biblical description of the final moments of human history.

The rise of a world leader with bizarre supernatural power, wide scale destruction not known since history began, and a final showdown between righteousness and evil, makes REVELATION arguably the Bible's most popular and most popularly misunderstood book.

The intent of this abbreviated series of sermons from Revelation is to provide an overview of the some of the highlights we find within this epistle.

The absolute bottom line of the book of Revelation is this: JESUS IS COMING AGAIN!

Revelation is a book of prophecy. God is sovereign. God is omniscient. God knows exactly how it all ends. Revelation, at a minimum, reminds and encourages us that all is under God's command, is well-planned, under control, and right on schedule.

Revelation reminds and encourages us that Satan, the great enemy of God, and all who believe, will soon realize his ultimate doom and destruction.

Adrian Rogers writes, "There is no devil in the first two chapters of God's Word or in the last two chapters of God's Word."[18]

Everywhere you look in the Bible you find JESUS. He is the heart of the entire Bible. Jesus is the hero, the central figure, of the entire canon of Scripture, and He is especially the hero in the Book of Revelation.

Note what Revelation's author, John, pens in the first two verses: "1:1 The revelation of Jesus Christ, which God gave him to show his servants what must soon take place. He made it known by sending his angel to his servant John, 2 who testifies to everything he saw-that is, the word of God and the testimony of Jesus Christ."

What you have here in essence is a chain of communication which was God the Father, to Christ, to an angel, to John, and to God' servants.

You may be asking this question: what is the purpose of Revelation? The clear purpose of Revelation was for God's Son, Jesus, to show His servants the future. Why do we have the Book of Revelation? Simple: to show us things which are to come.

Furthermore, Revelation contains a blessing within the book. Verse 3 states: "3 Blessed is the one who reads the words of this prophecy, and blessed are those who hear it and take to heart what is written in it, because the time is near."

The time for the Lord's return is imminent (I didn't say immediate), meaning simply that Christ could very well come at any moment!

---

18 Adrian Rogers, *Unveiling the End Times in Our Time: The Triumph of the Lamb in Revelation,* p. 2- Kindle edition

Friends, we live on the edge of eternity. And, there are definitive signs of Jesus' coming. Revelation tells us that horrific events
will happen, such as a one-world government and a merger of all the
world's religions headed up by Satan's strong man, the Antichrist.
There will be an exponential increase in knowledge. The world will
be systematized as every person will be given a mark, a number, and
they will not be able to buy or sell without that.[19]

As the end draws near, we will witness more and more moral
degradation and sin.

But, I want you to be encouraged, folks. God has given us His
Word to comfort, guide, and assure us. Almighty God has a sovereign
plan and He is bringing that plan to fruition.

Thus, with all that providing a backdrop and introduction, our
objective today is to gain "A Transcendent View of the Triumphant
Christ."

Revelation 1:4-20:

"4 John, to the seven churches in the province of Asia:

*Grace and peace to you from him who is, and who was,
and who is to come, and from the seven spirits before
his throne, 5 and from Jesus Christ, who is the faithful
witness, the firstborn from the dead, and the ruler of the
kings of the earth. To him who loves us and has freed us
from our sins by his blood, 6 and has made us to be a
kingdom and priests to serve his God and Father-to him
be glory and power for ever and ever! Amen.*

*7 Look, he is coming with the clouds,
and every eye will see him,
even those who pierced him;
and all the peoples of the earth will mourn because of him.*

So shall it be! Amen.

---

19 Ibid., p. 9.

8 "I am the Alpha and the Omega," says the Lord God, "who is, and who was, and who is to come, the Almighty."

9 I, John, your brother and companion in the suffering and kingdom and patient endurance that are ours in Jesus, was on the island of Patmos because of the word of God and the testimony of Jesus. 10 On the Lord's Day I was in the Spirit, and I heard behind me a loud voice like a trumpet, 11 which said: "Write on a scroll what you see and send it to the seven churches: to Ephesus, Smyrna, Pergamum, Thyatira, Sardis, Philadelphia and Laodicea." 12 I turned around to see the voice that was speaking to me. And when I turned I saw seven golden lampstands, 13 and among the lampstands was someone "like a son of man," dressed in a robe reaching down to his feet and with a golden sash around his chest. 14 His head and hair were white like wool, as white as snow, and his eyes were like blazing fire. 15 His feet were like bronze glowing in a furnace, and his voice was like the sound of rushing waters. 16 In his right hand he held seven stars, and out of his mouth came a sharp double-edged sword. His face was like the sun shining in all its brilliance. 17 When I saw him, I fell at his feet as though dead. Then he placed his right hand on me and said: "Do not be afraid. I am the First and the Last. 18 I am the Living One; I was dead, and behold I am alive for ever and ever! And I hold the keys of death and Hades.

19 "Write, therefore, what you have seen, what is now and what will take place later. 20 The mystery of the seven stars that you saw in my right hand and of the seven golden lampstands is this: The seven stars are the angels of the seven churches, and the seven lampstands are the seven churches."

For John's devotion to the Word of God and the testimony of Jesus Christ, he was marooned on the island of Patmos, as an act of Roman justice. John is given a revelation while "in the Spirit."

In this trance-like state, John heard a great voice, like the sound of a mighty trumpet.

John turns around to see the voice that was speaking to him, and He was privileged to see a Transcendent View of the Triumphant Christ! John describes what he saw.

First, Observe The Exalted Christ in His Royal Regalia (v. 12-13).

"12 I turned around to see the voice that was speaking to me. And when I turned I saw seven golden lampstands, 13 and among the lampstands was someone "like a son of man," dressed in a robe reaching down to his feet and with a golden sash around his chest."

The "son of man" in verse 13 is, of course a clear reference to Jesus Christ. Often, this description was one Jesus used for Himself. John intends to identify this "Son of Man" as the resurrected, glorified, triumphant Christ!

- Christ is the First and the Last. He is the Living One.
- He was dead, but now lives forevermore.
- He is the firstborn from the dead.
- He is the faithful witness.
- He is the holder of the keys to Death and Hades.
- He is Prophet, Priest, and King.
- He is the Ruler of the kings of the earth.

One day, when every knee bows, people will be bowing to a Righteous Judge and a Reigning King.

"At the name of Jesus every knee should bow—of those who are in heaven and on earth and under the earth—and every tongue should confess that Jesus Christ is Lord, to the glory of God the Father" (Phil. 2:10-11).

The reigning Christ rules with unrivaled majesty. No one will be able to hide or escape meeting King Jesus. It is inevitable. It is unavoidable. You cannot escape Jesus.

John saw Jesus dressed in royal regalia. His robe reached to His feet and a golden sash was draped around His chest.

Here, John sees a vision of the Majestic Lord Jesus walking among the seven churches to reprove, encourage, and to command and commend them.[20]

Folks, Jesus is King…now and forevermore! He is not only the Lamb of God, but also the Lion of Judah!

Transition: The Son of Man is divine, dwells in eternity, possesses ultimate authority, and is the sovereign of an indestructible Kingdom. His Royal Regalia (the long robe and golden sash) depict the dignity and high, royal standing of the Son of Man.

Second, Observe The Exalted Christ in His Righteous Radiance (v. 14-16).

14 His head and hair were white like wool, as white as snow, and his eyes were like blazing fire. 15 His feet were like bronze glowing in a furnace, and his voice was like the sound of rushing waters. 16 In his right hand he held seven stars, and out of his mouth came a sharp double-edged sword. His face was like the sun shining in all its brilliance.

20 Simon J. Kistemaker, *New Testament Commentary: Revelation*, p. 95.

John tells us that the head and hair of King Jesus were white look wool, as white as snow.

All through Revelation, the color white is symbolic of purity and sinlessness. Jesus is the radiance of God's glory, the exact representation of His nature (Heb. 1:3).

Jesus is not only the reigning Christ, but also He is the righteous Christ. He will not overlook our sin. He does not wink or excuse sin. Sin will not go unpunished.

Folks, there are truths we cannot forget or soften: 1). God is holy; and 2). We are sinful.

If you are without Christ as your Savior, you will die in your sins. If you refuse to repent and believe, you will be condemned to eternity without Jesus in a place the Bible calls hell.

You can plead for mercy now, but on the judgment day, when you stand before the radiant, righteous Judge Jesus, the time for pleading for mercy will have passed. The Scripture says, "27 And inasmuch as it is appointed for men to die once and after this comes judgment, 28 so Christ also, having been offered once to bear the sins of many, shall appear a second time for salvation without reference to sin, to those who eagerly await Him" (Heb. 9:27-28, NAS).

John goes on to say that Jesus' eyes were like "blazing fire." What does that mean? His eyes are piercing in fiery holiness. Our character is transparent to His eyes. Nothing escapes the penetrating gaze of the Righteous Judge.

John corroborates this in the letter to the church in Thyatira (2:18) where Jesus says that He is the One "who searches the minds and the hearts" (2:23).

"His feet were like bronze glowing in a furnace, and His voice was like the sound of rushing waters."

The Old Testament passage underlying this sentence is Ezekiel 43:2, where the prophet describes the glory of God and says, "His voice was like the sound of many waters" (NKJV). This passage is now ascribed to Jesus.[21]

[Scripture Reading: Psalm 29:3-5; 7-9]

Note, in verse 16 three physical features of Jesus' appearance: His right hand, His mouth, and His face.

The right hand may be interpreted as a source of power and protection.

The image of the sword symbolically represents Christ's spoken word. And, that Word is sharper than a two-edged sword and is able to discern the thoughts and intentions of the heart (Heb. 4:12; Eph. 6:17).

Furthermore, 2 Thessalonians 2:8 informs us that at His return, Jesus will overthrow the lawless one with the breath of His mouth. The great Bible teacher, John Phillips, says that Jesus will speak two words at the battle of Armageddon, and it will all be over. Jesus will look across the plains and say, "Drop dead!" Jesus is the triumphant Christ!

Transition: His face was like the noonday sun. One day, folks, we will see Jesus in His undimmed glory! We will see Him in His righteous radiance.

---

21 Kistemaker, p. 96-7.

Finally, Observe The Exalted Christ and Our Reverent Response (v. 17).

"17 When I saw him, I fell at his feet as though dead..."

If you are saved, if you have repented of your sin and believed in the Lord Jesus Christ, this transcendent view of the triumphant Christ will not cause you to fear.

No. It will compel you to feel enormous reverence, awe, respect, worship, and anticipation.

You will want to fall at His feet because Jesus is your Exalted King.

Illustration:

I read recently where John MacArthur shared a story about a man who was boasting about his intimacy with Jesus. This man said, "Jesus and I are good friends. Sometimes when I'm shaving, He comes in the bathroom with me."

> *John said, "Literally?"*
>
> *"Oh, yes! He comes in body."*
>
> *John asked, "What does He do?"*
>
> *The man replied, "He just puts His arm around my shoulder while I'm shaving."*
>
> *John said, "Is that right? What do you do then?"*
>
> *"I just keep on shaving."*
>
> *John responded: "Then that's not Jesus!"*

When we see Jesus, we won't keep on shaving. We will fall at His feet![22]

This "Son of Man" is the Exalted Christ, the Regal King, the Righteous Judge, the First and the Last, the Living One…the Triumphant Christ!

The book of Revelation is the revelation of One—the spotless, glorified Lamb, Jesus Christ.

The first time Jesus came, He came to a crucifixion; the next time He comes, He is coming to a coronation.

The first time He came, He came as a servant. The next time, He is coming as a Sovereign!

Have you bowed your knee to King Jesus? Is He your Savior? Have your turned from your sin?

Is the end close at hand? If so, why are we so casual about sharing Christ with our unsaved family, friends, neighbors, or co-workers.

We must be clear-headed. Disciplined in prayer.

Come to Jesus! Be saved! Today is the day of salvation!

---

22 Rogers, p. 34 of the Kindle version.

"DO YOU STILL LOVE JESUS?"

Revelation 2:1-7, ESV

Sometimes, things are NOT always as they might first appear. Think about it: a mule dressed up in a tuxedo is still a mule.

Illustration:

Maybe you have heard the story about the person who went to visit the local zoo one day and noticed one of the keepers sobbing quietly in a corner and on inquiry, was told that one of the elephants had died. "Fond of him, was he?" the visitor asked. "It's not that," came the reply. "He's the poor chap who has to dig the grave."

Right. Things are not always as they appear.

Such was the case with the historical church in Ephesus identified in the sermon text this morning.

By all outward appearances, things looked good. Yet, upon closer examination the Ephesians church had drifted, they had wandered from that which was most important: Christ and the Gospel. Their love for Jesus had grown cold.

Could the same be said of Field Street Baptist Church? Are we fooling others and ourselves? Has our love for Christ faded? Are we merely going through the motions?

The truth is: We do not and cannot fool THE ONE WHO WALKS among us and knows us so well.

Do you still love Jesus? Hold that thought.

> *Rev 2:1 "To the angel of the church in Ephesus write: 'The words of him who holds the seven stars in his right hand, who walks among the seven golden lampstands.*
>
> *Rev 2:2 "'I know your works, your toil and your patient endurance, and how you cannot bear with those who are evil, but have tested those who call themselves apostles and are not, and found them to be false.*
>
> *Rev 2:3 I know you are enduring patiently and bearing up for my name's sake, and you have not grown weary.*
>
> *Rev 2:4 But I have this against you, that you have abandoned the love you had at first.*
>
> *Rev 2:5 Remember therefore from where you have fallen; repent, and do the works you did at first. If not, I will come to you and remove your lampstand from its place, unless you repent.*
>
> *Rev 2:6 Yet this you have: you hate the works of the Nicolaitans, which I also hate.*
>
> *Rev 2:7 He who has an ear, let him hear what the Spirit says to the churches. To the one who conquers I will grant to eat of the tree of life, which is in the paradise of God.'*

Chapters 2-3 of Revelation address seven churches John greeted in chapter 1. They are each unique in their circumstances, makeup, and situation. Yet, each of their specific messages has a word of instruction and application for the all churches throughout the ages until Christ's return.

With that said, each of these churches is addressed in a common pattern. That pattern is identified in different ways by Bible commentators, so for our purposes, we will employ the pattern identified by Daniel Akin in his accessible work on Revelation.[23] That pattern consists of:

- A Commendation
- Criticism for their sins
- A word of Correction/warning
- A Challenge and promise

Look at verses 2-3 for Christ's COMMENDATION to the Church in Ephesus:

> *Rev 2:2 "'I know your works, your toil and your patient endurance, and how you cannot bear with those who are evil, but have tested those who call themselves apostles and are not, and found them to be false. Rev 2:3 I know you are enduring patiently and bearing up for my name's sake, and you have not grown weary.*

The first of these churches to be addressed by the Lord was the first-century church at Ephesus.

Ephesus was a city of great significance—politically, commercially, and religiously, though its prominence was beginning to wane.

Politically, Ephesus was the capital of Asia.

Commercially, the great highways converged there, and a major seaport was still in place. One commentator has referred to Ephesus as "the Vanity Fair of the Ancient World.[24]

23 Daniel L. Akin. *Christ-Centered Exposition: Exalting Jesus in Revelation*, location 802, Kindle Edition.

24 Akin, location 854 (primary source: Barclay, *Revelation*, p. 59).

Religiously, the city was the center for the worship of the Roman fertility goddess, Diana. The temple dedicated to Diana came to be known as one of the "Seven Wonders of the Ancient World" and was a source of extreme civil pride.

Oddly, one of Ephesus's own philosophers, Heraclitus, was known as the weeping philosopher, and he lamented over the immorality and wickedness of the city, saying that its citizens were "fit only to be drowned, and the reason he could never smile or laugh was because he lived amidst such terrible uncleanness."[25]

The church in Ephesus was founded by Paul and he strategically labored there for two years. Paul, Timothy, and now John had ministered to this church. It had quite a heritage and legacy.

While the past was notable, their present condition was spiritually perilous.

In verse 1, Christ is described as One who holds the seven stars in His right hand, and One who walks among the seven golden lampstands.

Christ holds His churches sovereignly in His hand. He has authority over His church. He is responsible for them. Jesus purchased the church with His own blood and is dear to Him. The Lord walks among His people. He is not disinterested or aloof. He is there. He is present. He is personally aware. He is a vigilant, tireless watchman.

He sees what we do. He hears what we say. He knows what we think. This is comforting and assuring, but also brings with it the reality of accountability.

The Ephesians church was busy and active in ministry. It's easy to imagine that their church calendar was full.

---

25 Ibid., location 854 (primary source: Johnson, *Revelation*, 1983, p. 41).

Christ commends the church for her work, labor and patient endurance (v. 2). He affirms them for their effort to steer clear of evil and their effort to be discerning about what they were hearing from those who called themselves apostles.

Furthermore, the church is commended for their patient endurance (v. 3). They labored in a culture which was hostile to the church's mission and vision.

Holiness and purity mattered to the church. Clearly, their effort to be discerning was guided by their commitment to Scripture.

The Lord was pleased with their good deeds. They had labored to the point of exhaustion and patiently endured the difficult external environment surrounding them. They refused to bow their knee to the false goddess, Diana or images of the emperor. No doubt this brought trouble and difficulty to their doorstep in their effort to be faithful to Christ. The Lord took special note of their dedication.

Note in verse 6 that they are commended because they "hate the works of the Nicolaitans, which I also hate." Now, we do not know with a high degree of certainty who the Nicolaitans were; however, it would seem that idolatry and immorality were at the root of their practices.

Transition: Christ commends the Ephesians, but He also levies against them a pointed, personal criticism.

In Verse 4 We Observe Christ's CRITICISM of the Church in Ephesus:

> Rev 2:4 But I have this against you, that you have abandoned the love you had at first.

The church in Ephesus looked good from the outside. The doctrine was accurate. The lifestyles of the membership were consistent with their profession. Apparently, they were doing the right things, but at some point the passion had diminished. The problem was not with their head, but with their HEART.

Hear this: their obedience to Christ was born out of a sense of duty as opposed to love.

Are YOU obedient to Christ out of duty or out of love for Him? This criticism must have been painful to hear.

Jesus is brutally honest.

Jesus is straightforward.

His words are sobering and piercing.

Verse 4 reminds us that Jesus has a jealous love for His church. The verse makes clear that the Ephesians church did not lose their first love, they walked away from it; they abandoned the love they once had.

What is the love they abandoned? It's hard to know for sure, but we can speculate. Daniel Akin offers four views in his commentary:

1. Their original love for one another?
2. Their love for God?
3. Their love for the Gospel?
4. Their love for Christ?[26]

I think you could make an argument that their passion for Jesus and the Gospel had slipped. Of course, Christ wants our OBEDIENCE, but He also wants our AFFECTION. It matters to Christ not only WHAT we do, but WHY we do what we do.

Transition: Criticism is rarely easy to receive, but Christ does not merely levy a critique against His church without offering some corrective path forward.

---

26 Akin, location 949, Kindle Edition.

In Verse 5. We Observe Christ's Plan of CORRECTION for the Church in Ephesus:

> *Rev 2:5 Remember therefore from where you have fallen; repent, and do the works you did at first. If not, I will come to you and remove your lampstand from its place, unless you repent.*

With the Lord's church, with Christ as the exalted Head, the church may not be well, but all is not lost.

The Lord, the Great Physician, has diagnosed the sickness. Now, Jesus charts a path forward.

Jesus articulates three imperatives:

1. Remember from where you have fallen-remember what you have abandoned. Go back to that time when your passion for Me and the Gospel was white hot.

2. Repent of your wrongdoing- to repent means to change, to think differently about one's sin. Repentance involves turning away from something and turning to something else, in this case turning from sin and turning back to Christ.

3. We are reminded that labor is not a substitute for love; purity is not a substitute for passion, and deeds are not a substitute for devotion.

4. We should resist the temptation to pat ourselves on the back for doing good deeds with the wrong motivation. Christ sees the heart behind the effort.

5. Return to the works you did at first- do you remember the first time you came to realize that God loved you? Do you recall the moment you came to an understanding that Christ loves you, not because you deserve or could earn it, but simply because He chose to love you and it pleased Him to do so?

6. Do you recall when you gave your heart to Jesus?

7. Can you harken back to the moment your love for Christ became something you thought about and talked about with anyone who would listen?

8. Friend, do you STILL love Jesus? Or, has your love grown cold and dutiful? Maybe it is high time to get back to the works which flowed from your life when you first came to love Christ.

Transition: All of us need a little "course correction" from time to time in our walk with Christ. Maybe, like the Ephesians, you need to remember, repent, and return. One final word…

In Verse 7. We Note Christ's CHALLENGE to the Church in Ephesus:

> *Rev 2:7 He who has an ear, let him hear what the Spirit says to the churches. To the one who conquers I will grant to eat of the tree of life, which is in the paradise of God. '*

To the one who conquers, who "overcomes," who perseveres, there is a promise to believe and receive.

We must actively trust in Christ, day-by-day to endure and remain faithful even in the most difficult of days.

We must be steadfast in our resolve to live for Christ!

The "tree of life" takes us back to Genesis 2:9 and 3:22-24 and forward to Revelation 22:2. What Adam and Eve forfeited through sin we regain in and through Christ. Heaven is a paradise recovered and so much more.

Paradise is the place where the righteous go to be with God. It is where sin has no place. God dwells there. Jesus is present. There we will live forever. We will be with Christ forever. How's that for a promise?

What do you love? Who do you love? How do we know?

What do you talk about?

What excites you?

What do you think about?

We know what we love by what we talk about, think about, and what gets us animated and excited. My hope for all of us is that the answer is Jesus. Do you STILL love Jesus? Are you good on the outside, but a mess on the inside? What changes do you need to consider in your heart? Let's pray about it.

"FAITHFUL UNTO DEATH"

Revelation 2:8-11, ESV

What are you reactions to the following words?

- Tribulation
- Poverty
- Slander
- Suffering
- Testing
- Prison
- Pain
- Death

I marvel with great admiration at some of the stories from church history regarding those who were martyred for their faithfulness to Christ and the Gospel.

For instance, you have heard me speak of John Rogers. Permit me to jog your memory. John Rogers was the 1st English Protestant to be executed by Queen Mary I, a.k.a., Queen Bloody Mary.

John Rogers was tied to a stake at Smithfield, near Oxford University, and burned alive in 1555. Among those who stood and watched him burned to death were his wife and nine children, one of them nursing at its mother's breast. His wife and children encouraged him as he faced the flames. After being tied to the stake, he was offered pardon if he would just give up his Protestant views. The Sheriff showed Rogers a document promising his full pardon if he would recant and go back to the Roman Catholic Church. He refused. Rogers answered, "That which I have preached with my lips will I seal with my blood." The fire was lit and Rogers reached out and washed his hands in the flames as his body was burned to ashes.

I want to ask you a very difficult question. Is there a spirit of a martyr residing in your heart? Is there a willingness, a readiness, to suffer and endure for your commitment to Christ Jesus?

It's been said that suffering, persecution, and martyrdom have indeed been the calling of the church of the Lord Jesus somewhere among the nations throughout her entire history.

Illustration:

In ancient Rome, crowds by the tens of thousands would gather in the Colosseum to watch as Christians were torn apart by wild animals. Paul Rader, commenting on his visit to this famous landmark, said, "I stood uncovered to the heavens above, where He sits for whom they gladly died, and asked myself, 'Would I, could I, die for Him tonight to get this gospel to the ends of the earth?'" Rader continued, "I prayed most fervently in that Roman arena for the spirit of a martyr, and for the working of the Holy Spirit in my heart, as He worked in Paul's heart when He brought him on his handcuffed way to Rome." Those early Christians "lived on the threshold of heaven, within a heartbeat of home, no possessions to hold them back."

Does that not give you goosebumps? I think you will find this morning's text quite challenging. Let's read it.

*Rev 2:8 "And to the angel of the church in Smyrna
write: 'The words of the first and the last, who died and
came to life.*

*Rev 2:9 "'I know your tribulation and your poverty (but
you are rich) and the slander of those who say that they
are Jews and are not, but are a synagogue of Satan.*

*Rev 2:10 Do not fear what you are about to suffer.
Behold, the devil is about to throw some of you into
prison, that you may be tested, and for ten days you will
have tribulation. Be faithful unto death, and I will give
you the crown of life.*

*Rev 2:11 He who has an ear, let him hear what the
Spirit says to the churches. The one who conquers will
not be hurt by the second death.'*

As clearly identified, this letter is specifically addressed to the church in Smyrna.

Smyrna is modern day Izmir. It is 35 miles north of Ephesus. Daniel Akin describes this city as proud and beautiful. Its coins were inscribed with the words, "First of Asia in beauty and size."[27] Temples of Apollos, Asclepius, Aphrodite, Cybele, and Zeus peppered the landscape of this beautiful pagan city.

Politically, the city was close to Rome and the imperial cult, which was marked by emperor worship. In AD 23, Smyrna beat out 11 other cities for the right to build the first temple to honor Tiberius Caesar, who reigned during the crucifixion of Jesus Christ.

Couple this allegiance to Rome with a large and influential Jewish population, and Smyrna had all the makings of a hostile environment for the church of the risen Christ.

---

27 Daniel Akin. *Revelation: Christ-Centered Exposition: Exalting Jesus in Revelation*, location 1066, Kindle Edition.

- This church needed encouragement.
- This church was suffering and persecuted.
- And, it was going to get worse.

This text follows a similar pattern to the letter written to the church in Ephesus.

In verse 8, we have a description of Jesus. He identifies Himself as "the first and the last, who died and came to life."

The emphasis here is upon Christ's eternality and sovereignty. Oh, dear friends, the victorious Christ gets the final word! He knew the situation of the church in Smyrna, and He knows our situation as we serve Him.

Furthermore, He is the crucified and resurrected Lord. Jesus experienced a suffering and death that is indescribable and more horrible then any human will ever know. He bore the wrath and judgment of God on behalf of GUILTY sinners.

In verses 9-10 Jesus COMMENDS the Church for Its Faith and Perseverance.

> Rev 2:9 "'I know your tribulation and your poverty (but you are rich) and the slander of those who say that they are Jews and are not, but are a synagogue of Satan.

> Rev 2:10 Do not fear what you are about to suffer. Behold, the devil is about to throw some of you into prison, that you may be tested, and for ten days you will have tribulation. Be faithful unto death, and I will give you the crown of life.

As the Lord makes His examination of the Smyrna church, they were a strong and wealthy people, at least by Jesus' estimation.

Imagine, if you would, hearing the pastor read these words from the risen Lord Himself. "I know your tribulation and your poverty (but you are rich)." They struggled just for basic necessities.

Christ knows. He knows the pressure. He knows the nature of the affliction. He knows the anguish. He knows the burden you bear and the trouble you face.

This church was enduring hardship—economic, physical, religious, and social. They were maligned and misrepresented. It cost them something to take their stand for Jesus. There was real sacrifice for remaining faithful to Jesus.

Yet, Christ saw them not as impoverished, but as wealthy. While it may be true that the Smyrna church was not materially affluent, nonetheless, they were spiritually rich.

This church was particularly harassed by the Jewish population in this city. They were slandered by those who claimed to be Jews, but were not, but rather were a synagogue of Satan. In other words, particular folks were tools in Satan's hands. They were under his influence.

Verse 10 contains a command from Christ to trust Him, but also a promise of suffering and difficulty.

Rev 2:10 Do not fear what you are about to suffer.

What were they about to suffer? Jesus states that Satan, the accuser, was about to throw some of them into prison to test them. He will try to harm them.

Scary, huh? Yet, Christ will use the devil's intentions to refine and prove them. Christ will reveal their faith, loyalty and for Him. Notice the duration—10 days—this is indicative of a definite, but limited period of time.

Jesus allows this and will control its duration.

Application: It would seem fitting at this point to make mention of the future of the church, especially here in the West, in America.

It is no secret that there are more and more people who oppose and reject Christianity, Christian ethics and values. Those who oppose biblical Christianity are going to oppose and reject us. It's happening already, and it is going to increase.

We will be portrayed and labeled as a crazy bag of nuts, bigoted, judgmental, dangerous, and even evil.

We will be slandered as:

- Anti-choice
- Anti-gay
- Anti-diversity
- Anti-inclusion
- Anti-intolerance.

We can anticipate economic boycotts, governmental restrictions, and social ostracism.

It is likely that a time is coming when we will experience severe persecution and even imprisonment for our fidelity to Christ and the Gospel.

This is already true for followers of Christ around the world, and it will come to America.

Alarming isn't it? How will we respond? We should pay close attention to what the Lord said to the church in Smyrna. "Do not fear. Expect it." We should ask God for the grace to receive this testing from the hands of a sovereign God who tests, prunes, and refines our faith.

Remember what James said, "Consider it great joy, my brothers, whenever you experience various trials, knowing that the testing of your faith produces endurance" (James 1:2-3.).

Transition: The Lord commends the Smyrna church for their faithfulness and perseverance.

In verses 10-11 Jesus CHALLENGES the Church by God's Reward and Reliable Promise.

> *Rev 2:10 Do not fear what you are about to suffer. Behold, the devil is about to throw some of you into prison, that you may be tested, and for ten days you will have tribulation. Be faithful unto death, and I will give you the crown of life.*
>
> *Rev 2:11 He who has an ear, let him hear what the Spirit says to the churches. The one who conquers will not be hurt by the second death.'*

You will note of course that Jesus does not say, "Hey, hard times are coming, suck it up buttercup!"

He does not say, "Hey, it stinks to be you. Good luck with all of that." It's not like that at all. Jesus encourages His people! He challenges the church in Smyrna.

It is true that men may kill the body, but they cannot destroy the soul (Matt. 10:28).

I like Daniel Akin's take on this--Yes, there are those who may kill our bodies. That means one truth for the devoted follower of Christ: instant heaven! What do we have to fear?[28]

Jesus exhorts this church, "Be faithful unto death, and I will give you the crown of life."

The King "will give you the crown of life." This is a victor's crown.

James 1:12 sets forth, "A man who endures trials is blessed, because when he passes the test he will receive the crown of life that God has promised to those who love Him."

---

28 Akin, location 1173, Kindle Edition.

Crowns are mentioned frequently in Scripture:

- Crown of life (Rev. 2:10)
- Crown of righteousness (2 Tim. 4:8)
- Crown of glory (1 Pet. 5:4)
- Crown of gold (Rev. 4:4)
- Crown of rejoicing (1 Thess. 2:19)
- Crown of incorruption (1 Cor. 9:25)

The latter part of verse 11 is interesting: "The one who conquers will not be hurt by the second death."

What does this mean? There is something worse than physical death: that is spiritual and eternal death, which is called here "the second death."

In Revelation 20:14 it is called "the lake of fire," another way to describe hell.

In Revelation 21:8 we are told who experiences the second death: "But the cowards, unbelievers, vile, murderers, sexually immoral, sorcerers, idolaters, and all liars—their share will be in the lake that burns with fire and sulfur, which is the second death."

Ladies & Gentlemen: It is the second death from which Christ came to rescue us.

The point simply is this: STAY WITH JESUS no matter what. Stay faithful unto death, for there is glory on the other side.

I close with this story. Some sixty years after John wrote these words to the church at Smyrna, the pastor of the Smyrna church, Polycarp, would indeed be a man who was faithful unto death.

The citizens and government of Smyrna would arrest, try, and burn at the stake and stab this steadfast pastor.

Listen to Polycarp's prayer after he had been tied up and prepared for the pyre.

"Lord God Almighty, Father of thy beloved and blessed Servant Jesus Christ, through whom we have received full knowledge of thee, 'the God of angels and powers and all creation' and the whole race of the righteous who live in thy presence: I bless thee, because thou hast deemed me worthy of this day and hour, to take my part in the number of the martyrs, in the cup of thy Christ, for 'resurrection to eternal life' of soul and body in the immortality of the Holy Spirit; among whom may I be received in thy presence this day as a rich and acceptable sacrifice, just as thou has prepared and revealed beforehand and fulfilled, thou that art the true God without any falsehood. For this and for everything I praise thee, I bless thee, I glorify thee, through the eternal and heavenly High Priest, Jesus Christ thy beloved Servant, through whom be glory to thee with him and Holy Spirit both now and unto the ages to come. Amen."[29]

Jesus said, "If the world hates you, understand that it hated Me before it hated you" (Jn. 15:18).

Dear God: grant us grace, courage, and strength to be faithful to Christ and the Gospel even unto death.

---

29 Akin, location 1253. Kindle Edition.

6

"THE SAVIOR'S SWORD"

Revelation 2:12–17, ESV

I want to share with you this morning, on Resurrection Sunday, a message about the Savior's Sword.

In our church, we speak often of Jesus, and rightly so, for He is the Exalted Head of His Church.

We speak of Him as:

- The eternal Son of God
- The incarnate Word
- Conceived by the Holy Spirit
- Born of the virgin Mary
- Taking upon Himself human nature
- Our substitute
- The crucified God
- The risen Lord
- The glorious Son
- The one Mediator between God and man
- The one who will visibly, victoriously return at the sovereign, perfectly timed command of God
- Today, we think of the Savior and His Sword.

Rev 2:12 "And to the angel of the church in Pergamum write: 'The words of him who has the sharp two-edged sword.

Rev 2:13 "'I know where you dwell, where Satan's throne is. Yet you hold fast my name, and you did not deny my faith even in the days of Antipas my faithful witness, who was killed among you, where Satan dwells.

Rev 2:14 But I have a few things against you: you have some there who hold the teaching of Balaam, who taught Balak to put a stumbling block before the sons of Israel, so that they might eat food sacrificed to idols and practice sexual immorality.

Rev 2:15 So also you have some who hold the teaching of the Nicolaitans.

Rev 2:16 Therefore repent. If not, I will come to you soon and war against them with the sword of my mouth.

Rev 2:17 He who has an ear, let him hear what the Spirit says to the churches. To the one who conquers I will give some of the hidden manna, and I will give him a white stone, with a new name written on the stone that no one knows except the one who receives it.'

As we look closely at this text of Sacred Scripture, I want you to see the following structure:

1. The Commendation (v. 13).
2. The Criticism (v. 14-15).
3. The Command/Consequence (v. 16).
4. The Conquerors (v. 17).

As clearly identified in verse 12, this letter is specifically addressed to the angel of the church in Pergamum.

Pergamum was an important religious center for the pagan religions of Athena, Asklepios, Dionysius (the god of drunkenness by the way), and Zeus. It was the first city in Asia to build a temple to Caesar and became the capital of the imperial cult of Caesar worship.

The risen Lord identifies Himself as He "who has the sharp two-edged sword."

I love that phrase. It is a bit of repetition from Revelation 1:16. It is an indispensable reminder that what proceeds from the mouth of Christ is piercing, cutting, separating, revealing, and irresistible.

The Bible states in Hebrews 4:12, "For the Word of God is living, active, sharper than any two-edged sword, piercing to the division of soul and of spirit, of joints of marrow, and discerning the thoughts and intentions of the heart." And, then the writer of Hebrews adds this statement, which is relevant for our purposes this morning: "And no creature is hidden from His sight, but all are naked and exposed to the eyes of Him to Whom we must give account" (v. 13). In other plain spoken words--we would do well to pay attention to Scripture, folks.

Why? Because the Lord's assessment, His judgment of our lives and of our church is thorough and true.

THE COMMENDATION (v. 13).

> Rev 2:13 "'I know where you dwell, where Satan's throne is. Yet you hold fast my name, and you did not deny my faith even in the days of Antipas my faithful witness, who was killed among you, where Satan dwells.

To begin with, Christ says He knows the situation in which the church in Pergamum exists. He knows where Satan's influence dwells. He knew they existed in a myriad of idols, thrones, shrines, and temples.

Christ knows that when a church seeks to carry out faithfully her mission in a context that is hostile to that mission, He knows it can be hard, excruciating even.

Let's not kid ourselves or sugar coat it, living for Jesus is difficult. Christ knows what the church in Pergamum faces. He knows the environment. He knows the circumstances in clear detail.

The Lord commends the church in Pergamum for faithfulness.

Daniel Akin points out in his commentary on Revelation that "Pergamum was obsessed with a love of the state. Patriotism had crossed the line into idolatry."[30] This is the major problem behind the book of Revelation, and frankly our lives—idolatry—anything we put ahead of our commitment to Christ, our love and affection for God.

You see, society expects that we not let our biblical convictions get in the way of being a part of a "progressive, secular" society.

It's ok to privatize your faith, but faith displayed in the public square is to be squelched, ridiculed, decried.

Illustration:

Let me offer you an example from the increasingly laughable, secular, cosmopolitan world of ethics.

Recently, a Washington Post columnist, Richard Cohen, summarily put forth that anyone who holds to biblical morality is a bigot. This columnist further called for the resignation of Vice President Mike Pence.[31]

---

30 Daniel Akin. *Exalting Jesus in Revelation: Christ-Centered Exposition*, Kindle Edition, Location 1350.

31 https://albertmohler.com/2019/02/07/knowing-stand-washington-post-columnist-

We know that the Pences are deeply religious Christians. They hold to a morality that is informed by Scripture, which means that they believe that LGBTQ behaviors and relationships are sinful. Mrs. Pence works at a school that discriminates against gays and lesbians.

Cohen basically paints anyone a bigot who would dare to even think of homosexuality as sinful.

This is clearly a clash between religious liberty and the newly defined sexual liberties.

Cohen's logic flows something like this: Homosexuality is not wrong, so if you believe that anything in the LGBTQ matrix is sinful, then you are bigoted. Consequently, you should be exiled from the public square, where there is no place for bigots.

What's scary about this is the idea that every man determines for himself what is right and wrong. Objective, unalterable truth, i.e. God's Word, is not the standard for truth in a culture that is "progressive."

*Devoted Christ-followers dare to say, "God hath said…"

We dare to say that morality is defined by God in the Bible. We dare to say that truth is fixed, eternal, and divinely revealed. We dare to believe that God has spoken, that the Bible is His Word, that Christ has the sharp two-edged sword.

As Al Mohler writes, "The secular elites believe that anyone who holds to a biblical morality is a bigot and anyone who believes in divine revelation must be an idiot."[32]

Jesus knows this. He knows the landscape in which we as His people exist. He knows hard times are coming.

says-anyone-holds-biblical-morality-bigot-calls-vp-pence-resign/

32 https://albertmohler.com/2019/02/07/knowing-stand-washington-post-columnist-says-anyone-holds-biblical-morality-bigot-calls-vp-pence-resign/

Like the believers in Pergamum, we cannot deny the faith. We must hold fast to the name of Christ. We must maintain our witness for Christ, living our lives in alignment with sacred Scripture in the example of the risen King Jesus!

We must remain faithful. Clearly, their faithful witness resulted in the martyrdom of one of their own.

Who was Antipas? We cannot know for sure.

Tradition says that he was roasted inside a brass bull during the reign of Domitian.[33] Christ describes Antipas as his faithful witness, which is exactly how Jesus is identified in Revelation 1:5.

Christ was God's faithful witness unto death. The Son honored His Father in death, and Antipas honored his Lord in death.

Did you know that some estimate that when it comes to deaths, "90% of all people killed on the basis of religious beliefs in the world today are Christians."[34]

Transition: The Lord commends the Pergamum church for their faithfulness to Him.

THE CRITICISM (v. 14-15)

Rev 2:14 But I have a few things against you: you have some there who hold the teaching of Balaam, who taught Balak to put a stumbling block before the sons of Israel, so that they might eat food sacrificed to idols and practice sexual immorality.

Rev 2:15 So also you have some who hold the teaching of the Nicolaitans.

---

33 Mounce, *Revelation*, 80 (primary source); secondary source, Akin, location 1367.

34 Akin, location 1376.

Christ criticized this church for their compromise. Many had been faithful, yes, but some compromised.

Compromise is a toxin that can easily poison the life of the church. Someone has once and rightly said that the greatest dangers to the church are almost never from the outside, but rather from the inside.

These are the Trojan horses we allow into our community of faith. It's when we compromise the truth to accommodate the culture and the world in which we live, or even to justify sin.

What happened in Pergamum? First, they compromised their morality. Evidently, some at Pergamum held to the teaching of Balaam. Specifically, the sin instigated by following Balaam was that related to food sacrificed to idols and the practice of sexual immorality.

The stumbling block refers both to immorality and idolatry. Regrettably, the church in Pergamum, some of them anyway, celebrated the idols of the culture and adopted their sexual ethics.

Compromise and accommodation were the calling cards. They attempted to serve God, but allowed these spiritual Trojan horses into the body life of the church.

What's interesting is that the word Pergamum means, "thoroughly married." Here was a church married to the world and its waywardness.

It's a heartbreaking reality when the church compromises her biblical morality and ethics.

Illustration:

May I offer you a real-time example of this kind of compromise, this kind of temptation to accommodate? On February 23rd of this year (2019) the United Methodist Church held a special conference in St. Louis to decide how to move forward in the debate over ordaining practicing homosexuals and blessing same-sex unions.[35] This is a war for the soul of the UMC, and it came from within the denomination. It's a moral and theological concession in what appears to be a misguided effort to remain relevant to culture.

Speaking of theology. Some at Pergamum held to the name of Jesus, and some held to the name of Balaam. Some at Pergamum held to the name of the Nicolaitans.

Do you remember them from chapter 2 verse 6? The Pergamum church embraced the Nicolaitans. It appears that doctrine mattered little and behavior mattered even less.

But, you cannot cleanly separate beliefs from behavior because generally speaking, beliefs inform behavior.

You could not distinguish between the lifestyle of a believer and unbeliever. How sad. Would this not describe the church in the Western world today?

Transition: The Lord sternly criticized the Pergamum congregation for their compromise, both morally and theologically.

THE COMMAND/CONSEQUENCE (v. 16)

Rev 2:16 Therefore repent. If not, I will come to you soon and war against them with the sword of my mouth.

You will notice right away that Christ commands His church to REPENT! This is an urgent imperative.

---

35 https://www.firstthings.com/web-exclusives/2019/02/sexuality-and-the-umc

What does it mean to repent?

I'm afraid the church has forgotten. It means to turn from sin. It is a heartfelt sorrow and brokenness for sin, a renouncing of it, and a sincere dead level best commitment to forsake it and walk in obedience to Christ.

Then, Jesus states the consequence the Pergamum congregation will experience if they do not return. This is dreadful! Jesus says, "If not, I will come to you soon and war against them with the sword of my mouth."

A failure to respond properly would result in a swift and serious response from Christ. Can you even imagine this—Christ fighting against His church?

And, the Savior's weapon of choice would be His Word, "the sword of my mouth."

His Word is the unchanging source of truth. His Word sets the standard for God's people. All of us should feel miserable about our sin when we are confronted by the Savior's Word. We are not supposed to be comfortable with our sin.

Transition: Christ commands the Pergamum body to repent, or ELSE…He would make war against them with the SWORD of His MOUTH.

THE CONQUERORS (v. 17)

> *Rev 2:17 He who has an ear, let him hear what the Spirit says to the churches. To the one who conquers I will give some of the hidden manna, and I will give him a white stone, with a new name written on the stone that no one knows except the one who receives it.'*

Christ says He will feed us, nourish us. As you recall Manna was given to the Israelites by God during the exodus and wilderness wanderings.

Christ says He will give a white stone. We are not sure what this means exactly, yet is points to acceptance and victory in Christ. What He gives us cannot be taken away.

Christ says further that He will give them a new name written on the stone. Marvelously, this points to the end-time supper in which intimate fellowship with the resurrected Lord will occur. A new name means a new status. The persevering believer can expect to be a part of the community of the redeemed. Without this new name entry into the "city of God" is impossible.

As I bring this message to a close, it's shocking to me that Christ is willing to go to war with His church if there is a refusal on our part to repent from sin.

I'll bet you didn't expect to hear that today on Resurrection Sunday.

Yet, what better Sunday to hear this declaration from the Lord's Word.

Sin is serious business—serious in the life of the unbeliever and serious in the life of those who follow Christ.

If you are looking for a Savior who will never confront you with your sin, you will not find that in Christ. He's willing to go to war with His own people, to combat us with the sword of His mouth.

You are a sinner. You must repent. God in His patience, grace, and mercy, has provided the ONLY way by which we can be right with Him—THE DEATH AND RESURRECTION OF JESUS CHRIST.

What will you do? What will be your response? Will you turn from your sin? Will you confess where you have compromised? Will you destroy the idols of your hearts?

Will you abandon the dopey, empty philosophies of this world and ground your thinking and acting in the Word of God?

7

"THE SIN OF TOLERANCE"

Revelation 2:18-29, ESV

TOLERANCE is defined in Webster's New World Dictionary as "1). a being tolerant of others' beliefs, practices, etc. 2). the amount of variation, [deviation] allowed from a standard, accuracy, etc."

The late Dr. D. James Kennedy, long-time pastor of Coral Ridge Presbyterian Church in Fort Lauderdale, Florida is said to have once made the following statement: "Tolerance is the last virtue of a depraved society."[36]

Furthermore, there are those who are careful observers and commentators (Josh McDowell and Bob Hostetler) on American culture who suggest that "tolerance has become the cardinal virtue, the sole absolute of our society."[37]

Decades ago, to be tolerant meant "to recognize and respect others' beliefs and practices without necessarily agreeing or sympathizing" with them. The attitude that everyone has a right to his or her opinion is essentially what tolerance ONCE meant. Not anymore, ladies and gentlemen. Not anymore.

---

36 http://literarytalk.blogspot.com/2009/06/tolerance-apathy-last-virtues-of-dying.html

37 http://www.bobhostetler.com/new-tolerance-no-virtue

The "new tolerance" is more nuanced and sophisticated. The new tolerance means to consider every individual's beliefs, values, lifestyles, and truth claims as equally valid. So, not only does everyone have an equal right to his beliefs, but all beliefs are equal. All values are equal. All lifestyles are equal. All truth claims are equal. The new tolerance goes beyond respecting a person's rights; it demands praise and endorsement of that person's beliefs, values, and lifestyle.[38]

Therefore, if I hold to a biblical perspective on homosexuality, then I am decried as "intolerant."

If I refuse to perform a wedding for a gay or lesbian couple, I am denounced as "intolerant."

If I think abortion is unscriptural and I cringe at and find morally repulsive this "culture of death" being lauded by the pro-abortion movement, and because I personally find it ghastly mortifying that our nation's leaders would fail to protect the lives of unborn children and now newly born children, then I am criticized as "intolerant, judgment, uninformed, and bigoted."

Watch out, dear people! The time is here when we as Christians are going to face an increasing pressure to privatize our biblically informed convictions—meaning simply that you can hold to your convictions, just be quiet about it. Why? Because the new tolerance says that all beliefs are equally valid.

If you speak out on the school campus, the workplace, or in the public square--be warned--you will be castigated as intolerant and judgmental of others' beliefs and lifestyles.

WHAT'S WORSE than when tolerance establishes itself in the broader culture, is when tolerance finds its way into the church. You say, "Oh, come on, preacher…that would NEVER happen." Wrong.

It's already occurred.

---

38 http://www.bobhostetler.com/new-tolerance-no-virtue

Permit me to Offer Exhibit A:

The LGBT debate has already divided major denominations and churches.

Most recently, the United Methodist Church, which is the third largest faith-group in the nation and the largest mainstream Protestant group. The issue at stake: many Methodist Pastors want to perform same-sex marriages and ordain gay men and women as clergy.[39]

Gratefully, the UMC conference recently voted to uphold biblical sexuality.

The Presbyterian Church (USA), the Evangelical Lutheran Church in America, and the Episcopal Church have long allowed gay weddings.

The Catholic Church is now battling the brutal nightmare of clergy sex abuse among their leadership ranks.

And, finally, the judgment of God seems to have fallen justifiably upon the Southern Baptist Convention when the Houston Chronicle detailed in three installments a report delineating hundreds of sexual abuses in Southern Baptist Churches.[40] GOD HELP US AND HAVE MERCY UPON US!

Put plain and simple all of the aforementioned is symptomatic and indicative of the sin of tolerance now existing in the church, which is why this morning's text is so crucial to hear and heed.

Listen closely…

---

39 https://www.washingtonpost.com/religion/2019/02/22/will-nations-third-largest-church-split-up-over-lgbt-debate-leaders-try-reach-an-answer/?noredirect=on&utm_term=.70b4ce5d780d

40 https://sojo.net/articles/people-have-been-crying-out-years-survivors-respond-sbcs-recommendations-abuse

Rev 2:18 "And to the angel of the church in Thyatira write: 'The words of the Son of God, who has eyes like a flame of fire, and whose feet are like burnished bronze.

Rev 2:19 "'I know your works, your love and faith and service and patient endurance, and that your latter works exceed the first.

Rev 2:20 But I have this against you, that you tolerate that woman Jezebel, who calls herself a prophetess and is teaching and seducing my servants to practice sexual immorality and to eat food sacrificed to idols.

Rev 2:21 I gave her time to repent, but she refuses to repent of her sexual immorality.

Rev 2:22 Behold, I will throw her onto a sickbed, and those who commit adultery with her I will throw into great tribulation, unless they repent of her works,

Rev 2:23 and I will strike her children dead. And all the churches will know that I am he who searches mind and heart, and I will give to each of you according to your works.

Rev 2:24 But to the rest of you in Thyatira, who do not hold this teaching, who have not learned what some call the deep things of Satan, to you I say, I do not lay on you any other burden.

Rev 2:25 Only hold fast what you have until I come.

Rev 2:26 The one who conquers and who keeps my works until the end, to him I will give authority over the nations,

Rev 2:27 and he will rule them with a rod of iron, as when earthen pots are broken in pieces, even as I myself have received authority from my Father.

Rev 2:28 And I will give him the morning star.

Rev 2:29 He who has an ear, let him hear what the Spirit says to the churches.'

The Central Idea of Text: The church in Thyatira was guilty of internal compromise, allowing sin and false teaching to be tolerated in the church.

As you can plainly see, this is the longest letter of the seven, written to the church in Thyatira. Furthermore, this text breaks down easily into five sections:

1. The Lord's Identity (v. 18).
2. The Lord's Praise (v. 19).
3. The Lord's Rebuke (v. 20-23).
4. The Lord's Exhortation (v. 24-25).
5. The Lord's Promise (v. 26-28).

Historical Background, Context, and Setting

Thyatira was a much smaller city than Pergamum and was situated in an area noted for its abundant crops and the manufacturing of purple dye. In Acts 16 we meet a woman by the name of Lydia, a seller of purple cloth, from the city of Thyatira.

Thyatira was a city with a stable center for manufacturing and marketing. One of the outstanding characteristics of Thyatira was the large number of guilds (similar to today's labor unions) that flourished there, from linen-workers to bronze smiths. Unlike Pergamum or Smyrna, Thyatira was not an important religious center. The primary god worshiped was the Greek sun god, Apollo.

The pressure faced by the Christians in Thyatira came from the guilds. To hold a job or run a business, it was necessary to be a member of a guild.

Each guild had a deity (and this is key) in whose honor feasts were held, including meat sacrificed to idols and sexual immorality.

How some in the Thyatira church were handling the situation caused Christ grave concern.[41]

First, Note the Lord's IDENTITY (v. 18)

> *Rev 2:18 "And to the angel of the church in Thyatira write: 'The words of the Son of God, who has eyes like a flame of fire, and whose feet are like burnished bronze.*

Interestingly, the expression "Son of God" appears only here in the entire book of Revelation. And, it is a designation of Christ as deity and His righteous indignation at their sins and His role as their divine just judge.

Christ's eyes are described as a "flame of fire."

Christ's discernment was penetrating of the false prophetess, Jezebel. Christ is not easily duped. He is nobody's fool. He sees things as they truly are.

His feet of burnished bronze trample out impurity and ongoing, unconfessed, and unrepentant of sin.

Second, Take Note of the Lord's PRAISE (v. 19)

> *Rev 2:19 "'I know your works, your love and faith and service and patient endurance, and that your latter works exceed the first.*

Christ praises the believers in Thyatira for four aspects: The believers were…

---

41   John MacArthur, *Because the Time Is Near*, p. 74.

1. Showing love for God and one another
2. Commended for their faith/faithfulness
3. Commended for service and perseverance
4. Growing and maturing in their application of grace

Third, Observe the Lord's REBUKE (v. 20-23)

Rev 2:20 But I have this against you, that you tolerate that woman Jezebel, who calls herself a prophetess and is teaching and seducing my servants to practice sexual immorality and to eat food sacrificed to idols.

Rev 2:21 I gave her time to repent, but she refuses to repent of her sexual immorality.

Rev 2:22 Behold, I will throw her onto a sickbed, and those who commit adultery with her I will throw into great tribulation, unless they repent of her works,

Rev 2:23 and I will strike her children dead. And all the churches will know that I am he who searches mind and heart, and I will give to each of you according to your works.

All was not well in the church at Thyatira. Their problem was not external persecution, but internal compromise.

The Lord's rebuke here is primarily concerned with a prophetess assigned the name of Jezebel, who was leading believers astray by teaching them to take part in sexual immorality which accompanied pagan religion and to eat food sacrifice to idols.[42]

Now, this woman's name was most likely not Jezebel. Rather, this name is a reference to the Old Testament infamous wife of King

---

42 *The Bible Knowledge Commentary, New Testament*, p. 937.

Ahab, whose evil influence lead to widespread Baal worship among the Israelites (1 Kings 16:30-31).

Whoever this woman was (as this name may function more as a characterization as opposed to an actual identity) she was evidently influencing considerable numbers of believers into a fatal tolerance and compromise of and with paganism.[43]

Furthermore, this Jezebel refuses to repent of her immorality, though given ample time and opportunity to turn from her sin.

Likewise, this woman at Thyatira succeeded in leading Christ's bond-servants astray so they committed acts of immorality and ate food sacrificed to idols.

Application:

The Bible teaches that true followers of Christ can fall into sexual immorality and idolatry (1 Cor. 6:15-20; 10:21).

Furthermore, to lead other believers into false doctrine or immoral living is a very serious sin, inviting the most severe judgment and punishment (Matt. 18:6-10).

This woman's refusal to repent was to invite the judgment of Christ not only on her life, but also those who committed adultery with her. She would face certain judgment. Refusal to repent is to invite the judgment of Christ. Period.

Christ graciously, mercifully warned her followers of impending judgment, unless they repented.

Notice, also, that Christ's judgment is based on each person's deeds. Those who were innocent would not be disciplined along with the guilty (Matt. 7:16; 16:27; Rev. 22:12).

---

43 Robert Mounce. *NICNT: The Book of Revelation*, p. 87.

God is the righteous judge "who will render to each person according to His deeds" (Rom. 2:6).

Listen: What you do reveals your spiritual condition. What does that say about you?

Fourth, Observe the Lord's EXHORTATION (v. 24-25)

> *Rev 2:24 But to the rest of you in Thyatira, who do not hold this teaching, who have not learned what some call the deep things of Satan, to you I say, I do not lay on you any other burden.*

> *Rev 2:25 Only hold fast what you have until I come.*

In these verses we read Christ's exhortation to the faithful remnant at Thyatira, to those who had not dabbled into the depths of Satan's domain. His instruction was simple: "only hold fast what you have until I come" (v. 25).

Christ did not command them to leave the church, but rather to remain as a godly testimony. In fact, Christ assures these faithful believers that they will not have any additional burden.

Finally, Observe the Lord's PROMISE (v. 26-28)

> *Rev 2:26 The one who conquers and who keeps my works until the end, to him I will give authority over the nations,*

> *Rev 2:27 and he will rule them with a rod of iron, as when earthen pots are broken in pieces, even as I myself have received authority from my Father.*

> *Rev 2:28 And I will give him the morning star.*

Two promises Christ makes:

1. Christ will "give them authority over the nations"
2. Christ will "give them the morning star."

The promise of authority is taken from Psalm 2:7-9, and is one of participation in the millennial kingdom.

The promise of the morning star is Christ promising the fullness of Himself to believers (1 Cor. 13:12).

The letter to Thyatira concludes by urging the Thyatiran believers to listen up and pay attention.

1. A church cannot practice and tolerate sin. God will judge sin in the church.

We must uphold the standard and the banner of God.

2. A pattern of obedience marks true believers.

Obedience is the great evidence of our love for Christ.

3. God's promise, in spite of struggles with sin and error in churches, is that faithful Christians will experience all the fullness of Christ as they reign with Him in His kingdom.

May God grant us grace to remain faithful to Him, His Word, and His standard of truth in a world that embraces destructive tolerance.

8

"DYING, BUT NOT YET DEAD"

Revelation 3:1-6, ESV

I would like to tell you a story about a dog named Sandy. Sandy, a yellow Labrador retriever, was a gift to me from my wife on the occasion of graduating from seminary in 1994.

Sandy was my first dog. Now, this sounds a bit pathetic, but she was one of my best buds. At the time, Beth and I were DINKWADS... you know...Dual Income, No Kids, With a Dog. When she was just a young pup, Sandy was staying at some friends' house until we moved. We were living in a one-bedroom apartment in Garland. It was a "no pets" allowed apartment complex. Our friends lived in Rowlett and had offered their backyard until we moved. I had been called recently as pastor to First Baptist Church, Quitaque, Texas and we were simply waiting to participate in graduation ceremonies just a few days away. Afterwards, we would load the UHaul, collect Sandy, and be on our way to make the move to Quitaque.

On several nights I would get in my small, blue Chevrolet S-10 pickup, drive over to our friends in Rowlett, sneak into their backyard undetected, check on my dog, and would even lay my head down on the back porch for a few hours to keep her company. I told you, it is borderline pitiful!

Fast forward a couple of years. We were in Beeville at Beth's parents, celebrating one of the holidays, I think it was Thanksgiving. By this time, we had added another dog to our family...a worthless, hell-bound Beagle named "Spud."

Sandy managed to get in more trouble because of that dog! Anyway, they wondered off and it occurred to me that I had not seen the two of them in a long while. Beth's parents live on a small ranch fronted by a busy highway. I got concerned because the sun was starting to set. So, Tim, my brother-in-law, and I loaded up in my truck and set out to find the two canines. We found Spud pretty quickly, but Sandy was not with her. I was modestly concerned. So, we continued the search driving here and there in hopes of finding Sandy. It was getting darker and harder to see. Just as we were about to give up the search and hope Sandy would return home on her own, I happened to notice, out of the corner of my eye, what looked like a brown paper bag out in a field. I guess on a whim, really, I decided to exit the truck and walk over there to see exactly what it was.

It was Sandy. She had been hit by a car. To this day, I will never forget her feeble effort to wag her tail when I called her name. Now, I'm not a veterinarian, but I knew as I leaned over her, Sandy was hurt badly. As it turned out, her abdomen was swelling. Her pelvis was shattered. Her leg was broken. Her spleen was lacerated. Her stomach was torn up. She was a pretty good mess. I had a lump in my throat which seemed the size of a tennis ball as I loaded her into the back of my truck.

I called Beth to inform her that I had found Sandy and asked if she would contact their vet and see if the vet would meet us at the clinic and take a look at her. We got Sandy to the vet quickly and this wonderful animal doctor did an initial examination of Sandy. It was obvious to her trained eye…Sandy was dying, but not yet dead. The vet said she would do everything she could to save her life. She said, "If she makes it through the night, she will probably be ok. But, she's in for a difficult few hours." Beth, myself, Tim, Ben, and Mr. Barris went home. Early the next morning, I drove to the vet clinic. All I could think about was that Sandy was dying, but not yet dead… with that said…that brings us to the text descriptive of the church in Sardis—a church dying, but not yet dead. Let's read about it.

> *Rev 3:1 "And to the angel of the church in Sardis write: 'The words of him who has the seven spirits of God and the seven stars. "'I know your works. You have the reputation of being alive, but you are dead.*
>
> *Rev 3:2 Wake up, and strengthen what remains and is about to die, for I have not found your works complete in the sight of my God.*
>
> *Rev 3:3 Remember, then, what you received and heard. Keep it, and repent. If you will not wake up, I will come like a thief, and you will not know at what hour I will come against you.*
>
> *Rev 3:4 Yet you have still a few names in Sardis, people who have not soiled their garments, and they will walk with me in white, for they are worthy.*
>
> *Rev 3:5 The one who conquers will be clothed thus in white garments, and I will never blot his name out of the book of life. I will confess his name before my Father and before his angels.*
>
> *Rev 3:6 He who has an ear, let him hear what the Spirit says to the churches.'*

By way of background and context, Sardis was an important commercial city located 30 miles southeast of Thyatira. The city's economy had been bolstered by the industries of jewelry, dye, and textiles. Religiously, Sardis was rampant with pagan worship, and was the site of a temple of Artemis.[44] Sadly, the city was a shell of what it once was; and the church, unfortunately, had become like the city which surrounded it—alive in name only. The church was on spiritual life support, if you will. The church was infected and infested with the disease of sin.

This church needed to listen to the Great Physician's accurate diagnosis and remedies for healing!

If you think of this text as a string, then I would like to hang three pearls of ideas on this string. They are:

1. Reputation Does Not Represent Reality (v. 1)
2. Immediate Imperatives (v. 2-3)
3. Promise to Those Who Persevere (v. 4-5)

In Verse 1 We Plainly See That Reputation Does Not Represent Reality.

> Rev 3:1 "And to the angel of the church in Sardis write: 'The words of him who has the seven spirits of God and the seven stars. "'I know your works. You have the reputation of being alive, but you are dead.

Christ in verse one is described as the One "who has the seven spirits of God and the seven stars." This is not some reference to a holy entourage; rather, it is a reference to the complete and perfect Holy Spirit; the Spirit in all His fullness. Having the Spirit, Christ is fully aware of His churches.[45]

---

44 *The Bible Knowledge Commentary*, Revelation 3:1-6, p. 938.

45 Daniel Akin. *Exalting Jesus in Revelation: Christ-Centered Exposition Commen-*

- He knows the church's condition.
- He knows their vital signs.
- He knows their health history.
- He sees things as they really are.
- In His omniscience, He knows all there is to know about the Sardis congregation.
- In Christ's perfect knowledge He diagnoses the Sardis church with having a reputation for life, but in actuality they were dead…spiritually dead. Christ is concerned.
- Hope is fading.
- Time is expiring.
- The seven stars are angels who direct report to Jesus.
- You will notice also in verse 1 there is NOT ONE word of commendation to the Sardis congregation, similar to the church of Laodicea.
- They were all style and no substance.
- They were all sizzle and no steak.

Charles Swindoll states the church in Sardis was a "morgue with a steeple."[46]

The church had a reputation of life and vitality—probably a church of size, money, and ministries that made others take notice.

In the past, no doubt, the Sardis church must have been something special. Surely, there was a time when reputation and reality were in sync. Probably there was a time in the church's esteemed past when she was white hot for God. They were doing great things for God.

Yet, Jesus says in actuality, "you are dead." Looks were deceiving. As one commentator mentioned, "they were a zombie church!"[47]

---

tary, Kindle Edition, location: 1812.

46 Akin, Kindle location- 1821. Primary Source: Swindoll- *Insights*, 64.

47 Akin, Kindle Edition location: 1830.

What happened? What caused the toxicity in this church?

It is suggested the church compromised their conviction, their public witness to Jesus to avoid the scrutiny, criticism, opposition, and persecution which comes when you try to blend in with a reprehensible culture.

Their allegiance to Christ had faded and drifted.

Transition: Put simply, their past reputation did not match their present reality. They were dying, but not yet dead.

In Verses 2-3 We Observe a Series of Prescriptive Immediate Imperatives

> *Rev 3:2 Wake up, and strengthen what remains and is about to die, for I have not found your works complete in the sight of my God.*
>
> *Rev 3:3 Remember, then, what you received and heard. Keep it, and repent. If you will not wake up, I will come like a thief, and you will not know at what hour I will come against you.*

Although the church was dying, and could be pronounced dead, it still had the possibility of restoration back to life and vitality. The church was not beyond hope.

In what is kind of a rapid-fire prescription, the Lord lays out five immediate imperatives the church must obey if she is once again to become the body of Christ which Jesus saved her to be.

First, Jesus says, "Wake up!" (v. 2)

It was interesting to learn that the city of Sardis had fallen twice due to military slothfulness. Jesus urges the church not to suffer the same fate. Stay alert! Stay at your post! Be vigilant! Wake up from your spiritual lethargy.

If I could utter ONLY one two-word sermon to the church today it would be without question, "WAKE UP!"

Second, Jesus says, "Strengthen what remains!" (v. 2)

Jesus indicates that the church's works were not complete in God's sight. Strengthen what remains. Do away with mediocre, half-hearted, convenient, comfortable Christianity. Be unique. Be resolute in your obedience to Christ. By the way, it may very well be better for a church to be hated by its surrounding community than to be ignored. The church in Sardis was of no real consequence. They were so inconsistent and compromising in their commitment to Christ that they bothered no one. It was time for them to strengthen what remained!

Third, Jesus says, "Remember what you have received and heard!" (v. 3)

What are they to remember? Good question. It is the GOSPEL. They need to recall continually the truth of the Gospel of Jesus Christ. Preach the gospel to yourselves once again! Remember what Christ has done for you through His cross and resurrection. Stop compromising gospel truth. Stop living like the world and live like those who have been transformed by the power of the Good News!

Fourth, Jesus says, "Keep it!" (v. 3).

Jesus encourages the church to hold on, to guard what they have received and heard. Don't lose the truths which flow from the gospel. Do not take for granted the gospel. Hold firm in the truth. Resist the temptation to drift and slide into error and theological liberalism. Stay with what you have received.

Fifth, Jesus says, "Repent!" (v. 3).

Listen closely. Do you know what biblical repentance is? Repentance results in change—a change in attitude, a change in action concerning sin. Repentance is not something we do one time and we are done. Like the church in Sardis, too many of modern Christians have forgotten the grace of repentance—a godly sorrow over the brokenness of one's sin. I fear that for many people today, believers and unbelievers alike, people don't appear to be too bothered by their sin.

Notice what Jesus states at the end of verse 3. Jesus says if the church doesn't wake up, He will come like a thief—they will get a surprise visit from God. This is not speaking here in this context to His second coming; rather, it speaks of His coming in judgment against His church. This is a powerful, grace-filled warning.

The warning could not be clearer: REPENT NOW! There is no promise of a later time. Now is the time.

Transition: Jesus examines His church. The Sardis church is dying, but not yet dead. Jesus prescribes five critical, immediate imperatives.

Finally, in Verses 4-5 We Observe a Promise to Those Who Persevere

> Rev 3:4 Yet you have still a few names in Sardis, people who have not soiled their garments, and they will walk with me in white, for they are worthy.
>
> Rev 3:5 The one who conquers will be clothed thus in white garments, and I will never blot his name out of the book of life. I will confess his name before my Father and before his angels.

Jesus identifies a small remnant which had stood strong for Christ—bucking the trends, swimming against the current. Their garments were not yet stained by the whims of the culture around them. They will walk with Christ in purity of white clothing provided by Jesus. This is symbolic of their holiness of life.

Those who conquer, that is, who persevere, will be clothed in white garments. Plus, note what else… "and I will never blot his name out of the book of life. I will confess his name before my Father and before His angels."

What a promise! Now, John references "the book of life" six times in Revelation [3:5; 13:8; 17:8; 20:12, 15; 21:27; the book of life is also mentioned in Daniel 12:1 and Luke 10:20]. I want to say much more about the "book of life" in a future sermon, so let me simply say here that the names in the book of life are those of the redeemed, the saved of God. And, the promise here in chapter 3 is that Christ affirms that their names will not be erased.

This idea of a divine register is first mentioned in Exodus 32:32-33, where Moses prays that if God will not forgive the sin of His people, he himself wants to be blotted out "of the book you have written."

Here, instead, their names will be acknowledged before God and the angels.

Could any affirmation and promise ring so sweet to the faithful follower of Jesus Christ? I think not.

When I arrived at the vet's office early that morning, I drove around back and there was my dog sitting up looking all forlorn. She had been saved by the quick actions of a competent, compassionate animal doctor.

Sandy would need lots of care and another surgery to put her shattered pelvis and leg back together, but she went on to live to the age of 14.

I wonder as I look out across the congregation this morning and across the denominational landscape…how many people in the pews are spiritual zombies or dead men walking.

I don't know. But, the Lord knows for certain. Are you dying, but not yet dead? Do you need to wake up, strengthen what remains, remember the gospel you once heard and responded to, guard the truth in your heart, and repent? If so, the Great Physician stands ready to apply His compassionate healing hand to your diseased, sin-ridden soul. Oh, won't you come to Jesus?

9

"FAITHFUL"

Revelation 3:7-13, ESV

Rev 3:7 "And to the angel of the church in Philadelphia write: 'The words of the holy one, the true one, who has the key of David, who opens and no one will shut, who shuts and no one opens.

Rev 3:8 "'I know your works. Behold, I have set before you an open door, which no one is able to shut. I know that you have but little power, and yet you have kept my word and have not denied my name.

Rev 3:9 Behold, I will make those of the synagogue of Satan who say that they are Jews and are not, but lie— behold, I will make them come and bow down before your feet, and they will learn that I have loved you.

Rev 3:10 Because you have kept my word about patient endurance, I will keep you from the hour of trial that is coming on the whole world, to try those who dwell on the earth.

Rev 3:11 I am coming soon. Hold fast what you have, so that no one may seize your crown.

Rev 3:12 The one who conquers, I will make him a pillar in the temple of my God. Never shall he go out of it, and I will write on him the name of my God, and the name of the city of my God, the new Jerusalem, which comes down from my God out of heaven, and my own new name.

Rev 3:13 He who has an ear, let him hear what the Spirit says to the churches.'

In chapters two and three we have the individual letters of Christ written to seven specific churches.

These letters, as we have considered them, have been instructive. These particular addresses have been revealing, convicting, encouraging, and challenging.

As we have been making our way through chapters two and three of Revelation, I have been thinking about this question: WHAT REALLY MATTERS TO JESUS WHEN HE EXAMINES A CHURCH?

Is it the EXTERNALS? That is—budgets, buildings, and slick, glossy bulletins.

Is it the INTERNALS? That is—a surrendered heart, an obedient will, an abiding love for God, a mind for the truth, and a passion for the souls of men.

I have come to at least one clear conclusion about what matters to Christ when He inspects one of His flocks as we have considered these churches. I believe it is significant to Christ that a church is FAITHFUL.

I recognize that, as a culture, even in the Christian community, we do not celebrate and laud faithfulness as much as perhaps we should.

Faithfulness is not stylish, fashionable, trendy, glitzy, dazzling, or alluring. A.W. Pink wrote, "Unfaithfulness is one of the most outstanding sins of these evil days."

Even so, there is much to be said for being FAITHFUL.

Having said that, when we think of God, we must remember that faithfulness is one of the glorious perfections of His being. He never falters. He never fails. He never forfeits. He never compromises. He never capitulates.

Lamentations 3:22-23 reads, "His compassions fail not, they are new every morning: great is Thy faithfulness."

Deuteronomy 7:9 says, "Know therefore that the Lord thy God, He is God, the faithful God, keeping His covenant of love to a thousand generations of those who love Him and keep His commandments."

- When the storm clouds gather, He is faithful.
- When afflictions beset us, He is faithful.
- When others walk away, He is faithful.
- If we are faithless, He remains faithful (2 Tim. 2:13).
- When we pray, He is faithful.
- When we have need, He is faithful
- There is no shadow of turning with God!

The city of Philadelphia (which means, "brotherly love") was 25 miles southeast of Sardis. It was an important commercial stop on a major trade route called the Imperial Post Road.[48] In AD 17, the city was destroyed by an earthquake and then rebuilt by Tiberius. Consequently, the city was loyal to Rome. In a sense, Philadelphia was something of a representative or "missionary city" for the spreading of Greek culture.[49]

Similar to the church in Smyrna, the righteous surveyor, the Lord Jesus has no word of criticism or condemnation for the Philadelphia church. Why?

---

48 John MacArthur. *MacArthur New Testament Commentary*, p. 909.

49 Daniel Akin. *Christ-Centered Exposition: Exalting Jesus in Revelation*, Kindle Edition, location 2003.

I think you could make the case that the church in Philadelphia was a model of a FAITHFUL church:

1. Faithful to Christ (v. 7).
2. Faithful to the Word (v. 8, 10).
3. Faithful to the Work (v. 8).
4. Faithful to the Finish (v. 10-12).

1st- The Church Was Faithful to Christ (v. 7)

> Rev 3:7 *"And to the angel of the church in Philadelphia write: 'The words of the holy one, the true one, who has the key of David, who opens and no one will shut, who shuts and no one opens.*

When a church has a high, exalted view of King Jesus, it helps to foster faithfulness to Christ. In verse 7 there are three apparent truths set forth about the Lord:

1. He is the holy one- Christ is pure and separate. He is separate from sin as our sinless Savior. Who God is, Jesus is, because Jesus is God. Christ is pure, holy, undefiled, spotless, without stain of any kind. Jesus is the Holy One who walked among us in the flesh and now walks among us by His Spirit.
2. He is the true one- Jesus is the true God, not a false god. What He says is true, accurate. What He says is true because it flows from Who He is…the True One. Christ is genuine, sincere, authentic; there is no falsehood or pretense with Him. His Word is certain and reliable.
3. He is the sovereign one- Jesus is in control. He holds the keys. He has the authority to admit or exclude who will come into the presence of the King. He alone has the key that permits people into the kingdom of God. You recall what Jesus said

in John 10:9: "I am the door. If anyone enters by Me, he will be saved and will come in and go out and find pasture." Paul said, "For there is one God and one mediator between God and men, the man Christ Jesus" (1 Tim. 2:5).

Transition: The Philadelphia church was a model church for their faithfulness to Christ.

2nd- The Church Was Faithful to the Word (v. 8, 10)

Twice in this particular text, Jesus affirms the Philadelphia church for their fidelity to His Word. What an affirmation for any church!

Look at verse 8:

> *Rev 3:8 "'I know your works. Behold, I have set before you an open door, which no one is able to shut. I know that you have but little power, and yet you have kept my word and have not denied my name.*

And, then verse 10:

> *Rev 3:10 Because you have kept my word about patient endurance, I will keep you from the hour of trial that is coming on the whole world, to try those who dwell on the earth.*

This church was loyal to the Gospel. From what I read about this church, it should be noted that they were small in number. This was not a large, strong church. They were not wealthy. They had no real stature in their community. In fact, they were looked down upon and persecuted.

Verse 9 informs us that the congregation faced relentless opposition from the Jews, which in a very real sense, was opposition from

Satan, for we know that ultimately our battle is not against flesh and blood.

The Philadelphia saints faced false accusations and lies, which were levied at them by those of "the synagogue of Satan…these false Jews."

There was no question that the church faced both opposition and opportunity. In fact, verse 8 informs the reader that it was Christ who opened the doors of opportunities. And, brothers and sisters, when Jesus opens a door for ministry, THERE IS NO ONE or NO THING that can shut that door!

Yet, this congregation endured. They loved Christ. They loved the Word of God. They kept God's Word and did not deny the name of Christ.

Their hearts were in the right place.

They persisted in their faithfulness to the Gospel.

Faced with constant aggravation and trials, they stayed true to the Word of God.

Faced with consistent opposition and ridicule, they remained faithful to the one and only name that saves (Acts 4:12; 1 Tim. 2:5). Opposition did not deter them from faithfulness to Christ and His Word.

Application

May I lovingly, yet truthfully remind you that secularists are already taking aim at biblical Christianity?

- We are now living in an age of infanticide.
- We are now living in an age where biblical standards for sexuality are under an all-out assault and re-definition.
- We are now living in an age of dreadful moral confusion. Moral absolutes are disappearing.

- We are now living in an age where religious liberty is now being questioned in American public life.
- We are witnessing in this era the active, as Al Mohler calls it, the "de-Christianization" of the American landscape.[50]
- Dr. Mohler writes, "The secular tides of modernity seek to erode the idea of Christian involvement in the public square. Christian symbols, prayers, and monuments stand in the crosshairs of the secular elites."[51]
- Just recently, the Supreme Court in British Columbia handed down an alarming decision essentially nullifying parental rights over their child and made it criminal for parents even to refer to their child as the gender assigned at birth. The court ordered that a 14-year-old girl receive testosterone injections without parental consent. The court also declared that if either of her parents referred to her using female pronouns or addressed her by her birth name, the parents could be charged with family violence. The judge ruled, "Attempting to persuade [their daughter] to abandon treatment for gender dysphoria, addressing [their daughter] by his birth name, or with female pronouns, *whether to him directly or to third parties* shall be considered to be family violence under Section 38 of the Family Law Act."[52]

Forgive me, but this is insanity. So many issues in our society demand our prayerful attention, church. But, sadly, too many Christians are absent from the pew, out on the lake, indulging themselves, asleep at the wheel, and busy obsessing over their smartphones! God help us.

Before I move on…Let me ask an even more chilling question: what will you do as a follower of Christ when all things Christian become

50 https://albertmohler.com/2019/03/01/scandal-peace-cross-secularists-take-aim-monument/

51 Ibid.

52 https://albertmohler.com/2019/03/04/end-parental-rights-chilling-case-canada/

criminal? What will you do when the courts drive a moral agenda that is in direct contradiction to the clear teaching of Holy Scripture?

I have a sneaking suspicion that a time is about to be upon us when we will see with clarity who is going to be faithful to Christ and His Word, and who is not. It just might be that the church is about to get much smaller in number. Believe me, I hope I'm wrong.

Transition: May we follow the example of the Philadelphia believers and remain faithful to the Word of God.

3rd- The Church Was Faithful to the Work (v. 8)

> Rev 3:8 "'I know your works. Behold, I have set before you an open door, which no one is able to shut. I know that you have but little power, and yet you have kept my word and have not denied my name."

Not only was this church faithful to the Word of God, but also they were faithful to the work of the Gospel.

They acted on the open doors which Christ set in front of them. He knew their works. They were moved to Gospel action because of their affection for Christ. As best as they could, they engaged their surroundings with the Good News of the Gospel. They were on mission with and for God. They were exemplary in their faithfulness to keep at it, to keep showing up, to keep plugging away at their assignment, against whatever the odds. We are to persevere in our Kingdom task as well.

Transition: The Philadelphia church was faithful to the work. One last idea.

Finally- The Church Was to Be Faithful to the Finish (v. 10-12)

> *Rev 3:10 Because you have kept my word about patient endurance, I will keep you from the hour of trial that is coming on the whole world, to try those who dwell on the earth.*
>
> *Rev 3:11 I am coming soon. Hold fast what you have, so that no one may seize your crown.*
>
> *Rev 3:12 The one who conquers, I will make him a pillar in the temple of my God. Never shall he go out of it, and I will write on him the name of my God, and the name of the city of my God, the new Jerusalem, which comes down from my God out of heaven, and my own new name.*

Jesus is very clear in verse 11. He is coming soon. He encourages the church to hold fast what you have. Jesus could come at any moment. His return is imminent. Hold on to Jesus, His Word, stay at your post, hold on, and remain faithful to the finish, for a crown awaits you at your finish line. Oh, the hope and assurance we have in Christ Jesus!

What is not so clear is a portion of verse 10. Give attention to that part which states, "I will keep you from the hour of trial that is coming on the whole world, to try those who dwell on the earth."

This might be our first interpretive challenge. The challenge is how to interpret the Greek verb tereo, which has the sense of "keep," and the Greek preposition ek, --does it mean "out of" or "from"?

The significance is this: Is this a promise that believers will be removed from the world prior to the great tribulation or a promise that believers, while enduring the tribulation, will be kept miraculously by God from the most difficult aspects of that tribulation?[53]

---

53 Paige Patterson. *The New American Commentary: An Exegetical and Theological*

The interpretive dilemma at this point speaks to the issue of the tribulation and when the church will be taken away—pre-tribulation, mid-tribulation, post-tribulation? (I'm choosing to address this issue in greater detail in a future message. I have leaped into the volume of material written to address what is popularly called "the rapture" and will share those findings later.)

So, the present question is: what does the text say? Honestly, what's present in the text does not help us resolve the question on the basis of vocabulary, syntax, or grammar. At best, the text is ambiguous. Frankly, scholarly, sincere interpreters are varied on how to understand this verse. This we can be sure of: Jesus will keep His church through this hour of trial coming on the whole world! This we can also be certain of: He is coming soon!

Important for us is to keep our eyes on Christ as we move to our finish line. There awaits for us a crown who no one can take from us.

Verse 12 concludes with a twofold promise: 1). God will make the one who conquers a pillar in the temple of God. In other words, the believer will be secure—nothing will disrupt or destroy that reality. 2). Christ will write on him the name of God and the name of the city of God.

At the end of Revelation, we will discover that Jerusalem is both a place and a people. The Philadelphians will have citizenship in the heavenly Jerusalem. The new name signifies, as Daniel Akin writes, "identification, character, ownership, and recognition."[54]

So, brothers and sisters—as Jesus examines us corporately and individually, what do you suppose He sees—will He observe a resolve to be faithful:

Exposition of Holy Scripture: Revelation, p. 131.

54 Akin, Kindle Edition, location, 2158.

- To Him
- To His Word
- To His Work
- To the Finish appointed for us
- If so, praise God! If not, what changes need to be made?
- Rev 3:13 He who has an ear, let him hear what the Spirit says to the churches.'

"THE SELF-SATISFIED, SMUG CHURCH"

Revelation 3:14–22, ESV

Today is Senior Recognition Sunday. Congratulations to our seniors and their families in light of reaching a significant milestone—graduating from high school.

Graduates, you are about to turn the page in the story of your life to an exciting new chapter. Your families are about to experience a mixed bag of emotions as you launch from your home into this next phase of your young adult life.

You are about to experience a newfound freedom. You will be away from the watchful eye of your parents. You will not be under your parents' "house rules"—you know, "as long as you live under my roof in my house, you will abide by my rules!" Sound familiar?

Soon, you will be confronted with what you will do regarding your involvement in a local church. You will be leaving, in a sense, the familiar of Field Street Baptist Church. You will decide even if you will attend a local church on the Lord's Day. Some of you will be faithful to a church; some of you will not. Sadly, many young people are leaving the church in droves and finding themselves no longer under the authority, spiritual watchcare, and godly influence of a Christ-centered, Bible-preaching church.

Will you read your Bible regularly?

Will you spend time with God regularly?

Will you spend time in prayer regularly?

Will you get involved with a local church?

So, as you think about what your habit and discipline will be relative to a church away from Field Street Baptist Church, I want to encourage you strongly to avoid a church like the one in Laodicea. I'm not sure there is anything worse than a self-satisfied, smug church.

> *Rev 3:14 "And to the angel of the church in Laodicea write: 'The words of the Amen, the faithful and true witness, the beginning of God's creation.*
>
> *Rev 3:15 "'I know your works: you are neither cold nor hot. Would that you were either cold or hot!*
>
> *Rev 3:16 So, because you are lukewarm, and neither hot nor cold, I will spit you out of my mouth.*
>
> *Rev 3:17 For you say, I am rich, I have prospered, and I need nothing, not realizing that you are wretched, pitiable, poor, blind, and naked.*
>
> *Rev 3:18 I counsel you to buy from me gold refined by fire, so that you may be rich, and white garments so that you may clothe yourself and the shame of your nakedness may not be seen, and salve to anoint your eyes, so that you may see.*
>
> *Rev 3:19 Those whom I love, I reprove and discipline, so be zealous and repent.*
>
> *Rev 3:20 Behold, I stand at the door and knock. If anyone hears my voice and opens the door, I will come in to him and eat with him, and he with me.*
>
> *Rev 3:21 The one who conquers, I will grant him to sit with me on my throne, as I also conquered and sat down with my Father on his throne.*

Rev 3:22 He who has an ear, let him hear what the Spirit says to the churches.'"

As we labor to unpack what Christ says to the church at Laodicea, there are four truths I want to put on your mind:

1. Three Affirmations about Christ (v. 14).
2. Two Key Analyses about Laodicea (v. 15-17).
3. One Critical Prescribed Action (v. 18).
4. An Exceptional Appeal (v. 20-21).

Look with me again at verse 14 and see how Christ identifies Himself. It's astounding.

Rev 3:14 "And to the angel of the church in Laodicea write: 'The words of the Amen, the faithful and true witness, the beginning of God's creation."

Three affirmations you will notice here: Christ is the Amen. Christ is the faithful and true witness. And, Christ is the beginning of God's creation. Now, before we identify what such an identity means, let's back up for a moment and gain some perspective on the context of Laodicea.

Laodicea was about 45 miles southeast of Philadelphia. Laodicea was a pivotal center of trade and communication. Laodicea was a wealthy city; it's wealth derived from the production of a fine quality of famous glossy black wool. The city had considerable banking assets and wealth; so wealthy was Laodicea that after the great earthquake of A.D. 17, which destroyed it, the people refused imperial help in rebuilding the city, choosing rather to do it entirely by themselves.

Laodicea had a famous school of medicine; and a special ointment known as "Phrygian powder," famous for its cure of eye defects.

Zeus was worshiped in this city. It was a city with a people who had learned to compromise and accommodate themselves to the needs and wishes of others.

Most interestingly, there was a six-mile-long aqueduct which brought Laodicea its supply of water from the south. The water came from hot springs and was cooled to lukewarm or came from a cooler source and warmed up in the aqueduct on the way. What's odd is that for all of its wealth, the city had poor water quality.[55]

Jesus identifies Himself as the speaker in verse 14. The word "Amen" means "so be it." In a sense this is an affirmation of that which is certain and binding. This reference alludes to Isaiah 65:16 which says, "Because he who is blessed in the earth will be blessed by the God of truth; and he who swears in the earth will swear by the God of truth…" In other words, all the promises of God are affirmed, guaranteed, and punctuated by the person and work of Jesus Christ.

Furthermore, Christ is the true and faithful witness-the perfect, complete witness to the truth of God. Jesus Himself said, "I am the way, and the truth, and the life; no one comes to the Father but through me" (Jn. 14:6).

Then we have the interesting expression of Jesus as the beginning of God's Creation. It was a popular heresy in Laodicea, as it was in Colosse, that Jesus was a created being. Instead, the testimony of Scripture is that Jesus is originator or initiator of creation; the firstborn of creation, that is to say (and, this is important) the most preeminent, supreme person ever born (Col. 1:15). John MacArthur writes, "As a man, He had a beginning, but as God, He was the beginning."[56]

---

55 Alan F. Johnson. *Revelation: The Expositor's Bible Commentary*, p. 456-457.

56 John MacArthur. MacArthur New Testament Commentary, p. 910.

Transition: Friends, you can't be a part of a church that gets it wrong about Christ. There is no room for tolerance when it comes to the person and work of Jesus Christ. The litmus test for churches/denominations is what it holds dear about Jesus. In each of these seven letters it is crucial to give attention to how Christ identifies Himself to that church. It adds up to give us a biblical sense of who Christ is.

As we move further into the text, you will notice two ANALYSES about the church in Laodicea in v. 15-17.

> *Rev 3:15 "'I know your works: you are neither cold nor hot. Would that you were either cold or hot!*
>
> *Rev 3:16 So, because you are lukewarm, and neither hot nor cold, I will spit you out of my mouth.*
>
> *Rev 3:17 For you say, I am rich, I have prospered, and I need nothing, not realizing that you are wretched, pitiable, poor, blind, and naked.*

Again, as with each of the churches, Christ knows fully, completely, and perfectly the condition of this Laodicean church. He says in verse 15, "I know your works: you are neither cold nor hot. Would that you were either cold or hot!" This is not a compliment or commendation. Their works are lukewarm, consequently, look at verse 16: "So because you are lukewarm, and neither hot nor cold, I will spit you out of my mouth."

Cleverly, this vivid portrayal has long been understood against the local background of the previously mentioned water source that came from the hot springs and was cooled to lukewarm as it made its way to the city, in effect rendering unusable for anything either refreshing or medicinal. Laodicea had dirty, tepid water that flowed for miles through an underground aqueduct. Visitors, unaccustomed to it, immediately spit it out.

In other words, this church was ineffective. Useless. Smug. Complacent. Self-satisfied. Indifferent.

They were not providing refreshment for the spiritually weary, nor healing for the spiritually sick.[57]

Yet, that was not the only analysis—that their works were neither hot nor cold. Notice verse 17: "For you say, I am rich, I have prospered, and I need nothing, not realizing that you are wretched, pitiable, poor, blind, and naked."

The bigger problem was the church was ignorant of their real condition. Sad. It's a heart-wrenching scenario to be ignorant of your own shortcomings and weaknesses.

They thought they were rich in possession and self-sufficient, much like the environment surrounding them.

In a way, the culture had crept into the congregation and had crippled their spiritual life and vitality.

The Lord's assessment must surely have shattered their self-delusion. He calls them to repentance. They were, in reality, wretched, pitiable, poor, blind, and naked. Spiritually, they were destitute and impoverished before the Lord.

Transition: The Lord's analyses were accurate. He therefore prescribes, as the Great Physician, a critical action.

Verse 18 identifies that One Prescribed Critical Action.

Rev 3:18 "I counsel you to buy from me gold refined by fire, so that you may be rich, and white garments

---

57 Robert Mounce. *NICNT: The Book of Revelation*, p. 109.

so that you may clothe yourself and the shame of your nakedness may not be seen, and salve to anoint your eyes, so that you may see."

Do you see the irony? The smug satisfaction of the Laodiceans is refuted with the Lord's prescription of making some purchases in the specific areas in which they thought they had no need.

Since they are poor, they need to buy gold from Christ refined in fire. That is spiritual wealth that has passed through the refiner's fire and has not been found lacking.

They needed white clothes to cover the shame of their nakedness. This is, of course, symbolic of righteousness. You know that nakedness in the biblical worldview is a picture of judgment and humiliation. They needed to acknowledge their shameful condition and clothe themselves with garments of righteousness.

Furthermore, the immediate cause of their many problems was spiritual blindness. Laodicea was known for a famous medical school and exported a widely used eye salve. They needed a spiritual eye salve to anoint their eyes so they could indeed see the truth about themselves. They were blind to their own spiritual bankruptcy and hypocrisy. It was a sad condition, but the prescription would indeed work for verse 19 tells us that "Those whom I love, I reprove and discipline, so be zealous and repent."

That's right. I occasionally hear believers say, "Well, Christ accepts me as I am and what I do, how come you won't? Why doesn't the church accept me for who I am and the choices I make? Why are you judging me?"

It is absolutely true that Christ accepts all of us just the way we are drawn to and come to Him. However, He DOES NOT, I repeat,

DOES NOT leave us in a state of rebellion and sin. He reproves us. He disciplines us. He urges us to repent. That's love, folks! He will not let us stay the same.

The first critical step to making a spiritual recovery is to acknowledge that things are not right and to repent. You must admit to the darkness of your heart. It is self-deluding to know you are not well spiritually, and act as if everything is good, great, fantastic!

Transition: The Savior in His accurate, precise, personal analysis will then offer a critical prescribed action to take.

Finally, Look at the Exceptional Appeal Stated in Verses 20-21.

> *Rev 3:20 Behold, I stand at the door and knock. If anyone hears my voice and opens the door, I will come in to him and eat with him, and he with me.*

> *Rev 3:21 The one who conquers, I will grant him to sit with me on my throne, as I also conquered and sat down with my Father on his throne.*

Verse 20 is so misunderstood by the Christian community. It is typical for us to understand verse 20 as an invitation and promise to the person outside the church. But, it should be noted that in the context of this passage, it speaks to believers, to the self-deluded members of this Laodicean congregation.

Christ was outside knocking on the door. Can you imagine jettisoning the Lord Jesus outside the church whereby He is knocking on the door to be let back inside?

In an act of remarkable humility and condescension, Christ is knocking on the door of His church requesting permission to enter and re-establish fellowship.

This, dear brother and sisters in Christ, IS AN EXCEPTIONAL APPEAL.

Take careful note of the address… "If anyone hears…and opens." The response of Christ is that He will enter and join in table fellowship! I read some time ago that in Oriental lands the sharing of a common meal indicated a strong bond of affection and companionship.[58] Then, in verse 21 we have the Lord's words of assurance to the overcomers, to the conquerors. We will share with Christ's reign in the future, eschatological kingdom.

Ladies and gentlemen, can you imagine? The high privilege and honor to share in the honor of Christ's elevated position. WOW!

> Rev 3:22 He who has an ear, let him hear what the Spirit says to the churches.'"

Concluding the Message & Calling for a Response

Does this text of Scripture pierce your heart? Is there any shred of fear and concern within you that perhaps these verses describe your heart?

I don't want to be a part of a church like this as described in this text. It's a dreadful dynamic to think you are one thing, but in reality you are altogether different.

Does your perception of yourself match the reality of yourself? Or, are you self-aware and recognize this morning your need to repent?

No Christian, no church should be so smug and self-satisfied as to accept a diagnosis of being lukewarm.

58 Mounce, p. 114,

Church, Christ knows our works—we must return to Him—making Him again the first affection of our hearts—we must be faithful, holding fast to the name of Christ—we must let love, faith, service, and patient endurance be what characterizes our fellowship—as we hold steady to the truth of God's Word—repenting of our sin—allowing the Lord to discipline and reprove us—leading to a greater obedience to his Lordship—and seizing upon the doors of opportunities He opens us.

May we never be a church He would want to spit from His mouth!

Rather, let us be found faithful, refined by His fire, clothed in His righteousness, and zealous for His Kingdom to come!

11

"THE SPLENDOR OF THE THRONE OF GOD"

Revelation 4:1-11, ESV

As we approach chapter four in the book of Revelation, what we have here is John's description of the splendor of God the Father and the throne room in heaven.

At the invitation of Jesus Himself, John is permitted to look through a door standing open in heaven to see the THRONE of ALMIGHTY GOD. The description of God's throne is awesome and awe-inducing. The throne of God is the very epicenter of the universe. To be clear, John was not the first mortal who was allowed to look into heaven. Jacob saw a stairway reaching to heaven from where God addressed him. Also Isaiah, Ezekiel, and Daniel were permitted to see God's celestial throne (Isa. 6:1; Ezek. 1:26; Dan. 7:9).[59]

This is John's second vision. His first vision was one of the triumphant Christ and encompassed the letters to the seven churches. This second vision begins in chapter four and concludes with the opening of the seventh seal in Chapter 8, verse 1. Listen closely...

---

59 Simon Kistemaker. *Revelation: New Testament Commentary*, p. 183.

Rev 4:1 After this I looked, and behold, a door standing open in heaven! And the first voice, which I had heard speaking to me like a trumpet, said, "Come up here, and I will show you what must take place after this." 4:2 At once I was in the Spirit, and behold, a throne stood in heaven, with one seated on the throne. Rev 4:3 And he who sat there had the appearance of jasper and carnelian, and around the throne was a rainbow that had the appearance of an emerald. Rev 4:4 Around the throne were twenty-four thrones, and seated on the thrones were twenty-four elders, clothed in white garments, with golden crowns on their heads. Rev 4:5 From the throne came flashes of lightning, and rumblings and peals of thunder, and before the throne were burning seven torches of fire, which are the seven spirits of God, Rev 4:6 and before the throne there was as it were a sea of glass, like crystal. And around the throne, on each side of the throne, are four living creatures, full of eyes in front and behind: Rev 4:7 the first living creature like a lion, the second living creature like an ox, the third living creature with the face of a man, and the fourth living creature like an eagle in flight. Rev 4:8 And the four living creatures, each of them with six wings, are full of eyes all around and within, and day and night they never cease to say, "Holy, holy, holy, is the Lord God Almighty, who was and is and is to come!" Rev 4:9 And whenever the living creatures give glory and honor and thanks to him who is seated on the throne, who lives forever and ever, Rev 4:10 the twenty-four elders fall down before him who is seated on the throne and worship him who lives forever and ever. They cast their crowns before the throne, saying, Rev 4:11 "Worthy are you, our Lord and God, to receive glory and honor and power, for you created all things, and by your will they existed and were created."

As we labor to unpack the meaning of this very special text, it is helpful to work a bit to arrive at what is meant by the phrase, "After these things," or as it is translated in the ESV and the KJV, "After this..."

On the one hand, some interpreters (dispensational in leaning) take the stance that 4:1 symbolizes the rapture of the church [this is the taking or snatching away of the church at the time of the coming of Christ]. They argue that the word "church" now disappears entirely from this book after chapter 3. Simply put, their position would be that 4:1 is a fulfillment of 1 Thessalonians 4:15-17.[60]

Yet, on the other hand there are interpreters who are more cautious and set forth that 4:1 IS NOT a cloaked reference to the rapture of the church. Hence, if you are looking for a pre-tribulation rapture of the church in Scripture, you will not find it here in Revelation 4:1.

So, to be honest with you, there just isn't any textual evidence for the rapture of the church to be found in Revelation 4:1. I will say more about the rapture, the tribulation period, and the millennium in future messages, unless of course, Jesus returns prior!

With that said, we turn our attention to the One who is seated on the throne. Look at verses 2-3:

> *4:2 At once I was in the Spirit, and behold, a throne stood in heaven, with one seated on the throne. Rev 4:3 And he who sat there had the appearance of jasper and carnelian, and around the throne was a rainbow that had the appearance of an emerald.*

In verse 2, John reports that he was in the Spirit, and what first catches his eye is a throne. If there is a word which dominates the landscape of chapter 4, it is the word THRONE. The word "throne" occurs thirteen times in 11 verses. In fact, the word occurs repeatedly in the Apocalypse--in total 37 times.

Chapter 4 describes the throne of God. Thus, the one sitting on the throne is the Sovereign of the universe. John intends to

---

60 Paige Patterson. Revelation: New American Commentary: Revelation, p. 149.

communicate that God is the Supreme Ruler of this universe. He governs everything. God is in full, complete, perfect control.

Folks, how do you dare to describe the One who is sitting on this throne? What we get in verse 3 is a sense of the majesty and beauty of the appearance of God and the throne. Rev 4:3 And He who sat there had the appearance of jasper and carnelian, and around the throne was a rainbow that had the appearance of an emerald. John references three precious stones: jasper, carnelian, and an emerald.

Jasper would be comparable to a diamond and would represent majesty, holiness, and purity.

Carnelian is dark red, orange-red, reddish-brown in color and represents wrath or judgment.[61]

A rainbow with the color of an emerald encircled the throne. An emerald as we know it is green.

John saw the entire rainbow as some shade of green. The rainbow, of course, is an important symbol of God's covenantal sign that He would not destroy the earth again with a flood (Gen. 9:15). Put all of this together and what you arrive at is a vision of God's majesty, beauty, glory, and faithfulness. Really, though, God transcends any human, earthly description in appearance. Scripture reveals God to be awesome, magnificent, glorious, spectacular, and totally reliable in His promises. There is no God like our God!!

Transition: Who's on the throne? God. Look now at verse 4:

> Rev 4:4 Around the throne were twenty-four thrones, and seated on the thrones were twenty-four elders, clothed in white garments, with golden crowns on their heads.

---

61 Daniel Akin. *Revelation: Exalting Jesus in Revelation (Christ-Centered Exposition Commentary*, Kindle Edition, location2477.

In verse 4, John describes who is around the throne of God. Surrounding the throne of God are 24 thrones, and seated on the thrones were 24 elders dressed in white and wearing crowns of gold.

Who are the 24 elders identified in verse 4? Truthfully, the identity of the 24 elders has been widely debated. Some of the options set forth by Greg Beale are:

1. Stars (from an astrological background)
2. Angels
3. OT saints
4. Angelic, heavenly representatives of all saints
5. Patriarchs and apostles representing the OT and NT saints together
6. Representatives of the prophetic revelation of the twenty-four books of the Old Testament[62]

Beale concludes that the 24 elders are angels. Robert Mounce would also suggest that the twenty-four elders are an exalted angelic order (Mounce, Revelation, p. 121). Respectfully, I would disagree for the simple reason that angels are not presented as elders, do not sit on thrones, nor do they wear victors' crowns.

What we do know is that they wear white garments symbolizing purity and wear crowns to indicate victory.

Who are they, though? Perhaps the best means to identifying the 24 elders is to consider their function. What do they do?

Throughout Revelation the elders are pictured as falling down before God in worship (5:14; 11:16; 19:4). Twice one of their number acts as a spokesman or interpreter (5:5; 7:13). On one occasion they

---

62 Greg Beale (primary source) *The Book of Revelation*, p. 322. Secondary source: Paige Patterson, *Revelation*, p. 152.

join the four living creatures in presenting the prayers of the saints to God (5:8). Adoration and praise are continually on their lips (4:11; 5:9-10; 11:17-18; 19:4) [Mounce, Revelation, p. 121].

Transition: With that said, a plausible argument can be made that the 24 elders represent the redeemed saints.

Look now at verse 5: Rev 4:5 "From the throne came flashes of lightning, and rumblings and peals of thunder, and before the throne were burning seven torches of fire, which are the seven spirits of God."

What John sees now is "flashes of lightning, and rumblings and peals of thunder." Appearing four times in Revelation, lightning and thunder are symbolic of incredible strength and power (4:5; 8:5; 11:19; 16;18).

John further sees "before the throne...seven torches of fire, which are the seven spirits of God."

The seven torches represent the abundance of light at God's throne, and of course, the seven spirits are representative of the Holy Spirit's fullness (Kistemaker, p. 188). This is such a prevailing, commanding, muscular scene. Who can contend with the Almighty?

In verses 6-8, dear church, we get a sense of the holiness of God.

> *Rev 4:6 and before the throne there was as it were a sea of glass, like crystal. And around the throne, on each side of the throne, are four living creatures, full of eyes in front and behind: Rev 4:7 the first living creature like a lion, the second living creature like an ox, the third living creature with the face of a man, and the fourth living creature like an eagle in flight. Rev 4:8 And the four living creatures, each of them with six wings, are full of eyes all around and within, and day and night they never*

cease to say, "Holy, holy, holy, is the Lord God Almighty, who was and is and is to come!"

Church, the Lord God is holy. He is separate. He is transcendent. Holiness is the very excellency of the divine nature. He is unstained even by the very shadow of sin.[63] His holiness is manifested in His law, His works, and the cross. One theologian I read stated that God's holiness is His attribute of attributes—meaning it is absolutely critical to labor to understand this particular attribute of God. In other words, to understand God and His "violent" and repulsive response to sin, you must strive to grasp as much as you can about His holiness.

This is an interesting vision. As such, there is no sea in heaven, but the crystal stretches out like a glistening sea.

Then, we are introduced in John's vision to four living creatures. In reference to the phrase "four living creatures," the number four is the numerical symbol for completeness in creation. These are the cherubim, those angels frequently mentioned in the Old Testament in connection with God's presence, power, and holiness.[64]

This imagery is from Ezekiel 1. These are messengers of God. They have eyes in the front and behind, so that nothing escapes their attention. Nothing escapes their scrutiny. In what is obvious, symbolic language in verse 7, we are told of a creature like a lion, a creature like an ox, a creature with the face of man, and a fourth creature like an eagle in flight.

- The likeness to a lion alludes to strength and power.
- The likeness to an ox alludes to the rendering of humble service to God.

63 Arthur Pink. *The Attributes of God*, p. 33.

64 John MacArthur. *MacArthur New Testament Commentary*, p. 913.

- The likeness to man demonstrates they are rational beings.
- The likeness to an eagle in flight means they execute their service to God with the speed of eagles' wings.

Then, verse 8. Rev 4:8 And the four living creatures, each of them with six wings, are full of eyes all around and within, and day and night they never cease to say, "Holy, holy, holy, is the Lord God Almighty, who was and is and is to come!"

The description continues. Each of the four living creatures had six wings, full of eyes, and did not rest. There are clear parallels with the visions of the prophets Isaiah and Ezekiel, except John does not give these beings specific names. These wings provide cover when the angels stand before God, and in flight they provide speed. The reference to their eyes is a reference to verse 6. They do not rest-- they sing praises to God continually. Now, there is no day and night in heaven; John is communicating in terms we would understand in expressing the concept of eternity.

They were saying, "Holy, holy, holy, is the Lord God Almighty, who was and is and is to come!"

Chapter four emphasizes the throne of God and the holiness of God. He is the Lord God Almighty—proclaiming the truth of God's omnipotence. Furthermore, God is timeless and eternal.

Finally, we look at verses 9-11: Rev 4:9 And whenever the living creatures give glory and honor and thanks to him who is seated on the throne, who lives forever and ever, Rev 4:10 the twenty-four elders fall down before him who is seated on the throne and worship him who lives forever and ever. They cast their crowns before the throne, saying, Rev 4:11 "Worthy are you, our Lord and God, to receive glory and honor and power, for you created all things, and by your will they existed and were created."

What we have here, church, is the second hymn of praise sung in heaven by the living creatures supported by the twenty-four elders at worship.

They give glory, honor, and thanks to God. The twenty-four elders fall down before God who is seated on the throne and worship Him who lives forever and ever. Numerous times in Revelation we have record of the twenty-four elders falling before the One seated on the throne to worship Him (5:8, 14; 7:11; 11:16; 19:4).

They also cast their crowns before the throne of God, rendering Him with the highest accolades in heaven and on earth. They had received these crowns from God for being overcomers, but now return them to God to assign to Him all glory and honor.

I want to close by reading verse 11: Rev 4:11 "Worthy are you, our Lord and God, to receive glory and honor and power, for you created all things, and by your will they existed and were created."

God created this universe. The sovereign will of God is the cause of creation. According to Scripture (John 1:1; Col. 1:15-18) Jesus is the agent of creation.

The testimony of Scripture both at the beginning and at the end is that this world did not come into being by evolving on its own, but God exercised His will and power. The Creator has made all things from the smallest particle, atom, and cell to the largest star.

This work of creation gives cause for the elders to render their praise to the Lord God.

By the will of Almighty God, who sits on His indescribable throne, you are here on this earth. You are in the pew in which you are sitting. You are here because it pleased God to put you here—to love Him supremely and to serve Him continually.

What a vision John was given of God and His throne. What is an appropriate response to this chapter in revelation?

I think it is our worship and our awe. I think it is to turn your life over completely to Him. That begins with a relationship with God through His Son, Jesus Christ.

Will you now give your heart to Christ?

Will you now declare the greatness of our God?

"THE INFINITE WORTHINESS OF THE LAMB"

Revelation 5:1-14, ESV

Please open your Bible to the Book of Revelation, Chapter 5, verses 1 through 14.

Chapter five is a continuation of John's vision from chapter four. By way of review, chapter 4 focused on God and His throne; whereas, chapter 5 focuses on God the Son and His infinite worthiness. The objective before us this morning is to consider the infinite worthiness of the Lamb.

> *Rev 5:1 Then I saw in the right hand of him who was seated on the throne a scroll written within and on the back, sealed with seven seals.*
>
> *Rev 5:2 And I saw a mighty angel proclaiming with a loud voice, "Who is worthy to open the scroll and break its seals?"*
>
> *Rev 5:3 And no one in heaven or on earth or under the earth was able to open the scroll or to look into it,*
>
> *Rev 5:4 and I began to weep loudly because no one was found worthy to open the scroll or to look into it.*

Rev 5:5 And one of the elders said to me, "Weep no more; behold, the Lion of the tribe of Judah, the Root of David, has conquered, so that he can open the scroll and its seven seals."

Rev 5:6 And between the throne and the four living creatures and among the elders I saw a Lamb standing, as though it had been slain, with seven horns and with seven eyes, which are the seven spirits of God sent out into all the earth.

Rev 5:7 And he went and took the scroll from the right hand of him who was seated on the throne.

Rev 5:8 And when he had taken the scroll, the four living creatures and the twenty-four elders fell down before the Lamb, each holding a harp, and golden bowls full of incense, which are the prayers of the saints.

Rev 5:9 And they sang a new song, saying, "Worthy are you to take the scroll and to open its seals, for you were slain, and by your blood you ransomed people for God from every tribe and language and people and nation,

Rev 5:10 and you have made them a kingdom and priests to our God, and they shall reign on the earth."

Rev 5:11 Then I looked, and I heard around the throne and the living creatures and the elders the voice of many angels, numbering myriads of myriads and thousands of thousands,

Rev 5:12 saying with a loud voice, "Worthy is the Lamb who was slain, to receive power and wealth and wisdom and might and honor and glory and blessing!"

Rev 5:13 And I heard every creature in heaven and on earth and under the earth and in the sea, and all that is in them, saying, "To him who sits on the throne and to the Lamb be blessing and honor and glory and might forever and ever!"

Rev 5:14 And the four living creatures said, "Amen!" and the elders fell down and worshiped.

As we sink our thinking into this extraordinary text, I think it will be helpful to employ the following headings:

1. The Sacred Scroll (v. 1-4).
2. The Conquering Lion (v. 5).
3. The Slain Lamb (v. 6-8).

The Sacred Scroll (v. 1-4).

This passage of Scripture opens with John informing the reader that he "saw in the right hand of Him who was seated on the throne a scroll written within and on the back, sealed with seven seals" (v. 1).

In chapter 5 the word "scroll" is used eight times. Clearly, this scroll is of unparalleled significance.[65]

From the text, we discover several details about this scroll:

1. It is held in the right hand of God-its author.
2. It is lengthy--written on the inside and on the back.
3. It is sealed with seven seals.
4. Evidently, no one is able, at first, to open the scroll, break its seals, and look into it.

So, the question is: what is written in this sacred scroll? What is the content of this divine scroll? As you might imagine, many answers have been offered. For example, some scholars suggest:

1. a title deed to the earth
2. a last will and testament
3. Ezekiel's lamentation, mourning, and woe (2:9-10)
4. the sealed book of the end time in Daniel 12:4[66]

65 Robert Mounce. *NICNT: The Book of Revelation*, p. 129).

66 Daniel Akin. *Exalting Jesus in Revelation: Christ-Centered Exposition Commen-*

5. Actually and technically, we are not informed of the content of the scroll in this chapter; we have to wait until chapter 6 when the seals are broken and the judgments of God are poured out on the earth.

What do I think? For me, Robert Mounce is helpful here as he writes, "Filled to overflowing and sealed with seven seals to insure the secrecy of its decrees, it contains the full account of what God in his sovereign will has determined as the destiny of the world."[67]

To put it yet another way, Alan Johnson writes, "It contains the announcement of the consummation of all history—how things will ultimately end for all people: judgment for the world and the final reward of the saints. Christ alone, as the Messiah, is the executor of the purposes of God and the heir of the inheritance of the world. He obtained this by his substitutionary and propitiatory death on the cross (5:9)."[68]

Transition: This sacred scroll is so significant indeed, and this leads us to verse 5.

The Conquering Lion (v. 5).

Rev 5:5 And one of the elders said to me, "Weep no more; behold, the Lion of the tribe of Judah, the Root of David, has conquered, so that he can open the scroll and its seven seals."

John is experiencing profound grief "because no one was found worthy to open the scroll and look into it" (v. 4).

tary, Kindle Edition, location 2673.

67 Mounce, p. 129.

68 Alan F. Johnson. *The Expositor's Bible* Commentary: Revelation, p. 467, General Editor: Frank E. Gaebelein.

The consequences of this scroll remaining sealed are catastrophic. For one, God's plan of salvation would not be executed and the human race would be condemned forever!

No human being was found worthy.

No angelic being was found worthy.

Then one of the elders, representative of the redeemed, addresses John. He instructs the apostle to stop his weeping. He instructs John to focus his attention on the Lion of the tribe of Judah, the Root of David, who has conquered. This is good news! The verb here relative to "overcome" or conquered indicates that Jesus is the conqueror over death and hell, the first fruits of the dead, and the King who ascended to heaven and sits at the magisterial right hand of God.

He is the Lion. He is the author of salvation. Remember Jacob's words? The patriarch blessed his twelve sons and singled out Judah as the tribe from which a ruler should come forth.

John calls Jesus "the root of David," which goes back to the prophets' saying that the Messiah will come up from the stump of Jesse and this root or branch of David will rule the peoples (Isa. 11:1, 10; Jer. 23:5; 33:15).

Jesus represents royalty, for these are messianic titles that attest to His royal, regal status.[69]

As a descendant of David (Matt. 22:41-45) Jesus is human, and as Messiah He is divine.

He is worthy because of His role as mediator, and He is able because of His divinity. He is the God-man. He is the incomparable, supreme, sinless Christ. Transition: Only Christ is worthy to open the scroll and its seven seals as the Conquering Lion. Not only is Christ

---

69 Kistemaker, p. 205.

depicted as the conquering Lion, but also as…

The Slain Lamb (v. 6-8).

> *Rev 5:6 And between the throne and the four living creatures and among the elders I saw a Lamb standing, as though it had been slain, with seven horns and with seven eyes, which are the seven spirits of God sent out into all the earth.*
>
> *Rev 5:7 And he went and took the scroll from the right hand of him who was seated on the throne.*
>
> *Rev 5:8 And when he had taken the scroll, the four living creatures and the twenty-four elders fell down before the Lamb, each holding a harp, and golden bowls full of incense, which are the prayers of the saints.*

The focus here is on the Lamb. What an image and contrast—from the Lion of Judah to the Slain Lamb. Of course, what comes to mind immediately is The Lamb is the symbol of the lamb slain for the Passover feast of the Israelites. You recall that the blood of the lamb had to be placed on the sides and top of the doorframes of their Hebrews' homes, so that the angel of death would "pass over" the Israelites and spare the lives of the firstborn (Exod. 12:1-13).

Also, the Lamb is symbolized in the lamb that was led to slaughter and stricken for the sins of His people (Isa. 53:7-8). Furthermore, John the Baptist twice identifies Jesus as the Lamb of God.

In John's vision, the Lamb was standing as though it had been slain—signifying a body brutally, fatally wounded, but was now healed and able to stand. The marks of the Lord's wounds are evidently still visible. Christ stands slain, yet triumphant, victorious!

Notice the threefold reference to the number 7—seven horns, seven eyes, and the seven spirits of God.

This emphasizes the symbol of completeness, perfection with respect to the Lamb. The horn symbolizes might, and with His power Jesus as King of kings promotes and exemplifies righteousness and justice.

With seven horns he possesses all authority to rule in heaven and on earth (Matt. 28:18; John 17:2).

Again, with seven eyes—perfect eyesight—He is able to observe all that happens in the universe; nothing escapes His notice. Because of His complete vision, he has perfect knowledge, discernment, and understanding.

John explains the significance of the seven eyes in the text. They are the seven spirits of God commissioned by Christ. The seven spirits refers to the Holy Spirit. Both the Father and the Son commission the Spirit to go forth into all the earth.

In verse 7 we are told that the Lamb came and took the scroll out of the right hand of Him who was seated on the throne. The right hand is interesting.

Did you know that the right hand in oriental culture signifies success, while the left hand denotes something sinister?[70]

The one and only person in the entire universe who is infinitely worthy to take the scroll from the hand of God is the Lamb. And, when He does, the four living creatures and the twenty-four elders fall down before the Lamb and worship.

They acknowledge His worship-worthiness. They are overjoyed that the contents of the scroll will soon be revealed. Each elder possesses a harp which accompanies their singing.

You will note that John provides an explanation as to the "golden bowls of incense." He states that these are "the prayers of the saints."

---

70 Kistemaker, p. 208.

The explanation for this could be taken from the Old Testament. In one of his Psalms, David prays to God and says, "May my prayer be set before you like incense" (Ps. 141:2.)

I would like to point out four statements regarding the Slain Lamb from this text.

The Slain Lamb is Worthy to Open the Scroll (v. 9).

> *Rev 5:9 And they sang a new song, saying, "Worthy are you to take the scroll and to open its seals, for you were slain, and by your blood you ransomed people for God from every tribe and language and people and nation...*

This is the first of three hymns that exalt the Lamb for His redemptive work on the cross. These twenty-eight voices sing a new song. This new song extols the Lamb of God who has accomplished His redemptive task.

Christ is worthy of a new song. The singers rejoice in the redemption of God's people through the substitutionary atonement of Jesus Christ. He is worthy of the highest praise. And only Jesus is worthy to take the scroll and open its seals. Why?

The Slain Lamb is Worthy to Ransom His People for God (v. 9).

> *Rev 5:9 ...for you were slain, and by your blood you ransomed people for God from every tribe and language and people and nation,*

This Lamb is worthy because He willingly, voluntarily, obediently laid down His life and purchased with His blood people for

God from every tribe, language, people, and nation. The selfless Christ paid for the sins of His people and set them free. He satisfied the justice of God, removed the curse, reconciled the world to God, and restored His people to fellowship with the Father.

Christ's death was not random.

His death was not an unavoidable tragedy.

Peter once stated, "Men of Israel, listen to these words: Jesus the Nazarene, a man attested to you by God with miracles and wonders and signs which God performed through Him in your midst, just as you yourselves know—this Man, delivered over by the predetermined plan and foreknowledge of God, you nailed to a cross by the hands of godless men and put Him to death. But God raised Him up again, putting an end to the agony of death, since it was impossible for Him to be held in its power" (Acts 2:22-24, NASB).

The phrase "from every tribe and language and people and nation," occurs frequently in Revelation. Simon Kistemaker suggests that this is an all-encompassing idiom (p. 211). In other words, Jesus calls His followers from every possible place on the face of this earth, and makes them a kingdom and priests to God, and they shall reign on the earth (v. 10).

The Slain Lamb is Worthy to Receive Adulation (v. 11-13).

> *Rev 5:11 Then I looked, and I heard around the throne and the living creatures and the elders the voice of many angels, numbering myriads of myriads and thousands of thousands,*
>
> *Rev 5:12 saying with a loud voice, "Worthy is the Lamb who was slain, to receive power and wealth and wisdom and might and honor and glory and blessing!"*

> *Rev 5:13 And I heard every creature in heaven and on earth and under the earth and in the sea, and all that is in them, saying, "To him who sits on the throne and to the Lamb be blessing and honor and glory and might forever and ever!"*

John observes countless angels surrounding the throne of God. He also observed the four living creatures and the elders around the throne. This specific wording is derived from Daniel 7:10. What were they doing?

Together, they said with a loud voice, "Worthy is the Lamb who was slain, to receive power and wealth and wisdom and might and honor and glory and blessing!" (v. 12)

The angels learn from the redeemed about the mystery of salvation and redemption. They rejoice when one sinner repents. They serve the saints. They, too, stand in wonder and awe at the redeeming love of God in Christ Jesus. In verse 12 we have a listing of seven intrinsic qualities which belong to God, but are now ascribed to the Lamb: power, wealth, wisdom, might, honor, glory, and blessing.

In verse 13, we have the rest of God's created beings, the totality of God's creatures join in the chorus of extoling praises to God the Father and to the Lamb. Nothing seems to be left out of this chorus of adulation.

This is an overwhelming chorus of praise, and defies human imagination. As God receives the adulation from His creatures, so does the Lamb, for He has accomplished the work God assigned to Him…He is the Lamb of infinite worth!

Finally, note verse 14: Rev 5:14 And the four living creatures said, "Amen!" and the elders fell down and worshiped.

Those closest to the throne utter, "So be it!" Theirs is the concluding act of praise and adoration.

The writer of the Apocalypse is now ready to record the breaking of the seals and the opening of the scroll, and reveal what is happening on the earth.

Jesus Christ is the Son of God, the Lion of Judah, the Lamb of God, the mediator between God and man, the one in whom we must place our faith to be saved. He is the infinitely worthy Lamb.

Perhaps you are asking this morning, "What must I do to be saved? What must I do to be numbered among the redeemed?"

The answer is simple: "Believe in the Lord Jesus, and you will be saved."

To do so, means to bow your knee to the infinitely worthy Lamb of God. It means to surrender your heart, your will to Christ. It means to give Him control of your life. It means to seek His forgiveness and cry out to Him for salvation.

When God's Spirit draws you to Christ and you experience the new birth, all the angels in heaven rejoice over your repentance.

The day God saved me there was a celebration in the hallowed halls of heaven. What about you? Have you come to a place where you recognize your greatest need for the Savior?

May today be that day! Oh, give your heart to the Lamb!

13

"THE GREAT TRIBULATION"

Matthew 24; Mark 13; Revelation 7:14

Before pressing ahead into chapter 6 of Revelation, it seems prudent to take a moment and define a "complex of events"[71] known as the great tribulation.

With certainty, the Bible sets forth that Christ is coming again. The Lord Himself promises that He will come again. Matthew 24:30 states, "Then will appear the sign of the Son of Man in heaven. And then all the peoples of the earth will mourn when they see the Son of Man coming on the clouds of heaven, with power and great glory." Additionally, the apostles make it abundantly clear that the first coming [His incarnation] will be followed by a second coming [His coronation] (Phil. 3:20; Titus 2:13; 2 Thess. 1:7, 10).

Bible scholars and theologians alike set forth that Christ's coming will be:

1. Personal- Jesus is the one triumphantly returning.
2. Physical- Jesus will return in body.
3. Visible- Not invisible, but clearly seen, obvious.
4. Sudden- Unexpected, people will be surprised.

---

71 Millard Erickson. *Introducing Christian Doctrine*, 3rd edition, p. 461.

5. Glorious and triumphant-in His glorified body clothed in royal apparel.[72]

That Christ is coming again is biblically indisputable. The Lord's promised return is the Christian's blessed hope.

An essential question to consider, then, is: what must take place "before" the Lord returns?

Interestingly, the disciples posed a similar inquiry: "Tell us, when will these things be, and what will be the sign of your coming and of the end of the age?" (Matt. 24:3).

Let me attempt to summarize briefly what Scripture teaches:

The Preaching of the Gospel to All Nations–Particularly, the Calling of Gentiles.

> "And the Good News about the Kingdom will be preached throughout the whole world, so that all nations will hear it; and then, finally, the end will come" (Matthew 24:14, NLT).

The Conversion of God's Elect among Israel. Thus, with the fullness of Gentiles will come also the fullness of Jews.

> "I want you to understand this mystery, dear brothers and sisters, so that you will not feel proud and start bragging. Some of the Jews have hard hearts, but this will last only until the complete number of Gentiles comes to Christ" (Romans 11:24-25, NLT).

---

72 Louis Berkhoff. *Systematic Theology*, Kindle Edition, p. 682.

The Great Apostasy and the Great Tribulation.

> *"For then there will be a great tribulation, such as has not occurred since the beginning of the world until now, nor ever will. Unless those days had been cut short, no life would have been saved; but for the sake of the elect those days will be cut short" (Matthew 24:21-22, NASB).*

> *"For that will be a time of greater horror than anything the world has ever seen or will ever see again. In fact, unless that time of calamity is shortened, the entire human race will be destroyed. But it will be shortened for the sake of God's chosen ones" (Matt. 24:21-22, NLT).*

The Revelation of Antichrist, the Lawless One.

> *"Don't be fooled by what they say. For that day will not come until there is a great rebellion against God and the man of lawlessness is revealed—the one who brings destruction. He will exalt himself and defy every god there is and tear down every object of adoration and worship. He will position himself in the temple of God, claiming that he himself is God" (2 Thess. 2:3-4, NLT).*

Signs and Wonders by False Christs and Prophets.

> *"Then if anyone says to you, 'Behold, here is the Christ,' or 'There He is,' do not believe him. For false Christs and false prophets will arise and will show great signs and wonders so as to mislead, if possible, even the elect" (Matthew 24:23-24, NASB).*

Unusual Natural Phenomena.

> *"Immediately after those horrible days end, the sun*
> *will be darkened, the moon will not give light, the stars*
> *will fall from the sky, and the powers of heaven will be*
> *shaken" (Matthew 24:29, NLT).*[73]

For a few moments I want to give due focus and emphasis upon what is commonly identified in Scripture as THE GREAT TRIBULATION. Our objective is to identify and address a couple of vital questions and answer them from the text of Sacred Scripture.

Our primary text for consideration is Matthew 24. In fact, chapters 24 and 25 in Matthew's Gospel are known as Jesus' Olivet Discourse. Why? Because Jesus "sat on the Mount of Olives" [v.3] when He spoke these words. Addressed to His disciples, it is intended to give them a prophetic overview of the events to take place in both the near and remote future. In this chapter Jesus addresses the subject of the Parousia, which means, "presence, or the coming."

The first and seemingly most obvious question to ask is, "What is the Great Tribulation?"

> *"For then there will be a great tribulation, such as has*
> *not occurred since the beginning of the world until now,*
> *nor ever will. Unless those days had been cut short, no*
> *life would have been saved; but for the sake of the elect*
> *those days will be cut short" (Matthew 24:21-22, NASB).*

The word tribulation in Scripture translates from the Greek word thlipsis.

73 Wayne Grudem. *Christian Beliefs: 20 Basics Every Christian Should Know*, p. 121.

The verb form means, "to press," "to press hard upon," from which we have the ideas of oppression, distress, and affliction.

The NASB uses eight different words to translate thlipsis: affliction, afflictions, anguish, distress, persecution, tribulation, tribulations, and trouble.

Biblically, the word thlipsis is used in two significant ways:

1. A time of suffering or affliction taking place any time in the existence of the church until Christ returns.
2. An unparalleled, unprecedented time of suffering under the Antichrist's persecution on God's people, beginning when the Antichrist commits the Abomination of Desolation, which is the image of the Antichrist being set up in the last days (predicted by Daniel) to when the elect of God are gathered.[74]

Transition: The latter use of the word is what is in view here in Matthew 24:21 and in Revelation 7:14.

The second and very significant, vigorously debated question to ask is, "Will Christ Return Before or After the Great Tribulation?"

A related question would be: "Will there be a SEPARATE coming of Christ to remove the church [referred to as the rapture] from the world prior to the GREAT TRIBULATION or will the CHURCH go through the tribulation and be united with the Lord only afterward?

There are those who believe that Christ will actually return twice: once in a secret return for His church when Christ suddenly takes

---

74 https://www.gotquestions.org/abomination-desolation.html

Christians out of the world and then seven years later in a second, public return, He will bring back Christians with Him to earth to reign with Him for the thousand years mentioned in Revelation 20:4-5.

This position and view is widely held and very popular. It is called pretribulationism or it is the pretribulational premillennial view.[75]

By definition, then, pretribulationism is the view that Christ will take the church to Himself BEFORE, PRIOR to the tribulation event.

Posttribulationism is the view that Christ will remove the church AFTER the tribulation.

And, a mediating position is the midtribulational view, which holds that the church will go through the less severe portion of the tribulation (usually the first half, or 3 ½ years), but then will be removed from the world.[76]

For sure Jesus is crystal clear in Matthew 24 that the great tribulation will be one of the indicators of His impending coming and of the end of the world.

So, how do we make some reasonable sense of the issue? What does the Bible say? Which view seems to garner the most support from the Scripture? Respectfully, I want to remind you that my only hermeneutical, exegetical objective is to investigate what the Scripture says. You are free to disagree with my eschatology. One's eschatological viewpoint is not a litmus test of fellowship. We can and do disagree on matters pertaining to the end times. My aim has been to labor in the biblical text—to go where the text leads. I have sought

---

75 Grudem, p. 126-27.

76 Erickson, p. 461-466.

to set aside my own presuppositions and preconceived ideas. I have made a choice to set aside what my favorite theologians, pastors, and authors say about these matters while examining the issues for myself. I would ask you to do the same. Let's strive to go where the Bible takes us.

First, there is no evidence in Scripture for a twofold coming of Christ.[77]

I am aware that there are some who might reject this idea, and they might base their argument on 1 Thessalonians 4:15-17 which says, "15For this we say to you by the word of the Lord, that we who are alive and remain until the coming of the Lord, will not precede those who have fallen asleep. 16For the Lord Himself will descend from heaven with a shout, with the voice of the archangel and with the trumpet of God, and the dead in Christ will rise first. 17Then we who are alive and remain will be caught up together with them in the clouds to meet the Lord in the air, and so we shall always be with the Lord."

There are those (Dispensationalists) whose opinion would be that this "coming for His saints" is followed by an interval of seven years, during which the world is evangelized, the great tribulation occurs, the Antichrist, or man of lawlessness is revealed, and then there is another coming of the Lord Jesus Christ with His saints, in which He comes down to earth, judges the nations, and ushers in the millennial kingdom.

This position would necessitate two distinct comings—one secret and one public. With respect, the difficulty with this view

---

77 Berkhoff, Kindle Edition, p. 676.

is that it is just not warranted by Scripture. It's difficult to find any Scriptures that indicate a "secret" return of Christ. The passages which speak of the Lord's return, always speak of it in very visible, public, can't miss it, terms! 1 Thessalonians 4:15-17 would be indicative of the public nature of Christ's return.

With that said, posttribulationists have a different understanding of Paul's reference in 1 Thessalonians 4:17 to those meeting the Lord in the air. The pretribulationist maintains that this event is the rapture; or Christ coming secretly for the church, catching believers up with Him in the clouds and taking them to heaven until the end of the tribulation.

However, some posttribulationists look at the usage of the Greek term (apantesis) translated "to meet" somewhat differently.

There are only two undisputed occurrences of this word in the New Testament. One of these references is in the parable of the wise and foolish virgins, an explicitly eschatological parable.

When the bridegroom comes, the announcement is made, "Here's the bridegroom! Come out to meet [apantesis] him!" (Matt. 25:6). What does the word mean in this context? The virgins do not go out to meet the bridegroom and then depart with him. Rather, they go out to meet and then accompany him back to the wedding banquet.

On the basis of this syntax and usage an argument could be made that the word apantesis suggests a welcoming party that goes out to meet someone on the way and accompanies them back from where they came. So our meeting the Lord in the air is not a case of being caught away, but of meeting Him and then immediately coming with Him to earth as part of His triumphant entourage. It is the church, not the Lord, that will turn around at the meeting.[78]

Furthermore, the Bible does not promise believers an exemption from adversities, but rather an enablement to endure and overcome them.

Scripture makes clear that believers will experience tribulation. (Matthew 24:9, 21, 29; Mark 13:19, 24; Rev. 7:14).

General tribulation has been the experience of the church throughout history!

Jesus said, "In this world you will have trouble" (John 16:33). Other text references would include: Acts 14:22; Romans 5:3; 1 Thess. 3:3; 1 John 2:18, 22; 4:3; and   2 John 7.

Posttribulationists draw a distinction between tribulation in general and the great tribulation in that the difference is one of degree or severity only, not of kind.

As you are likely deducing by now, posttribulationists set forth that the church WILL be present during and will experience the great tribulation.

Look at Matthew 24:29-31: "But immediately after the tribulation of those days the sun will be darkened, and the moon will not give its light, and the stars will fall from the sky, and the powers of the heavens will be shaken. And then the sign of the Son of Man will appear in the sky, and then all the tribes of the earth will mourn, and they will see the Son of the Man coming on the clouds of the sky with power and great glory. And He will send forth His angels with a great trumpet and they will gather together His elect from the four winds, from one end of the sky to the other."

Additionally, note again at Matthew 24:21-22: "For then there will be a great tribulation, such as has not occurred since the beginning

---

78 Erickson, p. 465. Primary source, George Ladd, *Blessed Hope*, p. 58-59.

of the world until now, nor ever will. Unless those days had been cut short, no life would have been saved; but for the sake of the elect those days will be cut short."

The term "elect" in Matthew 24, which means "chosen" should be understood in light of its usage elsewhere in the Bible, where it refers to "believers." Since Pentecost, the term "elect" has denoted the church.

Thus, the Lord will preserve the church during, but not spare it from, the tribulation.[79]

The Bible seems to indicate that believers will likely go through the great tribulation, which is distinguished by posttribulationists from the wrath of God.

The wrath of God is spoken of in Scripture as coming on the wicked, "whoever rejects the Son will not see life, for God's wrath remains on them" (John 3:36).

Believers will not experience the wrath of God—"we shall be saved from God's wrath through [Christ]" (Rom. 5:9; 1 Thess. 1:10; 5:9).

As I think about it, it does seem that a twofold coming of Christ is not plausible. I find Louis Berkhoff helpful here. He writes: "The distinction between a twofold gospel and a twofold second coming of the Lord is an untenable one. The gospel of the grace of God in Jesus Christ is the only gospel that saves and that gives entrance to the Kingdom of God. And it is absolutely contrary to the history of revelation, that a reversal to Old Testament conditions, including the absence of the Church and of the indwelling Holy Spirit, should be more effective than the preaching of the gospel of the grace of God

---

79 Erickson, p. 464.

in Jesus Christ and the gift of the Holy Spirit."[80] Wow! it seems, too, that a case can be made scripturally for any of the three tribulation positions.

**Put humbly, the tally of biblical support and evidence seems to favor and lean toward posttribulationism.

Now, I recognize that all of you have read the "Left Behind" series are collectively moaning! I get it. I prefer to be raptured out of here before the tribulation. The pretribulation position sells a lot of books! It would be hard to sell a book favoring posttribulationism.

Yet, I'm not selling a book. I'm preaching a gospel of repentance and faith in Jesus Christ.

Maybe the late Dan Crawford of Africa summed it up in a helpful and humorous way when he was distinguishing between the poets and the Bible. The poet says: "Cheer up! The best is yet to be!" The Bible says, "Cheer up! The worst is yet come!" The cheer for Christ-followers is not in earthly circumstances because Christ has overcome the world!

The Scripture says, "Therefore, we ourselves speak proudly of you among the churches of God for your perseverance and faith in the midst of all your persecutions and afflictions which you endure. This is a plain indication of God's righteous judgment so that you will be considered worthy of the Kingdom of God, for which indeed you are suffering" (2 Thess. 1:4-5, NASB).

Jesus said, "These things I have spoken to you, so that in Me you may have peace. In the world you have tribulation, but take courage; I have overcome the world" (John 16:33).

Do you have peace with God? You may only have such peace with God through faith in Christ.

---

80 Berkhoff, Kindle Edition, p. 674.

Do you want an easy way out? Most people do. Are you prepared to endure? Persevere? Remain faithful? Resolved? Will you be an overcomer?

Are you ready for the days which are ahead? If you do not know Christ, you are not ready? If you know Christ, then know that His peace and presence will sustain you when the time of tribulation presses in on all sides!

Let's pray.

14

"THE FOUR HORSEMEN"

Revelation 6:1-8, ESV

Open your Bibles please to the book of Revelation, chapter 6, as we look closely at verses 1-8.

By way of synopsis, in these verses the Lamb opens four of the seven seals on the scroll taken from the right hand of the Almighty.

With each seal undone, a horse and a rider are unleashed.

The four horsemen introduce us to the first of God's three series of judgments in Revelation: the SEAL judgments in chapter 6; the TRUMPET judgments in chapters 8 and 9, and the BOWL judgments in chapters 15 and 16.

Daniel Akin writes, "The Four Horsemen of the Apocalypse are the first harbingers of this judgment that is unparalleled in human history (Matt. 24:21)."[81]

Each horse is of a different color, and each color is highly symbolic. Each rider carries out a different judgment of God.

The horse colors are:

- A white horse
- A red horse

---

81 Daniel Akin. *Exalting Jesus in Revelation: Christ-Centered Exposition Commentary*, Kindle Edition, Location 2847.

- A black horse
- A pale horse

Let's examine this text more closely. We begin by reading Revelation 6:1-8:

> *Rev 6:1 Now I watched when the Lamb opened one of the seven seals, and I heard one of the four living creatures say with a voice like thunder, "Come!"*
>
> *Rev 6:2 And I looked, and behold, a white horse! And its rider had a bow, and a crown was given to him, and he came out conquering, and to conquer.*
>
> *Rev 6:3 When he opened the second seal, I heard the second living creature say, "Come!"*
>
> *Rev 6:4 And out came another horse, bright red. Its rider was permitted to take peace from the earth, so that people should slay one another, and he was given a great sword.*
>
> *Rev 6:5 When he opened the third seal, I heard the third living creature say, "Come!" And I looked, and behold, a black horse! And its rider had a pair of scales in his hand.*
>
> *Rev 6:6 And I heard what seemed to be a voice in the midst of the four living creatures, saying, "A quart of wheat for a denarius, and three quarts of barley for a denarius, and do not harm the oil and wine!"*
>
> *Rev 6:7 When he opened the fourth seal, I heard the voice of the fourth living creature say, "Come!"*
>
> *Rev 6:8 And I looked, and behold, a pale horse! And its rider's name was Death, and Hades followed him. And they were given authority over a fourth of the earth, to kill with sword and with famine and with pestilence and by wild beasts of the earth.*

You recall that in chapter 5 only Christ was the one found worthy to open the scroll. As Christ breaks the seven seals that secure the scroll, each seal unleashed a new demonstration of God's judgment on the earth in the future Tribulation period. By breaking the seals and opening the scroll, the Lamb inaugurates God's plan and reveals what must take place in the times before and at His coming.

The structure of this text focuses on the four horses and the riders upon each horse.

1. The WHITE horse (v. 1-2).
2. The RED horse (v. 3-4).
3. The BLACK horse (v. 5-6).
4. The PALE horse (v. 7-8).

The White Horse (v. 2)

> *Rev 6:1 Now I watched when the Lamb opened one of the seven seals, and I heard one of the four living creatures say with a voice like thunder, "Come!"*
>
> *Rev 6:2 And I looked, and behold, a white horse! And its rider had a bow, and a crown was given to him, and he came out conquering, and to conquer.*

John is still looking into heaven. He is watching the Lamb open one of the seven seals, and one of the four creatures says with a voice like thunder, "Come!" (v. 1).

No doubt this called everyone to attention. John beholds the summons of a white horse and its rider.

The question now before us is: Who is the rider on this white horse? First, let's identify what we can know for certain from the text. This rider holds a bow, is given a victor's crown, and rides out with the intent to conquer.

Beyond that, the opinions are all over the proverbial map: 1). Jesus Christ, 2). The advance of the gospel, 3). The Antichrist, 4). The spirit of conquest, 5). Government persecuting Christians 6). Satan's servants in general.[82]

John MacArthur writes, "The four horses and their riders do not represent specific individuals, but forces."[83]

Alan F. Johnson proved most helpful to me in resolving the issue. He boils it down to two interpretive options. Does the rider on the white horse represent Christ and the victory of the gospel or does he represent the Antichrist and the forces of evil?[84]

Another commentator argues that the answer is found in the context.[85] Therefore, the evidence of the text tends to lean toward the identity of the rider being the Antichrist and his forces that seek to conquer the followers of Christ. This makes some sense when you consider the parallelism with the other three horses, which are instruments of divine judgment.

Additionally, the parallels with the Olivet Discourse show that the first events mentioned are the rise of "false Christs and false prophets" (Matt. 24:24).

It is likely NOT Christ. Well, you say what about chapter 19. Chapters 6 and 19 show that the two riders have little in common beyond the fact that they are both mounted on white horses.[86]

Transition: No doubt this rider will be used of God to reveal that which is true and that which is false, the real from the inauthentic.

82 Akin, location 2883, Kindle Edition.

83 John MacArthur. *MacArthur New Testament Commentary*, p. 914.

84 Alan F. Johnson. *The Expositor's Bible Commentary, Volume 12, Hebrews-Revelation*, General Editor: Frank E. Gaebelein, p. 473.

85 Paige Patterson. *The New American Commentary: Revelation*, 179.

86 Robert Mounce. *The New International Commentary on the New Testament: The Book of Revelation*, revised, p. 142.

The Red Horse (v. 3-4)

> *Rev 6:3 When he opened the second seal, I heard the second living creature say, "Come!"*
>
> *Rev 6:4 And out came another horse, bright red. Its rider was permitted to take peace from the earth, so that people should slay one another, and he was given a great sword.*

The Lamb now opens the second seal, and the second living creature summons, in accordance with Christ's sovereign command, the next apocalyptic rider to come forth.

Out comes a fiery, bright red horse. The rider on this horse was given a great sword.

- His mission: to take peace from the earth.
- His mission: anarchy.
- His mission: slaughter and bloodshed.
- His mission: to allow people to turn their destructive instincts upon one another.
- His mission: to personify evil which will oppose God, God's Word, and God's people.

Wherever this evil rides, peace will disappear.

Jesus said in Matthew 24:10, "And many will turn away from me and betray and hate each other."

Transition: This rider and his horse symbolize bloodshed and anarchy.

The Black Horse (v. 5-6)

> *Rev 6:5 When he opened the third seal, I heard the third living creature say, "Come!" And I looked, and behold, a black horse! And its rider had a pair of scales in his hand.*
>
> *Rev 6:6 And I heard what seemed to be a voice in the midst of the four living creatures, saying, "A quart of wheat for a denarius, and three quarts of barley for a denarius, and do not harm the oil and wine!"*

At the command of Christ, there comes forth a black horse whose rider is holding a pair of scales in his hand.

Most commonly, the black horse and rider are interpreted to be symbolic of famine. Famine is implied by the balance and the exorbitant prices.

What we have here is somewhat of a logical progression: you have conquest, war, and now famine.

These three realities tend to show up together.

Apparently, there was a voice from the center of the throne room which announces famine prices for wheat and barley, and warns against harming oil and wine.

As you may recall, a denarius was a Roman silver coin equivalent to the daily wage of a working man (Matthew 20:2).

In essence, for a day's work a man could buy only enough wheat for himself or enough of the less nutritious barley for three. The price appears to be ten to twelve times what it should have been.[87]

Barley was the poor man's wheat, and it was normally fed to animals. It was low in nutritional value and occasionally mixed with wheat to increase the feeding amount.

---

87 Mounce, p. 144.

The phrase "do not harm the oil and wine" is seen as setting a limit to the deprivation caused by the horse of famine. Food will be scarce and in short supply.

Transition: The black horse and its rider will usher in a severe famine. Common staples of the food supply will become luxuries that will have to be carefully protected.

The Pale Horse (v. 7-8)

Rev 6:7 When he opened the fourth seal, I heard the voice of the fourth living creature say, "Come!"

Rev 6:8 And I looked, and behold, a pale horse! And its rider's name was Death, and Hades followed him. And they were given authority over a fourth of the earth, to kill with sword and with famine and with pestilence and by wild beasts of the earth.

This fourth horse, a pale horse, is mounted by a rider named Death, and Hades follows after him. Spooky!

Oddly, this is the only rider who is named. His name is Death. His companion is Hades.

Hades is the place where the souls of unbelievers are kept, while the souls of believers are and will be with Jesus in heaven (1:18).

This horse is the color of a corpse. Notice that power and authority are given them to kill twenty-five percent of the earth's population. Let me repeat: together, Death and Hades bring about the death of one-fourth of humankind. This is dreadful and will be devastating.

The four specific methods in which they kill are the four dreadful judgments referenced in Ezekiel 14:21—sword, famine, pestilence, and wild beasts.

Can you imagine how the first recipients of the Apocalypse heard these words?

They constantly faced death by sword, starvation, disease, and they knew the reality of death by wild beasts.

They lived constantly in the shadow of death. Roman power and corruption constantly threatened their existence.

Furthermore, throughout history the extermination of large numbers of the human race has been attributed to warfare, hunger, and disease.

The bubonic plague of the 14th century killed 26 million people in Europe.

During World War II, 20 million people in Europe lost their lives, as did an equal number in Asia.

With that said, the severity of eliminating human life from a fourth part of the earth refers to a future catastrophic event and is a dire warning of God's coming judgment.

By way of summary—four horses and four riders are called forth by the voices of four living creatures. These horses are white, red, black, and pale. Their riders are the Antichrist and his evil forces and deceptions, one permitted to remove peace from the earth, one who symbolizes the effects of famine, and one who is named Death followed by his companion, Hades.

How concerned should we be? On the one hand, the short answer is, "Very." I mean look around you this morning. This house of worship is not full. People are preoccupied with the affairs of this life. A lot of people could really care less about Christ and the condition of their souls.

Jesus was spot-on accurate long ago when He said, "However, no one knows the day or the hour when these things will happen, not even the angels in heaven or the Son Himself. Only the Father knows. When the Son of Man returns, it will be like it was in Noah's day. In those days before the Flood, the people were enjoying banquets and parties and weddings right up to the time Noah entered the boat. People didn't realize what was going to happen until the Flood came and swept them all away. THAT IS THE WAY IT WILL BE WHEN THE SON OF MAN COMES" (Matthew 24:36-39, NLT).

Too busy, too distracted, too glued to the need to be constantly entertained, too glued to your smart phone, too dependent on this world, too much in debt, too much chasing after the "American Dream" to even consider the real and present jeopardy which lurks around the corner. SCARY!

On the other hand, if you are in Christ Jesus and He is your Savior and Lord, then it is a great comfort that every horse and horsemen mentioned in this text is under the full, sovereign command of a just and holy Christ and God! Yes, scary times are ahead, but what an encouragement it is to know that God is going to judge evil. God is going to judge the ungodly. God is going to judge the rebellious and wicked. God is going to settle accounts.

So, you have to think about how you view Revelation 6:1-8. Are you scared? Are you comforted?

If you are unsaved, if you are in your sins without the Savior, you should be rightly terrified.

If you are saved, if your sins have been forgiven, your sin debt paid and cancelled by King Jesus, then your heart should be filled with hope. Let's pray.

"SOVEREIGN LORD-HOW LONG?"

Revelation 6:9-17, NLT

In the sermon text before us this morning, the Lamb [JESUS CHRIST] opens the fifth and sixth seals. In verses 1-8 of chapter six, we read of the wrath of God. In these verses, 9-17, we read of what sounds like a total contradiction, which is "the wrath of the Lamb" (6:16).

This Lamb, in judgment, pours out His wrath and fury on a sinful, unrepentant, rebellious humanity that has defiantly rejected His gracious offers of forgiveness, grace, and salvation.

It may be that this angle of the Bible's portrayal of Christ makes us uncomfortable. We have been conditioned to think only of Him as loving, meek, gentle, compassionate, patting little kids on the head, whistling with the birds, smiling all the time. Yet, while it is true that Christ is compassionate, meek, gentle, humble in heart, and the most loving man to ever walk the face of this earth, it is also accurate that the Bible portrays Jesus as a man who twice, in righteous anger, cleansed the temple (Matt. 21:12-17; John 2:13-22), angrily condemned the hypocrisy of the scribes and Pharisees (Matt. 23:13-36), even calling them "a brood of vipers," and said more about the eternal fire and judgment of hell than anyone else in Sacred Scripture. Thus, to have a balanced view of Jesus portrayed in the Bible, we must strive to hold in tension His love and His holiness, His compassion and justice, His grace and righteousness, and His mercy and wrath.[88]

Further, we are given a glimpse in this text as to what or who is under the altar of the throne in heaven. In verse 10, we have the question this group of people poses to the Lord. In a sense, it has the gravity of a question that is one for the ages. It's a substantive question.

God's response is recorded in verse 11. In verses 12-14, John witnesses certain signs heralding the final day of the Lord, so often alluded to and described in the Word of God. Finally, in verses 15-17, John describes a palpable terror experienced on the earth.

Let's examine this text more closely. We begin by reading Revelation 6:9-17:

> *9And when the Lamb broke the fifth seal, I saw under the altar the souls of all who had been martyred for the Word of God and for being faithful in their witness.*
>
> *10They called loudly to the Lord and said, "O Sovereign Lord, holy and true, how long will it be before you judge the people who belong to this world for what they have done to us? When will you avenge our blood against these people?"*
>
> *11Then a white robe was given to each of them. And they were told to rest a little longer until the full number of their brothers and sisters—their fellow servants of Jesus—had been martyred.*
>
> *12I watched as the Lamb broke the sixth seal, and there was a great earthquake. The sun became as dark as black cloth, and the moon became as red as blood.*

---

88 Daniel Akin. *Exalting Jesus in Revelation (Christ-Centered Exposition)*, Kindle Edition, location 3039.

13Then the stars of the sky fell to the earth like green figs falling from trees shaken by mighty winds.

14And the sky was rolled up like a scroll and taken away. And all of the mountains and all of the islands disappeared.

15Then the kings of the earth, the rulers, the generals, the wealthy people, the people with great power, and every slave and every free person—all hid themselves in the caves and among the rocks of the mountains.

16And they cried to the mountains and rocks, "Fall on us and hide us from the face of the one who sits on the throne and from the wrath of the Lamb.

17For the great day of their wrath has come, and who will be able to survive?"

To guide us in making our way through this amazing text, I want to organize our thinking in this way:

1. The cry (v. 10)
2. The cause (v. 9)
3. The costliness (v. 9)
4. The cosmos (v. 12-14).
5. The consequence (v. 15-17)

The CRY (v. 10)

10They called loudly to the Lord and said, "O Sovereign Lord, holy and true, how long will it be before you judge the people who belong to this world for what they have done to us? When will you avenge our blood against these people?"

The plural pronoun "they" refers back to those who are under the altar in verse 9. This is the altar of incense.

The identities of those under the altar in verse 9 are, according to the text, "those who had been slain, or martyred for the Word of God and for being faithful in their witness."

Paige Patterson states that the fifth seal, then, is the martyr's seal.[89]

Thus the Lamb opens the fifth seal and the scroll reveals an altar, together with souls who have been slain under that altar.

Now, it is a bit of a challenge to identify these martyrs. Who are they? Are they those who represent all those who are martyred during the entire history of the church or even all the dead saints of God? It would seem that based on context, the best explanation would be that the martyrs here are those who were killed during the tribulation period. Of course, it could also be those who gave their lives in faithfulness to God and the Gospel.

THEY CRY OUT TO THE LORD in verse 10. "O Sovereign Lord, holy and true, how long will it be before you judge the people who belong to this world for what they have done to us? When will you avenge our blood against these people?" Wow!

This is plain and simple a call for vengeance. How do we reconcile such a cry with teaching in Scripture that would instruct us to resist the urge to seek revenge and to avoid the desire to retaliate? These saints are practicing Romans 12:19.

Romans 12:19 states, "Do not take revenge, my friends, but leave room for God's wrath, for it is written: 'It is mine to avenge, I will repay,' says the Lord."

This cry sounds more like an imprecatory Psalm we would find in the Old Testament. An imprecatory Psalm contains curses or prayers for the punishment of the Psalmist's enemies (Ps. 7, 35,

89 Paige Patterson. *Revelation: The New American Commentary*, p. 182.

55, 58, 59). A Psalm of this nature would contain prayers for God's judgment to fall down on the psalmist's enemies.

Though we are forbidden to take revenge, we trust that God will vindicate His elect by punishing those who killed them. Their question is one of timing. They are assured of God's reckoning, retribution, and punishment. "O Sovereign Lord, how long…?"

Verse 11 informs us, by the way, that these martyrs were each given a white robe, as evidence of their righteousness, purity, and victory before the Judge. And, they are told to wait a little while longer until the full number of their brothers and sisters—their fellow servants of Jesus—had been martyred.

Application/Transition: Have you ever found yourself crying out to God in this fashion? How long, O Sovereign Lord before you judge the wicked, the rebellious, the perpetrators of such vile evil, those who slaughter your people…how long, indeed?

The CAUSE (v. 9)

> 9And when the Lamb broke the fifth seal, I saw under the altar the souls of all who had been martyred for the Word of God and for being faithful in their witness.

What was the cause for those who had been martyred? Why were these saints martyred?

The reason for their loss of life is clearly set forth in verse 9: the Word of God and the testimony they had faithfully maintained. In other words for their commitment to declare the Gospel and live the Gospel, they paid with their lives.

One man I read wrote this, and brothers and sisters, this will be difficult to hear: "Every believer in Christ ought to be prepared for martyrdom; for Christians…cannot express their priestly communion with their Lord more perfectly than when they accept the suffering and glory of martyrdom."[90]

Application:

Let's be really honest here for a moment: many modern, western Christians think they are doing God a favor when they manage to show up for church one out of four Sundays. They'll never miss a football game, soccer game, or gymnastics meet, but Sunday morning church is optional. Many modern Christians can't show up to church on time, but rarely are late for work, a hair appointment, or a movie. Instead of Sunday being the Lord's Day, for far too many, Sunday is a day to sleep in, relax, and recover from the demands of a busy week.

Many Christians think they have made enormous sacrifices for the Lord by giving Him a "tip" of their income. They pat themselves on the back when the throw a few dollars in the offering plate.

There's no denial of self; only the indulging of self.

Many Christians are annoyed with minor inconveniences when it comes to their "experience" with Christ.

Pastors are encouraged to accommodate to the whims of varying generations to "remain relevant." Simply loving Jesus and the Word of God are no longer enough to get people to participate in the life of the church. So, when we read in the Bible about those killed because of their commitment to the Word of God and living for Christ as a faithful witness, I might as well be speaking a foreign language in the western United States.

---

90 Alan F. Johnson. *Revelation: The Expositor's Bible Commentary*, Frank E. Gaebelein, General Editor, p. 475.

We can't even be inconvenienced, much less give our lives in martyrdom for the cause of Christ. All of us, we should surely be ashamed. My friend, you better inquire of yourself? What cause has captured your heart? Is it Christ? Is it anything and everything else? There are those who have and will give their lives for King Jesus. Incredibly, it is a precious fraternity.

The COSTLINESS (v. 9)

> *9And when the Lamb broke the fifth seal, I saw under the altar the souls of all who had been martyred for the Word of God and for being faithful in their witness.*

Not only was there a cause to which these martyrs were committed, but that commitment was costly. What did their commitment to the Word of God and their faithful witness cost them? THEIR VERY LIVES.

I simply ask: what does your commitment to Jesus and His Kingdom cost you?

What do you give up to follow Jesus?

What do you go without to follow Jesus?

What comforts do you forsake to follow Jesus?

What do you deny yourself to follow Jesus?

Illustration: Did you know?

> *Fifty-six men signed the Declaration of Independence. Their conviction resulted in untold sufferings for themselves and their families. Of the 56 men, five were captured by the British and tortured before they died. Twelve had their homes ransacked and burned. Two lost their sons in the Revolutionary Army. Another had two sons captured. Nine of the fifty-six fought and died*

*from wounds or hardships of the war. Carter Braxton
of Virginia, a wealthy planter and trader, saw his
ships sunk by the British navy. He sold his home and
properties to pay his debts and died in poverty.*

*At the battle of Yorktown, the British General
Cornwallis had taken over Thomas Nelson's home
for his headquarters. Nelson quietly ordered General
George Washington to open fire on the Nelson home.
The home was destroyed and Nelson died bankrupt.
John Hart was driven from his wife's bedside as she was
dying. Their thirteen children fled for their lives. His
fields and mill were destroyed. For over a year, he lived
in forest and caves, returning home only to find his wife
dead and his children vanished. A few weeks later, he
died from exhaustion.[91]*

Transition: I can assure you that if you give yourself to the cause of Christ, it is going to cost you something—time, money, effort, a few friends, ridicule, being misunderstood, and so forth. King David once said, "I will not sacrifice to the Lord my God burnt offerings that cost me nothing" (2 Samuel 24:24).

The COSMOS (v. 12-14)

*12 I watched as the Lamb broke the sixth seal, and there
was a great earthquake. The sun became as dark as
black cloth, and the moon became as red as blood.*

*13 Then the stars of the sky fell to the earth like green
figs falling from trees shaken by mighty winds.*

*14 And the sky was rolled up like a scroll and taken
away. And all of the mountains and all of the islands
disappeared.*

91 http://www.sermonillustrations.com/a-z/s/sacrifice.htm

In verse 12 the sixth seal is broken by the Lamb. This is the seal of the Day of the Lord when judgment falls on the unbelieving. Under the sovereign control and direction of Christ, what happens next is cosmic upheaval. Now, to be certain, some very fine, well-educated Bible scholars view these judgments as symbolic, say of political and social upheaval.

Yet, the Bible repeatedly indicates that such happenings will take place when our Lord draws history to a close (Isa. 13:9-10; Joel 2:10-11; 2:28-32; 3:14-16; Matt. 24:29-30; Mk. 13:24-37; Lk. 21:25-28).

A violent earthquake occurs. Earthquakes often accompany a divine visitation in Scripture.

The cosmic upheaval also impairs the light of the sun so that it is darkened like a dark cloth made from goat's hair and worn in times of mourning.

The moon is affected and appears like the deep, red color of blood.

Furthermore, stars fall from the sky to the earth. The word translated "stars" simply refers to any celestial body, large or small, having the appearance of a star.[92]

Verse 14 is difficult to understand, but whatever this describes we can only speculate. Make no mistake, though, there is a total cosmic meltdown.

The CONSEQUENCE (v. 15-17)

15 Then the kings of the earth, the rulers, the generals, the wealthy people, the people with great power, and every slave and every free person—all hid themselves in the caves and among the rocks of the mountains.

---

92 Akin, Kindle Edition, location 3134.

16 And they cried to the mountains and rocks, "Fall on us and hide us from the face of the one who sits on the throne and from the wrath of the Lamb.

17 For the great day of their wrath has come, and who will be able to survive?"

The nature of God's judgment is comprehensive. No one will escape. No one will be excluded or secluded. Those who get special treatment and status here on earth will get none. On this dreadful day all worldly status and privilege will matter not an iota.

Every king, every authority, every person of power, the wealthy, the poor, the slave and free will all have business with the righteous Lamb on that day. No one gets a pass. All must give account. There will be no place to hide. You would think that all of these phenomena would drive people to repentance. But, it doesn't. Tragically, there is no repentance, no sorrow, and no brokenness over sin.

Faced with the dread of God's judgment, people plead for death. Look at verse 16. People plead for the mountains and rocks to fall in on them and hide them from God and from the Lamb.

Consequently, people would foolishly rather die than repent and have a saving relationship with the One who was slaughtered on their behalf. There will be no place to hide, no place to run. You cannot escape the Omnipotent one.

Finally, verse 17 informs us that the great day of wrath has come.

The question in verse 10 was, "Sovereign Lord, how long…"

The question in verse 17 is, "Who will be able to survive or who can stand?" That is another question for the ages. Who can stand? What will you experience? Forgiveness or condemnation?

16

"FROM EVERY NATION"

Revelation 7:1–17, NASB

---

1 After this I saw four angels standing at the four corners of the earth, holding back the four winds of the earth, so that no wind would blow on the earth or on the sea or on any tree.

2 And I saw another angel ascending from the rising of the sun, having the seal of the living God; and he cried out with a loud voice to the four angels to whom it was granted to harm the earth and the sea,

3 saying, "Do not harm the earth or the sea or the trees until we have sealed the bond-servants of our God on their foreheads."

4 And I heard the number of those who were sealed, one hundred and forty-four thousand sealed from every tribe of the sons of Israel:

5 From the tribe of Judah, twelve thousand were sealed, from the tribe of Reuben twelve thousand, from the tribe of Gad twelve thousand,

6 from the tribe of Asher twelve thousand, from the tribe of Naphtali twelve thousand, from the tribe of Manasseh twelve thousand,

7 from the tribe of Simeon twelve thousand, from the tribe of Levi twelve thousand, from the tribe of Issachar twelve thousand,

8 *from the tribe of Zebulun twelve thousand, from the tribe of Joseph twelve thousand, from the tribe of Benjamin, twelve thousand were sealed.*

9 *After these things I looked, and behold, a great multitude which no one could count, from every nation and all tribes and peoples and tongues, standing before the throne and before the Lamb, clothed in white robes, and palm branches were in their hands;*

10 *and they cry out with a loud voice, saying,*

"Salvation to our God who sits on the throne, and to the Lamb."

11 *And all the angels were standing around the throne and around the elders and the four living creatures; and they fell on their faces before the throne and worshiped God,*

12 *saying, "Amen, blessing and glory and wisdom and thanksgiving and honor and power and might, be to our God forever and ever. Amen."*

13 *Then one of the elders answered, saying to me, "These who are clothed in the white robes, who are they, and where have they come from?"*

14 *I said to him, "My lord, you know." And he said to me, "These are the ones who come out of the great tribulation, and they have washed their robes and made them white in the blood of the Lamb.*

15 *"For this reason, they are before the throne of God; and they serve Him day and night in His temple; and He who sits on the throne will spread His tabernacle over them.*

16 *"They will hunger no longer, nor thirst anymore; nor will the sun beat down on them, nor any heat;*

17 *for the Lamb in the center of the throne will be their shepherd, and will guide them to springs of the bwater of life; and God will wipe every tear from their eyes."*[93]

93 *New American Standard Bible: 1995 update.* (1995). (Re 7:1–17). La Habra, CA: The Lockman Foundation.

As you recall, chapter six ended with the question: "...for the great day of their wrath has come, and WHO CAN STAND?" (Rev. 6:17)

In chapter 7, John provides the definitive answer: the 144,000 and a great multitude FROM EVERY NATION.

Let's pray. Ah, just kidding. Oh, how I wish it was that simple to understand chapter seven. This chapter has been the subject of vigorous discussion, interpretation, and disagreement.

For instance...

Who are the 144,000 referenced in verse 4?

1. Are these the 144,000 Jehovah's Witnesses who will reign in heaven?
2. Are these selected Sabbatarians who honor and worship on the seventh day of the week?
3. Does this number represent the church as the "new Israel" and thus the redeemed of all the ages symbolically?
4. Or, are they Jewish believers who are saved and sealed for service during what John calls "the great tribulation" (7:14) and "the great day of Their wrath" (6:17)?[94]

Trust me, the opinions among Bible scholars vary and the arguments are reasonable and solid for a variety of interpretive positions. Commentators are all over the map in their understanding of this chapter. So, to be dogmatic here would be unhelpful and foolish.

What one can conclude definitively is that both Jew and Gentile alike will be gathered around the throne of the Lamb in heaven. How marvelous! How wonderful!

94 Daniel Akin. *Exalting Jesus in Revelation (Christ-Centered Exposition Commentary*, Kindle Edition, location 3222.

Verse 9 makes this abundantly clear:

> *9 After these things I looked, and behold, a great multitude which no one could count, from every nation and all tribes and peoples and tongues, standing before the throne and before the Lamb, clothed in white robes, and palm branches were in their hands;*

In function, Revelation 7 serves as somewhat of an interlude between the sixth and seventh seals. As you can easily observe, there are two visions in this chapter; one in verses 1-8 and another in verses 9-17.

With that said, let's take a moment and review. In chapter 6 the Lamb begins to unfold the eschatological scroll introduced in chapter 5. Christ breaks six of the seven seals, and we are introduced to the Four Horsemen of the Apocalypse.

Massive destruction sweeps across the earth, martyred saints in heaven cry for out for justice, and those on the earth seek to hide from Him who is seated on the throne (God the Father) and from the Lamb (God the Son; 6:16).

It would appear that no one will survive, much less stand against the righteous wrath of God. Yet, in verses 1-3, we see the Lord showing mercy.

> *1 After this I saw four angels standing at the four corners of the earth, holding back the four winds of the earth, so that no wind would blow on the earth or on the sea or on any tree.*
>
> *2 And I saw another angel ascending from the rising of the sun, having the seal of the living God; and he cried out with a loud voice to the four angels to whom it was granted to harm the earth and the sea,*
>
> *3 saying, "Do not harm the earth or the sea or the trees until we have sealed the bond-servants of our God on their foreheads."*

In verse 1, the "four angels standing at the four corners of the earth," imply the four directional points on a compass. They are reported to be holding back the four winds of judgment which have the power to "to harm the earth and sea" (v. 2), "the earth or the sea or the trees" (v. 3).

Clearly, they are agents of judgment and destruction, ready to act. Yet, you will notice their hand of judgment is delayed...until... the bond-servants of God have received His seal.

This seal has its roots in the Old Testament (Ezekiel 9:4), and is a sign, a promise of divine possession and protection.[95] The seal indicates ownership.

The mark on the forehead of God's servants stands in direct contrast to the later marking on the right hand and foreheads on the followers of the "beast out of the earth" in chapter 13:16-17.

Now, in verse 4-8, we have the application of God's seal upon the 144,000 "from every tribe of the sons of Israel."

> 4 And I heard the number of those who were sealed, one hundred and forty-four thousand sealed from every tribe of the sons of Israel:

Then, in verses 5-8, an actual cataloguing of twelve tribes: Judah, Reuben, Gad, Asher, Naphtali, Manasseh, Simeon, Levi, Issachar, Zebulun, Joseph, and Benjamin.

12,000 from 12 tribes each. So, what you have in essence is 12 times 12 times a thousand. The number 12 in Revelation always refers to that which is perfect.

Now, this listing poses a few interpretive difficulties. For instance, Simon Kistemaker points out that the twelve tribes listed here differ considerably from those recorded elsewhere in the Old Testament.[96]

---

95 Akin, Kindle Edition, location 3247.

96 Simon Kistemaker. New Testament Commentary: Revelation, p. 250.

Furthermore there are other peculiarities with this text—like--why is Judah listed first? Why is Levi included? How do you explain the absence of the tribes of Dan and Ephraim?

There are some very plausible explanations addressing these peculiarities.

- There are some 19 different arrangements of the names of the tribes in the Old Testament, and this list is different from all of them.
- Judah is listed first because the Messiah, our Lord Jesus, comes from the tribe of Judah (Gen. 49:9-10; Rev. 5:5).
- Levi, though not allotted a portion of land, is rightly involved in this sealing for security and service.
- Ephraim is replaced by Joseph possibly because of its history of idolatry and its alliance with the enemies of Judah (Isa. 7:2,5).
- Dan is omitted, replaced by Levi, because of its practice of gross idolatry. They were the first to perpetrate the sin of apostasy.[97]

What all of this demonstrates is God's faithfulness. He maintains His covenant promises to His people.

Again, on the one hand, there are commentators who understand the 144,000 to be the church, the whole perfect number of the people of God. Put succinctly, the term Israel in verse 4 represents God's people (Kistemaker, p. 250).

On the other hand, there are commentators who are convinced that 144,000 sons of Israel represent Jewish believers who are included in the one people of God and the great multitude of verse 9 (Akin, location 3255).

What is to be understood without ambiguity is this: God has sealed us with the Holy Spirit and He maintains His covenant promises to His people. We are saved, safe, and secure in Christ Jesus!

---

97 Akin, Kindle Edition, location 3281.

Transition: Turn your attention now to the second vision in this chapter, verses 9-12.

> *9 After these things I looked, and behold, a great multitude which no one could count, from every nation and all tribes and peoples and tongues, standing before the throne and before the Lamb, clothed in white robes, and palm branches were in their hands;*
>
> *10 and they cry out with a loud voice, saying,*
>
> *"Salvation to our God who sits on the throne, and to the Lamb."*
>
> *11 And all the angels were standing around the throne and around the elders and the four living creatures; and they fell on their faces before the throne and worshiped God,*
>
> *12 saying, "Amen, blessing and glory and wisdom and thanksgiving and honor and power and might, be to our God forever and ever. Amen."*

This vision is in heaven and concerns "a great multitude which no one could count" (v. 9).

Notice the scope of God's salvation…it is GLOBAL. John sees a multitude no one could count, from every nation, tribe, people, and language. I love this image. In this massive sea of the redeemed, there is not a hint, not a smidgeon of bigotry, ethnocentrism, prejudice, socioeconomics, politicism, or racism. NONE!

I read that the IMB estimates that there are some 11,243 people groups in the world, and think about this, they will all be represented in the heavenly throng.

Some estimates indicate that there are still 3.7 billion people who have not had an adequate opportunity to hear the Gospel, yet the

Lamb is reaching out and calling them unto Himself by the Spirit, the Word, and through His people![98] Oh, one day, church, in the halls of heaven gathered around the throne of Holy God, the nations will rejoice and the nations will worship!

Four things are mentioned regarding these people in heaven:

1. Their location- they stand before the throne of God and the before the Lamb.
2. Their clothing-they are clothed in white robes, robes of victory and purity-they stand before God in the imputed righteousness of King Jesus!
3. Their instruments of worship- they have palm branches of joy and celebration.
4. Their confession-they cry out continually with a loud voice, "Salvation belongs to our God who sits on the throne, and to the Lamb!"

Also standing around the throne of God are the angels, the elders, and the four living creatures. They fell on their faces before the throne and worshiped God.

They say, "Amen! Blessing and glory and wisdom and thanksgiving and honor and power might be to our God forever and ever! Amen." The focus is one object: "to our God forever and ever."

In verse 13 you will notice that one of the elders addresses John, saying, "Who are these, clothed in white robes, and from where have they come?" John responds by saying, "Sir, you know." The elder answered, "These are the ones coming out of the great tribulation. They have washed their robes and made them white in the blood of the Lamb" (v. 14).

---

98 Akin, Kindle edition, location 3297.

The key here seems to be the definite article "the." Thus, the reference here specifically is the great tribulation associated with that final series of woes which immediately precedes the coming of Christ. Jesus speaks of this great tribulation in the Olivet Discourse, found in Matthew 24-25.

What is most intriguing is that they have washed their robes and made them white in the blood of the Lamb.

Corrie Ten Boom said of the cleansing and redeeming blood of the Lord Jesus, "The blood of Jesus Christ has great power! There is perhaps not a phrase in the Bible that is so full of secret truth as is 'the blood of Jesus.' It is the secret of His incarnation, when Jesus took on flesh and blood; the secret of His obedience unto death, when He gave His life at the cross of Calvary; the secret of His love that went beyond all understanding when He bought us with His blood; the secret enemy of and secret of our salvation (Quoted in Simcox, "The Greatest Sacrifice," 14-15).[99]

In verse 15, we are assured of God's presence with us forever.

> 15 *"For this reason, they are before the throne of God; and they serve Him day and night in His temple; and He who sits on the throne will spread His tabernacle over them.*

Not only His presence, but His protection are we promised in verse 15.

Verse 16 declares that God will meet our needs.

> 16 *"They will hunger no longer, nor thirst anymore; nor will the sun beat down on them, nor any heat;*

---

99 Akin, Kindle Edition, location 3367.

While hunger and thirst threaten much of the world's population today and in the past, not so in heaven. Starvation, thirst, and the brutal heat of the sun will have no place in heaven. Every need will be met by the Lamb who is, as we see in verse 17, our Shepherd.

> *17 for the Lamb in the center of the throne will be their shepherd, and will guide them to springs of the bwater of life; and God will wipe every tear from their eyes.* "[100]

The Lord is a Lamb, a Lion, and a Shepherd. He is the Good Shepherd who "will wipe away every tear from their eyes."

EVERYONE needs a shepherd of their soul. 1 Peter 2:25 says, "For you were like sheep going astray, but now you have returned to the Shepherd and Overseer of your souls."

Will you be among the redeemed? Have you turned from your sin and put your faith in Christ as Savior?

Who are you telling about Jesus? How are you moving the conversations of life to matters of the spiritual?

From every nation the redeemed of Christ will come. We do have a story to tell to the nations. May God renew our passion to make Him known by what we say and how we live!

---

100 *New American Standard Bible: 1995 update.* (1995). (Re 7:1–17). La Habra, CA: The Lockman Foundation.

17

"THE BOOK OF LIFE"

Revelation 13:8; 17:8, 3:5, ESV

This morning our objective is to investigate what the Scripture teaches about "The Book of Life."

Our investigation of this matter will include an examination of the most relevant Scripture verses.

Along the way, our survey of the related Scriptures will assist us in answering several VERY IMPORTANT questions. Questions such as…

1. What is the Book of Life?
2. Whose names are in the Book of Life?
3. When are those names placed in the Book of Life?
4. What is the fate of those whose names are not found in the Book of Life?
5. How can you be sure that your name is written in the Book of Life?

What is the Book of Life?

In the Old Testament the "Book of Life" was a register of the citizens of the theocratic community of Israel. To have one's name written in the book of life implied the privilege of participation in the temporal blessings of the theocracy, while to be erased or blotted out of this book, meant exclusion from those blessings. In other words, this book had reference to the rights of citizenship for the Jewish people (Ex. 32:32; Ps. 69:28; Isa. 4:3).[101]

There are eight references in the New Testament to the "book of life," and two of them refer specifically to the book of life that belongs to the Lamb, Jesus Christ.

It should be noted that the "book of life" and the "Lamb's book of life" in the NT are one and the same.

The Holman Bible Dictionary defines the "Book of Life" as:

> *"The heavenly record (Luke 10:20; Hebrews 12:23)
> written by God before the foundation of the world
> (Revelation 13:8; 17:8) containing the names of those
> who are destined, because of God's grace and their
> faithfulness, to participate in God's heavenly kingdom.
> Those whose names are in the book have been born into
> God's family through Jesus Christ (Heb. 12:12; Rev.
> 13:8); remain faithful in worship of God (Rev. 13:8;
> 17:8); are untouched by the practice of abomination
> and falsehood (Rev. 21:27); are faithful through
> tribulation (Rev. 3:5); and are fellow workers in the wok
> of Jesus Christ (Phil. 4:3). The book of life will be used
> along with the books of judgment at the final judgment
> to separate the righteous and the wicked for their
> respective eternal destinies (Rev. 20:12,15; 21:27).[102]*

Put simply, the Book of Life is the roll of those who are saved, those born again, regenerated by the Holy Spirit.

The Book of Life is the roll of those who have repented of their sin and put their faith in Jesus Christ alone for salvation. In essence,

---

101 https://www.crosswalk.com/faith/bible-study/10-things-to-know-about-the-lamb-s-book-of-life.html

102 Holman Bible Dictionary. General Editor: Trent C. Butler, 1991, p. 204-05.

by establishing what the Book of Life is, one also identifies whose names are written in it.

Whose Names Are in the Book of Life?

That's simple. To re-state and to be crystal clear, the answer is: the Book of Life is the roll of those who are saved, those born again, regenerated by the Holy Spirit.

The Book of Life is the roll of those who have repented of their sin and put their faith in Jesus Christ alone for salvation. The names in the Book of Life are the redeemed of God. Also, look at Philippians 4:3. Paul writes, "Yes, I ask you also, true companion, help these women, who have labored side by side with me in the gospel together with Clement and the rest of my fellow workers, whose names are in the book of life." (ESV) This identifies the book of life as a record of the names of those who have eternal salvation.

Transition: Thus far, I am assuming there is nothing problematic with the answers to the questions: what is the book of life and whose names are in the book of life. Yet, now it gets a bit more dicey, challenging, and sobering. Let's consider the next key question.

When Are Those Names Placed in the Book of Life?

Open your Bibles to the book of Revelation, chapter 13, verse 8. I want to read from three translations.

> *"All who dwell on the earth will worship him, everyone whose name has not been written from the foundation of the world in the book of life of the Lamb who has been slain." (Rev. 13:8, NASB)*

> *"Rev 13:8 and all who dwell on earth will worship it,*
> *everyone whose name has not been written before the*
> *foundation of the world in the book of life of the Lamb*
> *who was slain." (Rev. 13:8, ESV)*

> *"All inhabitants of the earth will worship the beast—all*
> *whose names have not been written in the book of life*
> *belonging to the Lamb that was slain from the creation*
> *of the world." (Rev. 13:8, NIV)*

I just read three different translations of this verse. Each transla-tion is distinct. In context, John is identifying that those whose names are not written in the book of life will worship the beast spoken of in chapter 13. I think the NASB and ESV are the more accurate translations of this verse. Yet, the word order is interesting because it does create the possibility for two understandings.

First, it might mean the names were written in the book of life before the foundation of the world.

Second, it could mean that the Lamb was slaughtered from the foundation of the world.

Simon Kistemaker's thoughts are valuable here. "How do we interpret these words? Should the phrase 'from the foundation of the world' be taken with 'slain' or 'written'?[103]

Therefore, you have to look elsewhere in Scripture to gain inter-pretive clarification.

Open your Bible to Revelation 17:8. This verse provides some assistance in understanding Revelation 13:8.

> *"Rev 17:8 The beast that you saw was, and is not,*
> *and is about to rise from the bottomless pit and go to*
> *destruction. And the dwellers on earth whose names*
> *have not been written in the book of life from the*

---

103 Simon J. Kistemaker. *New Testament Commentary: Revelation*, p. 384.

*foundation of the world will marvel to see the beast,
because it was and is not and is to come." (ESV)*

Here John omits the reference to the slain Lamb and thus indicates that God's elect were chosen in eternity AND they are eternally secure. God never blots a name from the Book of Life. Jesus makes this clear in Revelation 3:5.

Essentially, predestination simply identifies the point prior to time when God sovereignly determined that He would elect. In other words, election is the actual choice. Predestination simply identifies this as something that happened preliminary to time, in eternity past, "before the foundation of the world."

Yes, I recognize that election provokes controversy among the redeemed. Yet, the Bible does not shy away from the doctrine of election. Honestly, if you are going to be biblical in your theology, you must have some working doctrine of election and predestination, because the Bible—not Augustine, Martin Luther, or John Calvin—introduces the concept. In fact R.C. Sproul argues "that there is nothing in Calvin's doctrine of predestination that was not first in Luther's, and there is nothing in Luther's doctrine of predestination that was not first in Augustine's and Augustine's doctrine of predestination that was not first in Paul's. This doctrine has its roots not in the theologians of church history but in the Bible, which sets it forth explicitly."[104]

Paul also testifies that God chose His people in Christ before the creation of the world in Ephesians 1:4:

> *"Eph 1:4 even as he chose us in him before the
> foundation of the world, that we should be holy and
> blameless before him. In love Eph 1:5 He predestined
> us for adoption as sons through Jesus Christ, according*

---

104 R.C. Sproul. *Everyone's a Theologian*, Kindle Edition, page 222.

to the purpose of his will, Eph 1:6 to the praise of his glorious grace, with which he has blessed us in the Beloved. Eph 1:7 In him we have redemption through his blood, the forgiveness of our trespasses, according to the riches of his grace, Eph 1:8 which he lavished upon us, in all wisdom and insight Eph 1:9 making known to us the mystery of his will, according to his purpose, which he set forth in Christ." (ESV)

Yet, it should be carefully noted that God chose Christ for the task of redeeming His people before the world was created. 1 Peter 1:19-21 states, "Pet 1:19 but with the precious blood of Christ, like that of a lamb without blemish or spot. 1Pet 1:20 He was foreknown before the foundation of the world but was made manifest in the last times for the sake of you 1Pet 1:21 who through him are believers in God, who raised him from the dead and gave him glory, so that your faith and hope are in God." (ESV)

Listen to what Luke writes in Acts 2:23-24: "Acts 2:23 this Jesus, delivered up according to the definite plan and foreknowledge of God, you crucified and killed by the hands of lawless men. Acts 2:24 God raised him up, loosing the pangs of death, because it was not possible for him to be held by it." (ESV)

Transition: When are the names written in the book of life? According to the Scripture, the names are written in the book from before the foundation of the world.

What is the Fate of Those Whose Names Are Not Found in the Book of Life?

Please find Revelation 20:15. This verse states, "And if anyone's name was not found written in the book of life, he was thrown into the lake of fire." (ESV)

In the context of verse 15, this is from a passage which describes the final judgment of the unsaved, beginning in verse 11 of chapter 20.

The One seated on the GREAT WHITE THRONE is Jesus, the righteous judge. Those judged at this judgment are the UNSAVED dead of all ages, which would logically and textually speaking would be those whose names were not found written in the book of life.

According to Scripture, the FATE of those whose names are not found in the Book of Life is stated clearly in verses 14 and 15: "Then Death and Hades were thrown into the lake of fire. This is the second death, the lake of fire. 15 And if anyone's name was not found written in the book of life, he was thrown into the lake of fire." (ESV)

The Bible teaches that the resurrection of the unsaved dead to judgment will be a physical resurrection, whereupon receiving their judgment (John 5:28-29), they will be committed to an eternal, conscious punishment in the lake of fire (Matt. 25:41; Rev. 20:11-15).

Even death and Hades are cast into the lake of fire. Not only that, but Satan has already been cast into the lake of fire, as well (Rev. 20:10).

Transition: To be clear, then, the Great White Throne judgment, described in Revelation 20:11-15, is a judgment of unbelievers. This passage makes clear that no one at that judgment has his name in the Book of Life (12-14). The fate of the ungodly, the unsaved is sealed; their names are not in the Book of Life and their punishment is sure. That brings us to the final and extremely critical question.

How Can You Be Sure That Your Name is Written in the Book of Life?

God has not chosen to reveal to us the names written in the Lamb's Book of Life. This is hidden from us. The hidden, decretive will of God is none of our business.

To the question: how can you be sure that your name is written in the Book of Life? If it's true that names are inscribed in the Book of Life before the foundation of the world, is there something someone can do so that his/her name will be written in the book?

Oh, have I got GOOD NEWS for you. You must repent and believe in the Lord Jesus Christ.

Think about it: You don't repent and believe in Jesus in order to get your name in the book of life. You believe in Jesus BECAUSE your name has already been written down in the book.

Thus, to the unrepentant sinner, I boldly, confidently say based on the authority of God's Word, "Repent! Believe in the Lord Jesus!" And, if you do, it is because your name was written in the book of life before the foundation of the world.

And if you sit there wondering: am I among the chosen, the predestined, the called, the elect, is my name written in the Book of Life? Here's how you can know: Do you see Jesus as more to be desired than anything else, and all-sufficient to save you from your sin, and satisfy your heart forever? That is the mark of God's child. He who has the Son has life (1 John 5:12). To as many as received him, to them God gave the right to be become the children of God (John 1:12). Receive him!

There is no such thing as a person who doesn't want to be saved and God saves him anyway because he is elect.

Nor has any person ever existed who would like to be saved but cannot be because he is not elect.[105]

I do not know those that God will save. So, I preach the Gospel with all of my heart. We evangelize. We do missions. We proclaim, trumpet, and herald the Good News of the Gospel. I know in my heart that the gospel is to be preached universally to all men. I don't know who it is that God will save. That's not my job. I've never saved anyone. I'm not responsible for the results.

Charles H. Spurgeon, the venerable sovereign grace Baptist preacher of another generation, once said, "If God had painted a stripe down the back of the elect, I'd spend my days walking up and down the streets of London lifting up shirttails. But because He said, 'Whosoever wills may come,' I preach the Gospel to everyone, and I rely on Him to lead those to faith who are His."

God works in the lives of those who are to be saved, convicting them of sin by the work of His Spirit and giving them the faith to believe the gospel.

D.L. Moody once quipped: "The elect are the "whosoever wills" and the non-elect are the "whosoever won'ts."[106]

As I close, open your Bibles to John 3:16. Read this verse with me: "For God so loved the world that He gave His only begotten Son, that whosoever believes in Him should not perish but have everlasting life." Who said this? JESUS!

Do you know what this text teaches? It teaches that EVERYONE who believes in Christ will be saved!

Marvelously, God saves all who will believe!

---

105 Lutzer, *The Doctrines that Divide*, p. 191.

106 Ibid., p. 192.

How will you respond to God's gracious initiative to save you from your sin?

Then, to the saved I say as Peter said, "2Pe 1:10 Therefore, brothers, be all the more diligent to confirm your calling and election, for if you practice these qualities you will never fall. 2Pe 1:11 For in this way there will be richly provided for you an entrance into the eternal kingdom of our Lord and Savior Jesus Christ."

18

"THE COMING COSMIC CATASTROPHE"

Revelation 8:1-13, ESV

Rev 8:1 When the Lamb opened the seventh seal, there was silence in heaven for about half an hour.

Rev 8:2 Then I saw the seven angels who stand before God, and seven trumpets were given to them.

Rev 8:3 And another angel came and stood at the altar with a golden censer, and he was given much incense to offer with the prayers of all the saints on the golden altar before the throne,

Rev 8:4 and the smoke of the incense, with the prayers of the saints, rose before God from the hand of the angel.

Rev 8:5 Then the angel took the censer and filled it with fire from the altar and threw it on the earth, and there were peals of thunder, rumblings, flashes of lightning, and an earthquake.

Rev 8:6 Now the seven angels who had the seven trumpets prepared to blow them.

Rev 8:7 The first angel blew his trumpet, and there followed hail and fire, mixed with blood, and these were thrown upon the earth. And a third of the earth was burned up, and a third of the trees were burned up, and all green grass was burned up.

Rev 8:8 The second angel blew his trumpet, and something like a great mountain, burning with fire, was thrown into the sea, and a third of the sea became blood.

Rev 8:9 A third of the living creatures in the sea died, and a third of the ships were destroyed.

Rev 8:10 The third angel blew his trumpet, and a great star fell from heaven, blazing like a torch, and it fell on a third of the rivers and on the springs of water.

Rev 8:11 The name of the star is Wormwood. A third of the waters became wormwood, and many people died from the water, because it had been made bitter.

Rev 8:12 The fourth angel blew his trumpet, and a third of the sun was struck, and a third of the moon, and a third of the stars, so that a third of their light might be darkened, and a third of the day might be kept from shining, and likewise a third of the night.

Rev 8:13 Then I looked, and I heard an eagle crying with a loud voice as it flew directly overhead, "Woe, woe, woe to those who dwell on the earth, at the blasts of the other trumpets that the three angels are about to blow!"

Revelation 8 and 9 contain the second great series of judgments: the SEVEN TRUMPETS.

As you may recall, chapter 6 begins the account of the divine tribulation. Chapter 19 will bring it to its rightful conclusion with the second coming of Christ to the earth to establish His earthly millennial Kingdom.

Chapter 6 you remember contains the seal judgments and introduces us to the Four Horsemen of the Apocalypse.

Chapter 7 is a bit of an interlude, a break in the action, if you will, that informs us that even in the midst of extraordinary judgment; God is still extending mercy.

Now, in chapter 8 the judgment of God on planet Earth continues with the blowing of the trumpets. Thus, the seventh seal contains the seven trumpets.

As we wade into this chapter, notice first with me the opening statement. It's odd and found in verses 1-2.

> *Rev 8:1 When the Lamb opened the seventh seal, there was silence in heaven for about half an hour.*
>
> *Rev 8:2 Then I saw the seven angels who stand before God, and seven trumpets were given to them.*

The text informs us that the Lamb (Christ) opens the seventh seal, and upon so doing, there was silence in heaven for about 30 minutes.

It's almost as if this is the calm before the unimaginable, storm. For what follows is so great that when it is finished, one-third of God's magnificent creation will be gone, catastrophically destroyed by God Himself, who created it.[107]

Why is heaven silent? Robert Mounce suggests that "It is a dramatic pause that makes even more impressive the judgments about to fall upon the earth."[108]

The heavenly hosts wait with anticipation to observe what the Lord Jesus will do next as He judges the earth for its idolatries, immorality, and rebellion against His authority.

John MacArthur writes, "The hour of God's final judgment had come—the hour when the saints will be vindicated, sin punished, and Christ exalted."[109]

107 Daniel Akin. *Exalting Jesus in Revelation: Christ-Centered Exposition,* Kindle Edition, location 3524.

108 Robert Mounce. *The Book of Revelation: The New International Commentary on the New Testament,* p. 170.

109 Akin, location 3544. Primary Source: John MacArthur, Revelation 1-11, p. 238.

There is no question that God uses His angels to execute His divine will. And, sometimes it is in direct response to our prayers. This is quite clear in Daniel 10:12-14. In our focal text, the Lord gives seven trumpets to the seven angels who stand in the presence of the Almighty.

In Scripture, trumpets are used to call people together, announce war, or proclaim special times and events. For instance, trumpets were sounded at Mount Sinai when the law was given (Exod. 19:16-19). A trumpet will sound at the return of Christ (Matt. 24:31).

Transition: As we move beyond the opening two verses, we come to verses 3-6 where we find in part an emphasis upon the prayers of God's people.

Of all the spiritual disciplines, it would sure seem that the most difficult one for the majority of Christians is to engage in prayer.

Prayer is hard work—plain and simple. And, we often fail to see the immediate benefits of prayer. Oswald Chambers has written: "Prayer does not fit us for the greater work, prayer is the greater work."[110]

Alfred Lord Tennyson said, "More things are wrought by prayer than this world dreams of."[111]

Marvin Newell once stated, "Prayer lays hold of God's plan and becomes the link between His will and its accomplishment on earth."[112]

Another commentator wrote, "Prayer activates us and engages us in spiritual warfare in the present and also the future. And it is not a battle, a war, lightly to be entered."[113]

---

110 Oswald Chambers. *My Utmost for His Highest*, October 17.

111 Akin, location 3496.

112 Akin, location 3515.

113 Akin, location 3564.

Rev 8:3 And another angel came and stood at the altar with a golden censer, and he was given much incense to offer with the prayers of all the saints on the golden altar before the throne,

Rev 8:4 and the smoke of the incense, with the prayers of the saints, rose before God from the hand of the angel.

Rev 8:5 Then the angel took the censer and filled it with fire from the altar and threw it on the earth, and there were peals of thunder, rumblings, flashes of lightning, and an earthquake.

Rev 8:6 Now the seven angels who had the seven trumpets prepared to blow them.

Another angels stands at the altar with a golden censer, and what is unique about this censer containing much incense, is that it is mixed with the prayers of God's people. Thus, the incense and the prayers of the saints rise as a sweet fragrance before God from the hand of this angel. AMAZING! Our prayers enter the presence of God by way of the altar. Our prayers have not been voiced in vain. Those prayers have not fallen on deaf ears. Those prayers have been heard!

What's wild is that inexplicably and mysteriously in the providence of God, our prayers become the means by which God moves into action and ushers in His Kingdom.

William Hendriksen writes, "The Throne-Occupant sees the sighs and sufferings, he hears the request and the thanksgiving of his children who are in the midst of tribulation. The angel understands this: he realizes that the prayers are heard. Hence, he takes the censer, now emptied of its incense, and fills it with fire of the altar, and empties it upon the earth; that is God has heard the prayers of the saints, and the judgments upon earth are his answers to them."[114]

114 Akin, location 3584. Primary source: William Hendriksen, More than Conquerors,

Notice if you will that the angel takes the censer, fills it with fire from the altar, and throws it on the earth.

What follows? Thunder. Rumblings. Lightning. An Earthquake. This is reminiscent of Mount Sinai in the Old Testament.

The world trembles before the presence and power of its Sovereign Creator. The day of reckoning has arrived.

Transition: The seven angels prepare to blow their trumpets. Brace yourself. Look at verses 7-12.

> *Rev 8:7 The first angel blew his trumpet, and there followed hail and fire, mixed with blood, and these were thrown upon the earth. And a third of the earth was burned up, and a third of the trees were burned up, and all green grass was burned up.*
>
> *Rev 8:8 The second angel blew his trumpet, and something like a great mountain, burning with fire, was thrown into the sea, and a third of the sea became blood.*
>
> *Rev 8:9 A third of the living creatures in the sea died, and a third of the ships were destroyed.*
>
> *Rev 8:10 The third angel blew his trumpet, and a great star fell from heaven, blazing like a torch, and it fell on a third of the rivers and on the springs of water.*
>
> *Rev 8:11 The name of the star is Wormwood. A third of the waters became wormwood, and many people died from the water, because it had been made bitter.*
>
> *Rev 8:12 The fourth angel blew his trumpet, and a third of the sun was struck, and a third of the moon, and a third of the stars, so that a third of their light might be darkened, and a third of the day might be kept from shining, and likewise a third of the night.*

142, emphasis in original.

The seal judgments of chapter 6 saw the destruction of a fourth of the earth (6:8). The trumpet judgments will see the devastation of a third of the earth.

The word "third" occurs thirteen times in chapter 8, and each is like the tolling of a bell of judgment. As you will likely notice, the judgments recall the plagues of Exodus, which God exacted on Pharaoh and the Egyptians.

In verse 7, the first angel blows his trumpet, and with that trumpet blast hail and fire, mixed with blood followed. Consequently, a third of the earth was burned up, a third of the trees were burned up, and all the green grass was burned up.

Robert Mounce notes that a third indicates that "although God is brining punishment on the earth, it is not yet complete and final. The purpose of the visitation is to warn people of the full wrath of God yet to fall, and in so doing to bring them to repentance."[115]

Tragically, as we read in Revelation 9:20-21, most people will not repent.

In verse 8 the second angel blows his trumpet. John sees something he describes as a great mountain burning with fire, and this was thrown into the sea, and a third of the sea became blood. Verse 9 remarks that a third of the living creatures in the sea died, and a third of the ships were destroyed. This apocalyptic vision is devastating.

In verses 10 and 11 the third angel blows his trumpet. What transpires next sets into motion what could only be described as a cosmic catastrophe. A great star falls from heaven blazing like a torch and it falls on a third of the rivers and on the springs of water.

The name of this star is Wormwood. A third of the waters become wormwood, and many people die from the water, because it had been made bitter.

---

115 Akin, location 3621. Primary source: Mounce, *Revelation*, p. 178.

This word "wormwood" occurs only here in the New Testament. It is mentioned eight times in the Old Testament, where it is associated with bitterness, poison, and death (Deut 29:18; Prov. 5:4; Jer. 9:15; 23:15; Lam. 3:15, 19; Amos 5:7; 6:12).[116]

Look at verse 12:

> Rev 8:12 The fourth angel blew his trumpet, and a third of the sun was struck, and a third of the moon, and a third of the stars, so that a third of their light might be darkened, and a third of the day might be kept from shining, and likewise a third of the night.

The fourth angel blows his trumpet. And, again it is catastrophic. A third of the sun, a third of the moon, and third of the stars are struck so that a third of their light might be darkened, and a third of the day is kept from shining, and likewise a third of the night.

What do you suppose is the purpose of these trumpets and their results? That's a good question.

Maybe God desires to show His omnipotence to the world and the futility of turning and rebelling against Him.

Think of all the people who see Christianity as a crutch for the weak.

Think of all the people outside the church who view people inside the church as a bunch of hypocrites.

Think of all the people who actually consider the God of the Bible to be no different from other gods of other religions.

Think of all the people who view one religion as good as any other religion.

Think of all the people who say to themselves and to others, "You believe what you believe, and I will believe what I believe. Who am I to judge?"

---

116 Akin, location 3650. Primary: MacArthur, *Revelation 1-11*, p. 249.

Think of all the people who have convinced themselves they can have a good relationship with God without being involved in the church.

Think of all the people who would say simply, "You Christians just get on my nerves."

Think of all the people who have refused to engage their Bibles this year--rarely to never opening it.

Think of all the people who claim to be spiritual but not religious.

Think of all the people who identify as atheists, agnostics, have never made a faith commitment to Jesus, and have not read the Bible in days, weeks, months, or years.

Think of all the people who have shook their fist in the face of God and told Him to get lost.

Could it be that God is demonstrating that putting your hope in material wealth is not the answer?

Could it be that God is demonstrating that living only for what this world has to offer is in the end foolish and empty?

Listen carefully: The Book of Revelation makes crystal clear that a day is coming when you will either have the mark of the beast or the mark of the Lamb. Time is short. Judgment is coming. Salvation is as near as a prayer. Gratefully, the Bible says, "Everyone who calls on the name of the Lord will be saved" (Rom. 10:13).

Would you right now acknowledge your sin, repent, and put your faith in Christ? Would you right now ask Christ to be your Savior?

Believer, what prayer do you need to pray this morning? Who are you praying for to be saved? How are you praying for those who are persecuted for their faith? Are you fortifying your heart for the tough days ahead?

19

"CHASING DEATH"

Revelation 9:1-12, NLT

This morning we open our Bibles to the ninth chapter of the Book of Revelation.

In verses 1-12, we have a scary, mysterious account of the fifth angel sounding the Fifth Trumpet. These verses are dreadful in their statement of what happens next. Pay special attention, if you will, to verse six.

> *"Rev 9:1 Then the fifth angel blew his trumpet, and I saw a star that had fallen to earth from the sky, and he was given the key to the shaft of the bottomless pit. 2 When he opened it, smoke poured out as though from a huge furnace, and the sunlight and air turned dark from the smoke. 3 Then locusts came from the smoke and descended on the earth, and they were given power to sting like scorpions. 4 They were told not to harm the grass or plants or trees, but only the people who did not have the seal of God on their foreheads. 5 They were told not to kill them but to torture them for five months with pain like the pain of a scorpion sting. 6 In those days people will seek death, but will not find it. They will long to die, but death will flee from them! 7 The locusts looked like horses prepared for battle. They had what looked like gold crowns on their heads, and*

*their faces looked like human faces. 8 They had hair
like women's hair and teeth like the teeth of a lion. 9
They wore armor made of iron, and their wings roared
like an army of chariots rushing into battle. 10 They
had tails that stung like scorpions, and for five months
they had the power to torment people. 11 Their king is
the angel from the bottomless pit; his name in Hebrew
is Abaddon, and in Greek, Apollyon—the Destroyer. 12
The first terror is past, but look, two more terrors are
coming!"*

To assist us in seeking to gain a working understanding of this remarkable, frightening text of Scripture, I want to direct your thinking to three key words:

1. The word- STAR (v. 1)
2. The word- SMOKE (v. 2-4)
3. The word- STING (v. 5-10).

The Word- STAR (v.1)

*John writes in "Rev 9:1 Then the fifth angel blew his
trumpet, and I saw a star that had fallen to earth from
the sky, and he was given the key to the shaft of the
bottomless pit."*

Interesting! Who or what is this star? This star seems to be a personal being. The text says he is fallen. Furthermore, apparently, he is granted some level of authority. Combined, this star is clearly Satan himself.

One sturdy reason for identifying the star as Satan, comes from what Jesus stated to the disciples in response to reports of the returning disciples in Luke 10. Jesus noted, "I saw Satan fall like lightning from heaven" (Luke 10:18). Some commentators believe this reference is to a pre-cosmic confrontation referenced in Jude 6 and 2 Peter 2:4.[117]

Additional textual support as to the identity of this fallen star is found in verse 11:

> *11 Their king is the angel from the bottomless pit; his name in Hebrew is Abaddon, and in Greek, Apollyon— the Destroyer.*

This verse removes any confusion. A king, who is the angel of the abyss, or the bottomless pit, rules over an army of ominous locusts. His name in Hebrew is Abaddon, and in Greek- Apollyon—both names meaning "Destroyer."

As you know from your basic knowledge of Scripture, demons pay their allegiance to Satan. Jesus called Satan the "prince of this world" (John 12:31). Paul identified the Evil One as "ruler of kingdom of the air" (Eph. 2:2).

Simon Kistemaker points out that the New Testament assigns many names to Satan: devil, tempter, enemy, adversary, serpent, dragon, deceiver, accuser, evil one, Beelzebub, Belial, Apollyon.[118]

Summarily, the fall of Satan is presented as an event. A key is presented to this fallen star, and it is the key to the bottomless pit, or the Abyss. Notice that the text says specifically that "He was given the key..." This indicates a truth we should not too quickly dismiss. That truth is that he is given authority to unleash a horde of locusts awaiting in the bottomless pit. AND, that he is simultaneously under the authority of a superior.

---

117 Paige Patterson. *The New American Commentary: Revelation*, p. 215.

118 Simon Kistemaker. *New Testament Commentary: Revelation*, p. 292.

Translation: Even the fallen star operates under the sovereignty and authority of Almighty God!

Transition: The fallen star is most likely Satan who is given authority and is under authority at the same time. Notice that he opens the shaft of the bottomless pit and what comes from the shaft, or huge furnace, as the NLT identifies it? SMOKE.

The Word- SMOKE (v.2-4)

> John writes, "2 When he opened it, smoke poured out as though from a huge furnace, and the sunlight and air turned dark from the smoke. 3 Then locusts came from the smoke and descended on the earth, and they were given power to sting like scorpions. 4 They were told not to harm the grass or plants or trees, but only the people who did not have the seal of God on their foreheads."

What comes from this bottomless pit? Smoke. And, it would seem that the smoke is dark and black, as John describes the effect of the smoke—that is—the sunlight and the air were darkened.

Furthermore, the locusts, these demonic oppressors, come from the smoke and they are "given power" to sting like scorpions.

These beings-these locusts-are instructed to do no harm to the grass of the earth or to the trees or any green plant.

This instruction is odd because, as you know, the eighth Egyptian (Exodus 10:13-15) plague unleashed the destructive power of the locusts that devoured everything that was growing in the fields and stripped bare the trees, thus depriving people and animals of their food supply.

As Kistemaker correctly points out, these locusts in Revelation 9 are entirely different:

- They come forth out of the infernal smoke that arises from the Abyss
- They do not devour the green grass, plants, and trees
- They attack people who are not part of God's kingdom
- They strike the ungodly with the stings of scorpions[119]

Is this locust plague physical or spiritual in nature? I think an argument could be made that this plague could be torment on several levels—physical, mental, and spiritual.

I want you to be careful to note that God is sovereign over all of this demonic activity. God grants authority and establishes its limits, and at the same time, God protects His own people from harm-spiritual and otherwise. Clearly, God is in charge, not Satan.

The locusts are told that they may not harm those with the seal of God on their foreheads.

Transition: Thus, out of the bottomless pit comes the smoke like that of a great furnace. Out of the smoke appears a horde of demonic locusts given permission to torment those who do not have the seal of God on their foreheads. That brings us now to the final word that is guiding our thinking.

The Word- STING (v.5-10)

Verse 5 reads: "5 They were told not to kill them but to torture them for five months with pain like the pain of a scorpion sting."

These beings are "allowed" to torture, but not to kill. They are permitted to torture, torment, and aggravate for a limited time of five months.

---

119 Kistemaker, p. 286.

The specific mission of these demonic locusts is to inflict suffering upon the wicked.[120]

John describes their torment as that of a scorpion when it stings someone.

Give your attention please to verse 6: "In those days people will seek death, but will not find it. They will long to die, but death will flee from them!"

John foretells here that people will seek death, people will chase death, but death will flee from them.

It would seem that in this eschatological plague, it is actual pain that drives people earnestly to pursue death.

Do you see the irony? It is ironic that in that day death, which the wicked inflicted upon Christian martyrs, will be eagerly desired, yet people will find that death eludes them.[121]

These demonic creatures cannot kill these folks, but they sure can and vex the bodies and minds of the sufferers and drive them to utter despair.

By contrast, the followers of Christ have the seal of God on their foreheads and are safe. They are protected by the Lord Himself, who has given His angels charge over them.

What did these locusts look like, by the way? The answer is found in verses 7-10:

> "7 The locusts looked like horses prepared for battle.
> They had what looked like gold crowns on their heads,
> and their faces looked like human faces. 8 They had
> hair like women's hair and teeth like the teeth of a lion.

120 Robert H. Mounce. *The New International Commentary on the New Testament: The Book of Revelation*, p. 188.

121 Mounce, p. 188.

*9 They wore armor made of iron, and their wings roared
like an army of chariots rushing into battle. 10 They
had tails that stung like scorpions, and for five months
they had the power to torment people."*

Up to this point, we know the origin and mission of these
locusts, but now John describes them.

Essentially, the description of the locusts compared to horses
prepared for battle is AWESOME.

Human faces…

Crowns of gold…

Women's hair…

Lions' teeth…

Iron like breastplates…

Wings that sound like horse-drawn chariots rushing into battle.

John describes what he saw, but does not interpret each char-
acteristic. He borrows imagery from Joel, who compares an invasion
of locusts to a mighty army which destroys everything in its path.

To say the least, this is a multifaceted symbol depicting demonic
creatures seeking to wage war and overpower anyone and anything
standing in their way.

Can you imagine locusts having the appearances of horses,
galloping like a calvary?

Can you imagine the noise they make being as that of a caval-
cade of chariots? The thundering hooves and the wheels of chariots
would be exceedingly intimidating.

Can you envision these creatures charging like highly motivated
warriors?

Again John draws from Joel's account of swarming locusts who
appear as horses (Joel 2:4) and whose sound is like the noise of chariots in battle or the raging fury of a prairie fire (Joel 2:5).

Mounce points out that the demonic beings contain human and bestial qualities combined in a figure both unnatural and diabolical.[122]

They are invincible, protected, and intent on their mission to inflict agony and misery. They are of considerable size. No person on earth is a match for these creatures. They have tails and stings like scorpions, and they are granted power to hurt people for a period of five months. They have the power to punish. Miserable.

One commentator I read reminded me that though Satan is sometimes portrayed as an angel of light, here Satan and his demons are seen for what they really are, destroyers of people.[123]

Look with me now, finally, at verse 12: "The first terror is past, but look, two more terrors are coming!"

Now, if the reader makes the assumption that with the release of the demonic locusts the plagues have somehow come to an end, John announces that this is only the first woe, the first terror.

These woes grow in intensity.

Two woes are still to come. One translation captures the idea this way: "The first disaster is now past, but I see two more approaching."

THE APPEAL:

As I bring this message to a close, I must appeal to you this morning to commit your life to Jesus Christ.

I want to ask you a personal question: Do you know the Lord Jesus as your Savior?

I want to urge you to commit your life to Jesus Christ. I want to urge you to do it now. Don't put off this decision to trust Christ

---

122 Mounce, p. 189.

123 Walvoord and Zuck. The Bible Knowledge Commentary: Revelation, p. 953.

as your Savior any longer. The Bible makes clear that each of us is a sinner, separated from God because of our sin. God so loved this world that He gave His Son, who lived a perfect life, and laid down His life as the atoning sacrifice for our sin.

Without Christ in your life as Savior and Lord, do you not sense the spiritual emptiness which exists?

How can you be saved? Simple. By repentance and by placing your trust in Jesus Christ. To be certain walking an aisle in any Baptist church never saved anyone! Never. It is Jesus Christ who saves when a man comes under conviction by the Holy Spirit and the Spirit draws and compels that man to come to Jesus Christ for salvation. Listen, a time is coming that is too awful for words. We read only a portion of this reality this morning from the sermon text.

You must identify yourself with Christ. You must turn to Christ. You must respond to the Gospel. Even not responding is a response. You cannot be neutral about Christ. It is a very dangerous game to play to presume you can do this at a later time. I appeal to you this very moment to come to Christ.

If you are a believer, I suspect you know someone who needs to be saved. Pray for them this very moment. If you are a believer, but you are not particularly serious about your walk with Christ, maybe this morning you would apologize to Jesus for being a mere accessory in your life rather than Lord.

No one in good conscience can leave this room this morning and not offer some response to Christ. Oh, may God be pleased with your response this morning.

20

"THE DEMONIC CAVALRY"

Revelation 9:13–21, NLT

This morning we open our Bibles to the concluding verses of the ninth chapter of Revelation, verses 13-21.

The sixth angel blows his trumpet and thus we have a detailed account of what is set loose. This is the second woe, the second terror. This intense text introduces us to a demonic cavalry of unparalleled number and ferocity—200,000,000—and they come charging across the eschatological scene of history.

> *13 Then the sixth angel blew his trumpet, and I heard a voice speaking from the four horns of the gold altar that stands in the presence of God.*
>
> *14 And the voice said to the sixth angel who held the trumpet, "Release the four angels who are bound at the great Euphrates River."*
>
> *15 Then the four angels who had been prepared for this hour and day and month and year were turned loose to kill one-third of all the people on earth.*
>
> *16 I heard the size of their army, which was 200 million mounted troops.*
>
> *17 And in my vision, I saw the horses and the riders sitting on them. The riders wore armor that was fiery*

red and dark blue and yellow. The horses had heads like lions, and fire and smoke and burning sulfur billowed from their mouths.

18 One-third of all the people on earth were killed by these three plagues—by the fire and smoke and burning sulfur that came from the mouths of the horses.

19 Their power was in their mouths and in their tails. For their tails had heads like snakes, with the power to injure people.

20 But the people who did not die in these plagues still refused to repent of their evil deeds and turn to God. They continued to worship demons and idols made of gold, silver, bronze, stone, and wood—idols that can neither see nor hear nor walk!

21 And they did not repent of their murders or their witchcraft or their sexual immorality or their thefts.

Embedded within this biblical text are three ideas I want to put upon your minds:

1. The Unleashing of the Four Angels (v. 13-15).
2. The Unrelenting Army of Death (v. 16-19).
3. The Unrepentance of the Depraved (v. 20-21).

The Unleashing of the Four Angels (v. 13-15).

13 Then the sixth angel blew his trumpet, and I heard a voice speaking from the four horns of the gold altar that stands in the presence of God.

14 And the voice said to the sixth angel who held the trumpet, "Release the four angels who are bound at the great Euphrates River."

15 Then the four angels who had been prepared for this hour and day and month and year were turned loose to kill one-third of all the people on earth.

When the sixth angel blows his trumpet, a voice is heard FROM the golden altar unleashing the four angels who are bound at the great Euphrates River.

What's interesting and of note is that the prayers of God's people seem to play a key and active role in the eschatological drama.[124] This dynamic continues to be prevalent in the book of Revelation.

We do not have a good handle on the identity of the four angels. They are NOT mentioned anywhere else in the apocalyptic writings.

Yet, in the context of this passage the four angels appear to have charge over a limitless cadre or force of demonic horsemen who gallop across the pagan landscape and wreak terror and death.

The Euphrates is one of the four rivers which flowed through the Garden of Eden. The Euphrates was also the eastern boundary of the Roman Empire, and the mention of the invading horsemen from that quarter, would immediately suggest the much-feared Parthian warriors. But, I think Mounce in his reputable commentary is wisely measured and conservative in his view here. He makes clear that John at this point is recounting a vision given to him in the Spirit, not describing a Parthian invasion.[125] Nonetheless, the 200,000,000 demonic horsemen and their plague of death is an event of epic proportion!

These formerly bound demonic angels are unleashed at just the right, divinely appointed moment. It is written that they have been kept ready for this specific task and time.

The use of the perfect tense strengthens the argument of their existing state of readiness.

124 Robert H. Mounce. *NICNT: The Book of Revelation*, p. 193.

125 Mounce, p. 194.

What we cannot miss here is that in apocalyptic thought, God has fixed the exact time of every event.

Look at verse 15. Note the use of the definite article for all four time designations: "the hour, the day, the month, and the year." At the precise moment decreed by Almighty God, the angels of destruction and their demonic horde will be released upon the human race. These angels are turned loose for the purpose of killing one-third of the world's population.

You recall that under the fourth seal, a fourth of the human race was put to death (6:8). Now, a third of people are to be killed. Yet, as in the previous Woe, so also here, believers are to be spared (9:4; 20-21).

**The assault will be upon those who are hostile toward God. G.E. Ladd makes a careful distinction here between John's version and similar expectations of prophets and apocalyptists: "The latter always envision the foreign invasion as an attack against the people of God by pagan hosts while John sees it as a divine judgment upon a corrupt civilization."[126]

Transition: Thus, with the blowing of this sixth trumpet, these four angels are unleashed. But, notice what is said next in verses 16-19:

The Unrelenting Army of Death (v. 16-19)

> 16 I heard the size of their army, which was 200 million mounted troops.
>
> 17 And in my vision, I saw the horses and the riders sitting on them. The riders wore armor that was fiery red and dark blue and yellow. The horses had heads like lions, and fire and smoke and burning sulfur billowed from their mouths.

126 Mounce, p. 195. Primary source: Ladd, 135.

18 One-third of all the people on earth were killed by these three plagues—by the fire and smoke and burning sulfur that came from the mouths of the horses.

19 Their power was in their mouths and in their tails. For their tails had heads like snakes, with the power to injure people.

John hears the size of this army—it is massive, almost unimaginable—200,000,000 in number, be it literal or figurative—either way, this is colossal.

They are well-outfitted in almost impenetrable, colorful armor. The horses upon which these warriors ride are intimidating in and of themselves—they are terrifying, daunting, and fear-inducing.

Their heads are like lions, and fire and smoke and burning sulfur billow from their mouths.

John seems to interrupt his description of these horrific creatures of death with a declaration of their mission and imminent, devastating result in verse 18.

Three plagues are set free: fire, smoke, and burning sulfur.

John writes, "18 One-third of all the people on earth were killed by these three plagues—by the fire and smoke and burning sulfur that came from the mouths of the horses."

John then continues his description in verse 19: 19Their power was in their mouths and in their tails. For their tails had heads like snakes, with the power to injure people."

Ladies and gentlemen: I have one word for you in response to reading verse 19- CREEPY!!

TAILS with HEADS LIKE SNAKES…enough said. Man, I hate snakes with a passion! Period. According to John, these creatures have power in their mouths and tails, and their tails have the power to injure and wound.

Illustration: I hate snakes. So much so, that I will not even enter into our chicken coop now because we have found several snakes in there helping themselves to our chicken eggs. Big snakes which are probably harmless, but creepy nonetheless. I tell Beth, "Send one of the girls in there to get the eggs. If something happens to one of them, hey, we can always adopt another one…!!" Oh, come on, I'm just kidding…mostly!

What's odd is that the riders on these creatures do not play an active role in carrying out the plague. It appears to be accomplished by the horses.

They are grotesque.

They are destructive.

They are terrifying.

They are demonic in origin and intent.

They are scary and lethal.

As an interesting footnote: it may very well be that this vision is linked with Ezekiel's prophecy of the invasion of Israel by God (Ez. 38-39).

Transition: This unrelenting demonic army will be responsible for the death of one third of the earth's population. This vision is almost beyond comprehension. Yet, what is the response of the unbelieving?

John tells us in verses 20-21. This stubborn refusal to repent will take your breath away and break your heart.

The Unrepentance of the Depraved (v. 20-21)

> *20 But the people who did not die in these plagues still refused to repent of their evil deeds and turn to God. They continued to worship demons and idols made of gold, silver, bronze, stone, and wood—idols that can neither see nor hear nor walk!*
>
> *21 And they did not repent of their murders or their witchcraft or their sexual immorality or their thefts.*

Remarkably, though this judgment was devastating and obviously from God, it did not bring men to a place of repentance.

Is this not astounding? Can you believe the hardness of heart? Not even the scourge of death could lead these depraved people to a place of repentance.

- Notice they continued to worship demons.
- They continued to worship man-made idols.
- They did not repent of their murders.
- They did not repent of their witchcraft.
- They did not repent of their sexual immorality.
- They did not repent of the stealing.
- Instead, they continued in evildoing and rebelling against God.

Keep in mind (and this is extremely important) that God's purposes behind these plagues are judgment and a call to repentance.

Judgment for what? Simple--for a refusal to repent of their evil actions and a refusal to turn to God.

These unrepentant people stubbornly, willfully choose to continue in idolatry and all the corruption which comes with godless living.

The concept of repentance means "to change one's mind." In essence repentance calls for a change of one's mind which leads to a change in one's actions.

The Bible makes clear that sinners must repent.

Acts 17:30 states: "The times of ignorance God overlooked, but now He commands all people everywhere to repent."

Instead, men persisted in evil and sin.

Thus far, by way of a bit of summary, the two demonic woes of chapter 9 have passed.

God has meted out punishment on those who do not bear the seal of God on their foreheads.

It is important to remember that God's own people are protected during this time from the plagues that fall on the rest of the human race (v. 4).

Believers will endure the tribulation that comes from a world controlled by a different set of values, but THEY WILL NOT BE TOUCHED BY THE WRATH OF GOD.[127]

It is entirely the case that the protection of God's people is not physical but spiritual. Locusts from the Abyss will be unable to harm them, and the life-destroying cavalry will sweep by, leaving them intact.

The Bible makes crystal clear that God will vindicate His cause and the judge the enemies of righteousness.

This should bring us a great deal of hope as the people of God faced with the prospect of impending persecution and difficulty.

Transition: Though the sixth judgment and trumpet produced dread, it did not produce repentance among the depraved.

As I close, I would like to share with you a statement attributed to Oswald Chambers:

---

127 Mounce, p. 199.

"It is not repentance that saves me; repentance is the sign that I realize what God has done in Christ Jesus. The danger is to put the emphasis on the effect instead of on the cause. Is it my obedience that puts me right with God? Never! I am put right with God because prior to all else, Christ died. When I turn to God and by belief accept what God reveals, instantly the stupendous atonement of Jesus Christ rushes me into a right relationship with God. By the miracle of God's grace I stand justified, not because of anything I have done, but because of what Jesus has done. The salvation of God does not stand on human logic; it stands on the sacrificial death of Jesus. Sinful men and women can be changed into new creatures by the marvelous work of God in Christ Jesus, which is prior to all experience."

Oh, I plead with you to decide for Christ today. Now!

For whom must you pray today that they might be saved in Christ Jesus?

Oswald Chambers quoted in So Great Salvation, Charles Ryrie, Victor Books, 1989, p. 91ff.

21

"SWEET & SOUR"

Revelation 10:1–11, ESV

Before launching into the 10th chapter of Revelation this morning, I would like to share the Gospel with you. I want to make an urgent appeal to you to trust Christ to be your Savior.

When you pause to consider it, the Gospel of Jesus Christ contains both sweet and sour truths.

The ugly, honest, sour truth is that man is a sinner and is in desperate need of the Savior.

The Bible declares with great clarity that we are corrupt, depraved sinners in the sight of a HOLY GOD and doomed to be the objects of the righteous judgment and wrath of God. The Bible makes clear that all have sinned and fallen short of the glory of God (Rom. 3:23). The sour news is that the wages of sin is death, but the sweet news is that the free gift of God is eternal life in Christ Jesus (Rom. 6:23).

While God has no obligation to save even one single sinner, and owes salvation to no man, God nonetheless loved the world so much (Jn. 3:16) that He sent His one and only Son, Jesus Christ, to this earth to save His people from their sins (Matt. 1:21) and to redeem them from the wretched curse of the law.

This is the sweet news! We call it the Good News! The very name "Jesus" means "Savior." Not only that, but also, He is a conquering, victorious Savior who was tempted in every way as we are, yet was without sin.

The only begotten Son of God trod the winepress of God's holy wrath alone; none were with Him on Calvary's cursed tree. No man helped Jesus out of the cold tomb and no man can assist the exalted Lord Jesus save a sinner.

The sour news: man is fallen and sinful; the sweet news: God is free and sovereign. Salvation is not of man; rather, salvation is of the Lord (Jon. 2:9).

As much as you might like, you play not a solitary role in your salvation, with the exception of bringing Him your sin and mess. Christ is the only Savior of the whosoever(s) who repent and believe (Rom. 10:13).

Yet, the question: "What must I do to be saved?" is one of the greatest inquiries which might be asked by a sinner. Scripture teaches that YOU must repent (Acts 17:30) and believe (Acts 16:31).

Therefore, the saving power of God regenerates and quickens a dead sinner. Union with the crucified, resurrected, and glorified Christ is only possible by the work of the Holy Spirit. Oh, friend, please hear me when I tell you that man cannot be his own savior, for God alone in mercy and grace saves the sinner.

Oh, how you need Jesus to be your Savior this very morning. He left heaven's glory and came to Bethlehem as a Babe. He lived a sinless life, having done the will of God perfectly. He fulfilled and honored God's holy law in every detail, then suffered on the cross the very wrath of God which we should have suffered.

Jesus redeemed us from the curse of a broken law. He died for our sins and rose again for our justification (Rom. 4:25). He ascended to the right hand of the Father, and there He sat down, waiting until all His enemies should be made His footstool (Heb. 10:12-13).

And there He sits, this position of authority and privilege, bestowing salvation upon sinners, and interceding for those who come unto God by Him (Heb. 7:25).

So, poor and wretched sinners, BOW DOWN. Cast yourself upon the Lord's tender mercy. Be assured He will not cast you out (Jn. 6:37) for He cast none out who were given to Him by the Father! Oh, won't you call on His name for salvation.

Prayer:

Chapter 10 is an interlude between the sixth and seventh trumpets. You may recall that there was an interlude in chapter 7 between the sixth and seventh seals. Chapter 10 has its focus on a mighty angel, a little scroll, and the eating of the little scroll, if you will.[128]

> *Rev 10:1 Then I saw another mighty angel coming down from heaven, wrapped in a cloud, with a rainbow over his head, and his face was like the sun, and his legs like pillars of fire.*
>
> *Rev 10:2 He had a little scroll open in his hand. And he set his right foot on the sea, and his left foot on the land,*
>
> *Rev 10:3 and called out with a loud voice, like a lion roaring. When he called out, the seven thunders sounded.*
>
> *Rev 10:4 And when the seven thunders had sounded, I was about to write, but I heard a voice from heaven*

---

128 Daniel Akin. *Exalting Christ in Revelation: Christ-Centered Exposition Commentary*, Kindle Edition, location 3942.

saying, "Seal up what the seven thunders have said, and do not write it down."

Rev 10:5 And the angel whom I saw standing on the sea and on the land raised his right hand to heaven

Rev 10:6 and swore by him who lives forever and ever, who created heaven and what is in it, the earth and what is in it, and the sea and what is in it, that there would be no more delay,

Rev 10:7 but that in the days of the trumpet call to be sounded by the seventh angel, the mystery of God would be fulfilled, just as he announced to his servants the prophets.

Rev 10:8 Then the voice that I had heard from heaven spoke to me again, saying, "Go, take the scroll that is open in the hand of the angel who is standing on the sea and on the land."

Rev 10:9 So I went to the angel and told him to give me the little scroll. And he said to me, "Take and eat it; it will make your stomach bitter, but in your mouth it will be sweet as honey."

Rev 10:10 And I took the little scroll from the hand of the angel and ate it. It was sweet as honey in my mouth, but when I had eaten it my stomach was made bitter.

Rev 10:11 And I was told, "You must again prophesy about many peoples and nations and languages and kings."

I want you to see three key moments occurring in this chapter.

1. The Introduction of the Mighty Angel (v. 1-4).
2. The Announcement of the Impending End (v. 5-7).
3. The Eating of the Scroll (v. 8-11).

The Introduction of the Mighty Angel (v. 1-4)

> *Rev 10:1 Then I saw another mighty angel coming down from heaven, wrapped in a cloud, with a rainbow over his head, and his face was like the sun, and his legs like pillars of fire.*
>
> *Rev 10:2 He had a little scroll open in his hand. And he set his right foot on the sea, and his left foot on the land,*
>
> *Rev 10:3 and called out with a loud voice, like a lion roaring. When he called out, the seven thunders sounded.*
>
> *Rev 10:4 And when the seven thunders had sounded, I was about to write, but I heard a voice from heaven saying, "Seal up what the seven thunders have said, and do not write it down."*

John identifies another mighty angel coming down from heaven. Who is this mighty angel? From the text, we have no concrete idea as to the specific identity of this creature.

Some commentators identify this angel as being the person of Christ. I don't think that is warranted.

Why? Well, perhaps the most compelling reason is that Christ does not appear in Revelation as an angel. Furthermore, there is just nothing in these verses that give us the ability to identify with certainty the identification of this angel.

What, then, do we know about this angel?

- Mighty-an angel of high rank and honor
- He comes down from heaven
- Clothed in a cloud-speaking of his adornment
- A Rainbow is about his head as if it was a crown
- His face is radiant like the sun
- His legs are like pillars of fire

- He has a little scroll open in his hand
- His right foot is on the sea
- His left foot is on the land
- He has the voice of a lion roaring
- When he speaks, the response is that of seven thunders sounding.

What the text tells us about this mighty angel is interesting on several levels. For instance, the observation that he has his right foot on the sea and his left foot on the land. What does this imagery mean? It means simply that his authority encompasses all the earth—that is, the entire cosmos.

Furthermore, the mighty angel speaks with a commanding, loud voice such as when a lion roars.

This scene is really quite awe-inspiring, church. When this angel shouted, the voices of the seven thunders spoke. That's pretty cool!

What did the seven thunders say? This is clearly more than just the rumbling of crashing molecules caused by lightning. The seven thunders spoke and their message must have been discernible because John was going to record what was said, but a voice from heaven instructed John to seal up what the seven thunders said, and he was not permitted to write it down.

Transition: And with that we have the introduction in verses 1-4 of the Mighty Angel. Very intriguing.

The Announcement of the Impending End (v.5-7)

> *Rev 10:5 And the angel whom I saw standing on the sea and on the land raised his right hand to heaven*

> *Rev 10:6 and swore by him who lives forever and ever, who created heaven and what is in it, the earth and*

what is in it, and the sea and what is in it, that there would be no more delay,

Rev 10:7 but that in the days of the trumpet call to be sounded by the seventh angel, the mystery of God would be fulfilled, just as he announced to his servants the prophets.

What follows the introduction of this mighty angel is a pronouncement.

In verse 5, the mighty angel raises his right hand to heaven and swears by omnipotent God, the eternal Creator, that THERE WILL BE NO MORE DELAY (v. 6).

This announcement carries with it tremendous, unparalleled authority. The angel acknowledges in his oath the superiority of the one true God whom he serves.[129]

The judgment of God will not be delayed any longer. The prayers of the saints will be answered.

Look at verse 7: Rev 10:7 but that in the days of the trumpet call to be sounded by the seventh angel, the mystery of God would be fulfilled, just as he announced to his servants the prophets.

Oh, this speaks of the final judgments of the tribulation period and the establishment of the kingdom with the coming of Christ to the earth.

Thus, when the seventh angel, who is about to trumpet his message, sounds his instrument, then the mystery of God preached through the prophets will be accomplished or completed.

Prophetic literature stretching back 750 years before Christ envisioned the coming of an awesome day of judgment.

Paige Patterson writes, "…the Prophets envisioned a golden daybreak, a utopian era, God's earthly reign, which would ultimately reverse and restore all the iniquity had cost the race and the cosmos."[130]

---

129 Paige Patterson. *The New American Commentary*: Revelation, p. 232.

130 Patterson, p. 233.

Transition: Without delay, and perfect in sovereign timing, the announcement is made that all God has promised through the prophets and the apostles will not be delayed any longer, but will come to pass in rapid sequence, following the sounding of the trumpet of the seventh angel.

The Eating of the Scroll (v. 8-11).

> *Rev 10:8 Then the voice that I had heard from heaven spoke to me again, saying, "Go, take the scroll that is open in the hand of the angel who is standing on the sea and on the land."*
>
> *Rev 10:9 So I went to the angel and told him to give me the little scroll. And he said to me, "Take and eat it; it will make your stomach bitter, but in your mouth it will be sweet as honey."*
>
> *Rev 10:10 And I took the little scroll from the hand of the angel and ate it. It was sweet as honey in my mouth, but when I had eaten it my stomach was made bitter.*
>
> *Rev 10:11 And I was told, "You must again prophesy about many peoples and nations and languages and kings."*

John receives a threefold command:

1.   Go and take the open scroll from the hand of the angel standing on the sea and the land (v. 8).
2.   Take and eat the scroll (v. 9).
3.   Go and prophesy (v. 11).

Another way to frame the commands would be:

- Take the Word
- Feed on the Word
- Proclaim the Word[131]

---

131 Akin, Kindle Edition, Location 9973.

Furthermore, John was told that the little scroll would be bitter in his stomach, but sweet as honey in his mouth (v. 9).

Ladies and gentlemen, let us affirm what God says in His Word about His Word in Isaiah 55:11: "So my word that comes from My mouth will not return to Me empty, but it will accomplish what I please and will prosper in what I send it to do."

It is not an understatement to declare the importance of God's Word for any and every generation. Each of us must be committed to take it, read it, feed on it, and then go and proclaim it by what you say and how you live.

John is told to take and eat. This book is bread, honey, and milk—necessary for our spiritual health and development.

Yet, it is often sweet in our mouths, and bitter in our stomachs. It is sweet in our mouths because it reveals the gospel—which I shared with you from the beginning of this message.

It is bitter in our stomachs because it is a word of judgment to unbelievers.

John MacArthur has this to say: "All who love Jesus Christ can relate to John's ambivalence. Believers long for Christ to return in glory, for Satan to be destroyed, and the glorious kingdom of our Lord to be set up on earth, in which He will rule in universal sovereignty and glory while establishing in the world righteousness, truth, and peace. But they, like Paul (Rom. 9:1-3), mourn bitterly over the judgment of the ungodly."[132]

Finally, John is told to go and prophesy to the nations. The declaration of the Gospel is as Paul wrote: "For the message of the cross is foolishness to those who are perishing, but to us who are

---

132 Primary Source: John MacArthur, *Revelation 1-11*, 288. Secondary source: Akin, Kindle Edition, Location- 4051.

being saved, it is the power of God" (1 Cor. 1:18). Indeed, the gospel is both sweet and sour!

The gospel of Jesus Christ is Good News…sweet news! Yet, if you remain in a stubborn state of unrepentance and disbelief, the gospel of Jesus Christ is sour news and bitter to the stomach.

Have you come to a place where you are certain that your eternal destiny and home is heaven?

How can you know for sure…by trusting in Christ to be your Savior. To follow Jesus as your Lord.

Will you do that right now? Don't delay any longer.

Believer…are you building your life on the foundation of the Word of God? Do you read it? Do you share it with others by your words and lifestyle?

Would you join with me in prayer?

22

"WHEN MANKIND DEIFIES EVIL"

Revelation 11:1-14 ESV

The verses before us this morning are universally accepted as some of the most difficult to interpret in the entire Apocalypse.

The challenge is, as it has been in the previously reviewed chapters of Revelation, to determine what should be considered literal and what should be considered figurative, or symbolic. In these present verses we have times, persons, events, and places to consider. My aim will be to interpret literally where it makes sense to do so. The most common, largely agreed upon and applied hermeneutical principle is known as the literal grammatical-historical method of interpretation. As always, we ask and depend upon the Holy Spirit to enlighten our understanding of all Scripture not just that found in the Revelation.

Nonetheless, the task before us is considerable.

> *Rev 11:1 Then I was given a measuring rod like a staff, and I was told, "Rise and measure the temple of God and the altar and those who worship there,*
>
> *Rev 11:2 but do not measure the court outside the temple; leave that out, for it is given over to the nations, and they will trample the holy city for forty-two months.*

Rev 11:3 And I will grant authority to my two witnesses, and they will prophesy for 1,260 days, clothed in sackcloth."

Rev 11:4 These are the two olive trees and the two lampstands that stand before the Lord of the earth.

Rev 11:5 And if anyone would harm them, fire pours from their mouth and consumes their foes. If anyone would harm them, this is how he is doomed to be killed.

Rev 11:6 They have the power to shut the sky, that no rain may fall during the days of their prophesying, and they have power over the waters to turn them into blood and to strike the earth with every kind of plague, as often as they desire.

Rev 11:7 And when they have finished their testimony, the beast that rises from the bottomless pit will make war on them and conquer them and kill them,

Rev 11:8 and their dead bodies will lie in the street of the great city that symbolically is called Sodom and Egypt, where their Lord was crucified.

Rev 11:9 For three and a half days some from the peoples and tribes and languages and nations will gaze at their dead bodies and refuse to let them be placed in a tomb,

Rev 11:10 and those who dwell on the earth will rejoice over them and make merry and exchange presents, because these two prophets had been a torment to those who dwell on the earth.

Rev 11:11 But after the three and a half days a breath of life from God entered them, and they stood up on their feet, and great fear fell on those who saw them.

Rev 11:12 Then they heard a loud voice from heaven saying to them, "Come up here!" And they went up to heaven in a cloud, and their enemies watched them.

Rev 11:13 And at that hour there was a great earthquake, and a tenth of the city fell. Seven thousand people were killed in the earthquake, and the rest were terrified and gave glory to the God of heaven.

Rev 11:14 The second woe has passed; behold, the third woe is soon to come.

This particular text unfolds in the following sections:

1. The Measuring of the Temple (v. 1-2).
2. The Ministry of the Two Witnesses (v. 3-6).
3. The Death of the Two Witnesses (v. 7-10).
4. The Resurrection of the Two Witnesses (v. 11-12).
5. The Resulting Judgment of God (v. 13-14).

The Measuring of the Temple (v. 1-2)

Rev 11:1 Then I was given a measuring rod like a staff, and I was told, "Rise and measure the temple of God and the altar and those who worship there,

Rev 11:2 but do not measure the court outside the temple; leave that out, for it is given over to the nations, and they will trample the holy city for forty-two months.

The text informs the reader that John was a given a "measuring rod" the equivalent of a modern yardstick.

He is told to go and measure the "temple of God and the altar and those who worship there…"

The Old Testament background is Ezekiel 40-42. The idea here is one of ownership and protection.[133]

Yet, in verse 2, John is instructed not to measure "the court outside the temple; for it is given over to the nations, and they will trample the holy city for forty-two months."

---

133 Daniel Akin. *Exalting Jesus in Revelation: Christ-Centered Exposition Commentary*, Kindle Edition, location 4144.

This references what Jesus said in Luke 21:24: "And Jerusalem will be trampled by the Gentiles until the times of the Gentiles are fulfilled."

Right away we have three key issues with which to contend:

1. What is God's sanctuary?
2. What is the holy city?
3. How do we understand 42 months?

I think the 42 months is simply 3 ½ years. Although, there are Bible scholars who view this time frame to mean simply a "short period of time."

Furthermore, John's 1st century audience would have understood the holy city to be Jerusalem, though there are quite a few others who believe it represents the church (Mounce, Revelation, 215).[134]

Yet, what about the identity of God's sanctuary or temple? This question poses some significant degree of difficulty to answer.

Historically, two temples have been built on the Temple Mount in Jerusalem. The first, King Solomon's. The second, Zerubbabel's temple that was later enlarged by Herod the Great. Spiritually, the idea of the temple is varied and developing.

Jesus used the image of the temple to refer to Himself.

The church is called the sanctuary of God in 1 Corinthians 3:16 and Ephesians 2:21-22. Believers in Christ are a sanctuary of the Holy Spirit (1 Cor. 6:19-20).

The Sanctuary in Revelation is referred to as both the place where God is present and even God Himself (3:12; 7:15; 11:19; 14:15,17; 15:5-6, 8; 16:1, 17; 21:22).

---

134 Akin, Kindle Edition, location 4153. Primary source: Robert Mounce. *NICNT: The Book of Revelation*, p 215).

So, how do we understand the sanctuary in 11:1-2? Good question. Some fine scholars believe it represents the church, the Christian community. Robert Mounce writes, "For John, the temple was not a literal building but "the Christian community who worship God." It is the church, the people of God.[135] However, other scholars, based on what Jesus says in Matthew 24:15, and Paul in 2 Thessalonians 2:4, believe a future physical temple will be built during the last days.[136]

The arguments for the various options seem solid to me. Yet, I would suggest that the temple of God is a symbol of the true church that worships the triune God.

Furthermore, Russell Bradley Jones writes, "The court outside the sacred sanctuary represents the lost people of the earth, who will tread the holy city under foot, but will ever be apart from God's separated people in their spiritual relationship to Him. This is a picture of spiritual conditions in the earth from God's point of view."[137]

Transition: In short, the measuring of the temple is indicative of God's ownership and divine, spiritual protection of His people.

The Ministry of the Two Witnesses (v. 3-6).

> *Rev 11:3 And I will grant authority to my two witnesses, and they will prophesy for 1,260 days, clothed in sackcloth."*
>
> *Rev 11:4 These are the two olive trees and the two lampstands that stand before the Lord of the earth.*

---

135 Robert Mounce. *NICNT: The Book of Revelation*, 213.

136 Akin, Kindle Edition. Location 4162. (Also MacArthur would be included in this camp.)

137 Russell Bradley Jones. *The Triumphant Christ and His Church: An Expositio of the Revelation*, p. 53.

Rev 11:5 And if anyone would harm them, fire pours from their mouth and consumes their foes. If anyone would harm them, this is how he is doomed to be killed.

Rev 11:6 They have the power to shut the sky, that no rain may fall during the days of their prophesying, and they have power over the waters to turn them into blood and to strike the earth with every kind of plague, as often as they desire.

First, who are these two witnesses? Are they two literal individuals or do they symbolize the witnessing church in the last days before the end of the age?

Honestly, the suggestions as to the identification of the two witnesses are almost endless. The suggestions include:

- Elijah and Enoch
- Elijah and Moses
- Jeremiah and Elijah
- Joshua and Caleb
- Peter and Paul
- John the Baptist and Jesus of Nazareth
- James and John
- Law and gospel
- Israel and the church
- Israel and the Word
- Churches of Smyrna and Philadelphia
- Spirit of Elijah and Moses
- The witnessing church

To put it succinctly, the text does not identify the two witnesses, so we cannot be dogmatically certain.

I find myself leaning in the direction of the two witnesses being symbolic of the witnessing church. Why? Well, Simon Kistemaker's argumentation was very helpful to me here.

1. The witnesses must address all the inhabitants of the world: peoples, tribes, languages, and nations (v. 9), which can hardly be done by two individuals.
2. The pairing of the witnesses harkens back to Jesus' sending out his disciples two by two (Mk. 6:7). The apostles also went out two by two.
3. In Israel a verdict was confirmed on the testimony of two or three witnesses (Deut. 17:6; 19:15). The witness of one man can be disregarded, but on the testimony of two men truth is validated (Jn. 8:17).[138]

Look at verse 4. John relies here on an Old Testament prophecy, for he describes the two witnesses as olive trees and lampstands. The prophet Zechariah mentions two olive trees and a solid gold lampstand (4:2-3); olive oil placed in the lampstand functions to spread light and dispel the darkness. And, symbolically, a lampstand is the church (1:20) made up of believers who live by the word of God and testimony of Jesus.

John notes they are clothed in sackcloth. Symbolically dressed in sackcloth as a sign of repentance, the church has been called to prophesy the Word of God, the content of the little scroll, to the world. It is the duty of the church to call people everywhere to repentance and faith in Christ (10:11).

The two witnesses will have power to prophesy for 1,260 days or 42 months, or 3 ½ years, which is the same period of time during which the Gentiles profane the outer court mentioned in verse 2.

What will these witnesses do? Prophesy. Preach. Proclaim the Word of God. And, ladies and gentlemen, until their work is done, they are untouchable. They will be protected as indicated in verse 5.

---

138 Kistemaker, p. 329.

They will be protected by supernatural powers for the period of their prophetic activity. Verse 6 indicates the two witnesses also have the power to shut up the sky so that it will not rain during the time of their prophecy. The background, of course, is reminiscent of Elijah's day. They can turn water into blood and smite the earth with whatever kind of plague they wish.[139]

Transition: The two witnesses prophesy the Word of God to call people to repentance and faith in Christ.

The Death of the Two Witnesses (v. 7-10)

Rev 11:7 And when they have finished their testimony, the beast that rises from the bottomless pit will make war on them and conquer them and kill them,

Rev 11:8 and their dead bodies will lie in the street of the great city that symbolically is called Sodom and Egypt, where their Lord was crucified.

Rev 11:9 For three and a half days some from the peoples and tribes and languages and nations will gaze at their dead bodies and refuse to let them be placed in a tomb,

Rev 11:10 and those who dwell on the earth will rejoice over them and make merry and exchange presents, because these two prophets had been a torment to those who dwell on the earth.

When the church has completed her task of proclaiming the gospel of the Kingdom to all the nations of the world (Matt. 24:14), the beast rises up from the bottomless pit makes war with them, conquers them, and kills them!

Listen, folks, as you know…whenever and wherever the gospel is proclaimed, there will be opposition. The Antichrist is constantly

139 Mounce, p. 219.

opposing and seeking to thwart Christ and His church every step of the way.

Here, the witness of the church has come to an end. The beast's attack is on the message and the messengers.

He kills the messengers to silence the message.

Richard Bauckham offers a haunting insight here: "It is not a literal prediction that every faithful Christian will in fact be put to death. But it does require that every faithful Christian must be prepared to die."[140]

The bodies will lie in the street of the great city as objects of contempt and scorn (v. 8).

Now, here is where the text gets tricky—you have to make a choice between a literal interpretation or a figurative interpretation. Literal Jerusalem? Spiritual Jerusalem? Note, too, that the great city is identified with Sodom and Egypt...one a place of rampant immorality, and the other a land symbolizing the enslavement of the Israelites. The great city is the place where people, living contrary to the will of God, have crucified and continue to crucify the Lord all over again (Hebrews 6:6).

In verse 9, citizens from all over the world (people, tribes, languages, and nations) view the corpses of the witnesses. These people represent the world set against the saints. They view and rejoice in the demise of the church; they spurn God and His Word.

In verse 10, we are told they rejoice, celebrate, and exchange gifts. They gloat. They are filled with wicked satisfaction. They celebrate victory over God's people.

Why? Because the two prophets had been a torment to those who dwell on earth.

140 Richard Bauckham, *The Theology of the Book of Revelation*, New Testament Theology, p. 93.

How twisted is this mindset? The world demonstrates this twisted thinking in that God's messengers spiritually tormented unbelievers.

- The Word of God exposed their sin.
- There were told the truth.
- They were called to repentance and faith in Christ.
- They were told of God's Wrath and the Day of Judgment.

Transition: This is a tragic account of the two witnesses' death.

The Resurrection of the Two Witnesses (v. 11-12)

Rev 11:11 But after the three and a half days a breath of life from God entered them, and they stood up on their feet, and great fear fell on those who saw them.

Rev 11:12 Then they heard a loud voice from heaven saying to them, "Come up here!" And they went up to heaven in a cloud, and their enemies watched them.

The demise of the Christian witness is of short duration due to the intervention of God. The world gloats for three and half days. When this period comes to an end, God as the author of life breathes life into the corpses of these two witnesses. He makes the dead come alive. He possesses ultimate authority over life and death.

Furthermore, a loud voice summons the two witnesses to heaven. God's enemies watch them go up to heaven in a cloud. This triumph over evil is openly visible to all.

Finally, we have…

The Resulting Judgment of God (v. 13-14)

> *Rev 11:13 And at that hour there was a great earthquake, and a tenth of the city fell. Seven thousand people were killed in the earthquake, and the rest were terrified and gave glory to the God of heaven.*
>
> *Rev 11:14 The second woe has passed; behold, the third woe is soon to come.*

As the witnesses are taken up into heaven, a great earthquake devastates a tenth of the city and 7,000 people are killed. The rest were terrified and ironically gave glory to the God of heaven. This is an odd response in the context of this chapter, especially after such a deification of evil.

Yet, is it conceivable that the resurrection of these martyrs strike terror in their hearts leading to giving glory to God?

In short, Revelation 11 is a very concerning chapter. It is an exceedingly difficult text to interpret. Yet, what I do know for certain is that there is still time to repent and believe in Christ.

The Bible says, "The times of ignorance God overlooked, but now He commands all people everywhere to repent."- Acts 17:30

You need Christ.

You cannot be your own Savior.

Will you turn to Christ this very morning?

23

"THE GREAT ANNOUNCEMENT"

Revelation 11:15-19, ESV

This morning we fix our attention on the final five verses of Revelation 11.

What we have here is essentially the trumpet blast of the seventh angel.

The FIRST SIX trumpets were harbingers or forerunners of six devastating judgments, yet the seventh trumpet introduces the reader to a great announcement.

When you pause to reflect upon the subject, you begin to realize that there are a number of significant announcements in the New Testament as related to Christ.

For instance, we have a record of the angelic announcement regarding the birth of the Savior, the Anointed One, in Luke 2:11: "The Savior—yes, the Messiah, the Lord—has been born today in Bethlehem, the city of David!" [NLT]

God announced the birth of His Son, conceived of the Holy Spirit, born of the virgin Mary, and lying in a manger, to a collection of shepherds staying in a field nearby guarding their flocks by night.

The angels were joined by the armies of heaven in lifting their voices in praise to God by saying: "Glory to God in highest heaven, and peace on earth to those with whom God is pleased." [Luke 2:13-14, NLT]

The content and substance of that announcement shook the world in such a way that the universe has never been the same.

Yet another proclamation took place the day of Jesus' baptism. Matthew records the event this way: "After being baptized, Jesus came up immediately from the water; and behold, the heavens were opened, and he saw the Spirit of God descending as a dove and lighting on Him, and behold, a voice out of the heavens said, "This is My beloved Son, in whom I am well-pleased." [Matthew 3:16-17, NASB]

Can you imagine? The very voice of holy God announcing and affirming the eternal Sonship of the Lord Jesus! It gives me goose-bumps, folks!

Finally, the declaration of Christ on the cross. The disciple whom Jesus loved wrote, "Therefore when Jesus had received the sour wine, He said, 'It is finished!' And He bowed His head and gave up His spirit." [Jn. 19:30, NASB] Christ on the cross putting the exclamation point on His redemptive work to redeem repentant, believing sinners from their sin and save them from the wrath and condemnation of God. It was an announcement no doubt heard by very few people, but the import of that statement cannot be overstated.

Thus, here in Revelation 11:15-19 we have yet another great announcement. Give special attention to verse 15.

> *Rev 11:15 Then the seventh angel blew his trumpet, and there were loud voices in heaven, saying, "The kingdom of the world has become the kingdom of our Lord and of his Christ, and he shall reign forever and ever."*
>
> *Rev 11:16 And the twenty-four elders who sit on their thrones before God fell on their faces and worshiped God,*
>
> *Rev 11:17 saying, "We give thanks to you, Lord God Almighty, who is and who was, for you have taken your great power and begun to reign.*

> *Rev 11:18 The nations raged, but your wrath came, and the time for the dead to be judged, and for rewarding your servants, the prophets and saints, and those who fear your name, both small and great, and for destroying the destroyers of the earth."*

> *Rev 11:19 Then God's temple in heaven was opened, and the ark of his covenant was seen within his temple. There were flashes of lightning, rumblings, peals of thunder, an earthquake, and heavy hail.*

As we unpack this text, I hope that you might find the following headings helpful:

1. The Great Announcement (v. 15).
2. The Great Response (v. 16-17).
3. The Great Judgment (v. 18).
4. The Great Temple (v. 19).

The Great Announcement (v. 15)

> *Rev 11:15 Then the seventh angel blew his trumpet, and there were loud voices in heaven, saying, "The kingdom of the world has become the kingdom of our Lord and of his Christ, and he shall reign forever and ever."*

The announcement is made that "The kingdom of the world has become the kingdom of our Lord and his Christ, and he shall reign forever and ever."

Multiple loud voices proclaim this announcement.

Now, to be sure, there has never been a time when the entire universe, including this earthly kingdom, has not belonged to the Lord. He reigns. He rules supreme.

With that said, under the sovereignty of God, the enemy has been allowed to have dominion over this world.

Scripture says, "The god of this age has blinded the minds of unbelievers, so that they cannot see the light of the gospel that displays the glory of Christ, who is **the** image of God." [2 Cor. 4:4]

It is set forth in Scripture that the god of this age is Satan. The current depraved mindset of the world and its godless, false philosophies blind the people of this age to the truths of God. Satan's leadership and deceptions pander to the depravity of unbelievers and only serves to deepen the moral darkness in which people actively, willingly participate. Satan's rule is over a system of darkness.

Nonetheless, a day is coming when the long rebellion of the world kingdom will end when Christ establishes His eternal reign and rule! Oh, glorious day!

Note the expression: "…the kingdom of our Lord and of his Christ…" Interesting. Clearly, the reference to "our Lord" is to God the Father, and the terminology "…and of his Christ…" serves as a reference to the Messiah or the Anointed One, the Lord Jesus Christ.

While there is no identification of the Spirit in this specific text, we can be sure, as one Bible scholar stated that the eternal Kingdom is a Kingdom of God the Father, of the Lord Jesus Christ, and of the Holy Spirit, the one God in three persons![141]

Transition: Dear church, this is a glorious, grand, great announcement.

The Great Response (v. 16-17).

> *Rev 11:16 And the twenty-four elders who sit on their thrones before God fell on their faces and worshiped God,*

---

141 Paige Patterson. *The New American Commentary: Revelation*, p. 253.

*Rev 11:17 saying, "We give thanks to you, Lord God
Almighty, who is and who was, for you have taken your
great power and begun to reign.*

Clearly, the great announcement incites a great response!

The 24 elders vacate their thrones and fall prostrate before
God and worship Him. Frankly, this is an appropriate, astonishing
response...one we might do well to consider for a moment.

Application: In the modern era, the worshiper is so different
when one discovers he or she is in the presence of God.

Some of the contemporary worshiper's responses might include:

- Indifference
- Ho-hum-I've heard it all before.
- Can we be done already?!?
- Ambivalence.
- Distraction/preoccupation.
- Boredom (this one drives me bonkers). How can the worship of
  God, who is holy, holy, holy, be boring? Worship is a thrilling
  and moving experience.
- Very little desperation for God.
- Very little recognition of our brokenness before Christ and our
  great need for Him.
- Very little desire to repent of sin.

For starters, we must reclaim that hunger in worship for God
and for His Word. There must be a renewed appetite to hear the
Bible expounded. As one of my favorite authors [Dr. Steven Lawson]
aptly put it: "It is the man of God opening the Word of God and
expounding its truths so that the voice of God may be heard, the
glory of God seen, and the will of God obeyed."[142]

142 Steven J. Lawson. *Famine in the Land: A Passionate Call for Expository Preaching*, p. 18.

Along those same lines, Martyn Lloyd-Jones wrote: "Wanting to listen to the Word is inevitable if men and women are born again and have become Christians. A babe…has an instinct for milk. He wants it!…He is alive and wants the mother's milk, and rightly so. The point is clear. One simply cannot be a Christian and have no desire for a knowledge of this truth—it is impossible."[143]

Additionally, remember Isaiah's response when He encountered God in the temple? It's recorded in Isaiah 6. When Isaiah entered the temple, he saw another King, the Ultimate King--the One who sat forever on the throne of Judah. He saw the Lord.

- He knew he had been in the presence of God, the sovereign One. He saw God seated on the throne.
- The Temple shook down to its very foundations.
- The entire building was filled with smoke.
- Yet, do you know what quaked the most in the Temple that day? ISAIAH.
- When Isaiah saw the living God, the reigning monarch of the universe on display before his very eyes, he became acutely aware of his sin.[144] He was a man of unclean lips.
- Isaiah knew he had an impure heart. He knew he was undone, ruined.
- Isaiah was exposed, made naked under the gaze of God's utter holiness.
- His glimpse of the Almighty shattered Isaiah's self-esteem and ego.
- He became acutely aware that he dwelled among sinners.
- God showed to Isaiah his corruption all at once and Isaiah was

---

143 Ibid., p. 43. Primary source: D. Martyn-Lloyd Jones, *Authentic Christianity* (Wheaton, Ill.: Crossway, 2000), 1:105-6.

144 R.C. Sproul. The Holiness of God, Kindle Edition, location 274.

undone. He trembled before the Holy One. There was nowhere to hide. He was alone before God. He mourned over his sin. No half-baked appreciation for God's grace.

No boredom.

No indifference.

No ho-hum.

No preoccupation with the affairs of today.

No indulging of self.

No casual, flippant attitude before God.

Yes, we have much to learn about how to approach and respond to the God we worship and who reveals Himself in the Sacred Scripture.

Transition: The 24 elders fell down on their faces before God and worshiped. They gave thanks to Him, the Almighty, for His power and His reign and rule. What a lesson for us to learn. A right response before God is always to honor Him with our lips and our lives.

The Great Judgment (v. 18)

> *Rev 11:18 The nations raged, but your wrath came, and the time for the dead to be judged, and for rewarding your servants, the prophets and saints, and those who fear your name, both small and great, and for destroying the destroyers of the earth."*

The time has come for the judging of the dead. The Bible makes clear: "It is appointed for man to die once and after that comes judgment" (Heb. 9:27, ESV).

I would like to identify three key aspects of this judgment:

1. The time has come for judging the dead. Those who rejected God's gracious invitation to salvation through Christ are now to face their final judgment.

2. The time is also appointed to rewarding the servants, the prophets and saints, and those great and small who have honored and feared the name of God. The Bible speaks of rewards promised to believers (Matt. 5:12; Lk. 6:23, 35; 1 Cor. 3:14; 9:18). Certainly, the greatest of all eternal rewards is the very presence of God for all eternity. Rewards will be given by the Father to those who were "high profile" followers of Christ as well as those largely unnoticed, but highly esteemed by the Lord for going about their faithful service to Him. Oh, what a great and faithful God we have who promises to bless and reward our faithful service to Him.

3. Third, we have an odd phrase, "and for destroying the destroyers of the earth." God is going to destroy those who are destroying the earth. This would seem to be a reference at least to the beast and the false prophet of chapter 13, and the scarlet woman of chapter 17.

Transition: True to God's Word, a great judgment is coming.

The Great Temple (v. 19)

> Rev 11:19 Then God's temple in heaven was opened, and the ark of his covenant was seen within his temple. There were flashes of lightning, rumblings, peals of thunder, an earthquake, and heavy hail.

This is the concluding verse of chapter 11. Here John notes that the temple of God in heaven was opened. The ark of the covenant was seen inside.

With that we are given a description of lightning, rumblings, peals of thunder, an earthquake, and heaven hail.

This portion of the vision is interesting. Why? Well, as Paige Patterson points out it is because there is a sense in which the Lamb is the temple (Rev. 21:22), and another sense that there is a temple that is open in heaven and within that temple is found the ark of God.[145]

In Scripture, the ark represented the presence of God. It symbolized God's atonement and covenant with His people. That earthly ark was only a picture of this heavenly one.[146]

There is much happening in the world today, especially in the United States, that surely causes each of us a moment of pause and great concern.

As we continue our march through Revelation, I am convinced that we are living in the last days. Or, at a minimum we are seeing elements of the last days. Other Scriptures seem to confirm this reality. Specifically, listen to what Paul wrote to Timothy:

> "But realize this, that in the last days, difficult times will come. For men will be lovers of self, lovers of money, boastful, arrogant, revilers, disobedient to parents, ungrateful, unholy, unloving, irreconcilable, malicious gossips, without self-control, brutal, haters of good, treacherous, reckless, conceited, lovers of pleasure rather than lovers of God, holding to a form of godliness, although they have denied its power; avoid such men as these."- 2 Tim. 3:1-5

Yet, God is patient giving people more time to repent and believe in His Son Jesus Christ.

A day is coming, though, when rebellion will end and Christ will set up His eternal reign.

You and those you love must repent and be saved before it is too late.

---

145 Patterson, p. 256.

146 John MacArthur. MacArthur New Testament Commentary, p. 925.

24

"THE CHRISTMAS STORY IN REVELATION"

Revelation 12:1-6, ESV

We find ourselves this morning in the very center of the book of Revelation, and are now entering into the second half of this the final book of Holy Scripture.

Revelation has essentially two parts:

1. Chapters 1-11 - Christ's church persecuted by the world.
2. Chapters 12-22 - Christ's church persecuted by Satan.

Additionally, chapter 1 contains an introduction to the Apocalypse, and chapter 22 a fitting conclusion.

Chapter 12 is intriguing and encouraging on virtually every level. Why? In part, John emphasizes in this chapter the beat-down and defeat of Satan.

Bible Scholar, Simon Kistemaker, identifies Satan as a five-time loser in chapter 12, whereas Christ and His church are victorious!

- In verse 5, the devil attempted to devour the male child, but God snatched him up to his throne.

- In verse 9, Satan fought against Michael and his angels and lost.
- In verses 6 and 14, the dragon pursued the woman, but God prepared a place for her in the desert.
- In verses 15-16, the serpent wanted the woman to drown in a torrent, but the earth swallowed the river.
- In verse 17, Satan lost when he waged war against the woman's offspring, who kept on obeying God's commands and holding on to Jesus' testimony.[147]

With that said, concerning the specific text before us today, Daniel Akin writes, "This is an apocalyptic Christmas story."[148] Now, that assertion caught my eye and my interest right away. We do not tend to equate anything in Revelation with the Christmas story in Matthew and Luke. However, as we will see, you can make a case that the Christmas story does exist in Revelation. Revelation 12:1-17 accounts for us, in part and in summary, the grand story of redemption in the Bible. In this chapter we encounter, in fantastic imagery and vision, the true story of the entire world. This is the Christmas story in Revelation. Let's begin…

> *Rev 12:1 And a great sign appeared in heaven: a woman clothed with the sun, with the moon under her feet, and on her head a crown of twelve stars.*
>
> *Rev 12:2 She was pregnant and was crying out in birth pains and the agony of giving birth.*
>
> *Rev 12:3 And another sign appeared in heaven: behold, a great red dragon, with seven heads and ten horns, and on his heads seven diadems.*

147 Simon Kistemaker. *New Testament Commentary: Revelation*, p. 353.

148 Daniel Akin. *Exalting Jesus in Revelation: Christ-Centered Exposition: Revelation*, Kindle Edition, location 4335.

Rev 12:4 His tail swept down a third of the stars of heaven and cast them to the earth. And the dragon stood before the woman who was about to give birth, so that when she bore her child he might devour it.

Rev 12:5 She gave birth to a male child, one who is to rule all the nations with a rod of iron, but her child was caught up to God and to his throne,

Rev 12:6 and the woman fled into the wilderness, where she has a place prepared by God, in which she is to be nourished for 1,260 days.

Two key ideas I want to ask you to consider as we think about the opening verses of chapter 12:

1. The Origins of Christmas (Genesis 3:15)
2. The Characters of Christmas (Rev. 12:1-6)

The Origins of Christmas (Genesis 3:15)

Please open your Bibles to the first book of the Scripture, the book of beginnings, that is, Genesis. Please locate chapter three, verse 15.

The book of Genesis is included in a section of Scripture known as "The Pentateuch." The designation Pentateuch refers to the first five books of the Bible.

The Jewish designation for the Pentateuch is the Hebrew word, "Torah." Usually, we translate this word to mean "law," but it means significantly more. It comes from a word for "teach" and is better understood as "instruction."

In effect, the first five books of the Bible establish and instruct us regarding historical and theological foundations important for the rest of the Bible.

The word Genesis means "beginning" or "generation."

For our purposes this morning, it's important to understand the full import of Genesis 3:15 by understanding how humanity changed after the first sin.

1. Man lost his original innocence—their eyes were opened and they had a sudden awareness of nakedness, signifying their shame and guilt (3:7).
2. Man's relationship with God was distorted—they lost their immediate and easy access to God's presence.
3. Adam and Eve "knew good and evil" (3:21)—they now knew evil as participants.
4. They lost the peaceful paradise and freedom of the Garden of Eden (3:23).
5. The effects of the Fall carry on to future generations.[149]

In Genesis 3 we have a detailed account of the fall of man. In short, man rebels against God yet God shows remarkable mercy.

Look at verses 14-19:

> *Gen 3:14 The LORD God said to the serpent, "Because you have done this, cursed are you above all livestock and above all beasts of the field; on your belly you shall go, and dust you shall eat all the days of your life. 15 I will put enmity between you and the woman, and between your offspring and her offspring; he shall bruise your head, and you shall bruise his heel." 16 To the woman he said, "I will surely multiply your pain in childbearing; in pain you shall bring forth children. Your desire shall be for your husband, and he shall rule over you." 17 And to Adam he said, "Because you have listened to the voice of your wife and have eaten of the tree of which I commanded you, 'You shall not eat of*

---

149 Lecture notes on the Old Testament: The Promise and the Blessing RELI 1301 Old Testament Survey, compiled by Steve Mullen, Ph.D., p. 44-45.

*it,' cursed is the ground because of you; in pain you
shall eat of it all the days of your life; 18 thorns and
thistles it shall bring forth for you; and you shall eat
the plants of the field. 19 By the sweat of your face you
shall eat bread, till you return to the ground, for out of
it you were taken; for you are dust, and to dust you shall
return."*

In a very real sense, Genesis 3:15 provides a glimpse of the origin of Christmas. The Christmas story actually begins in Eden, not in a city called Bethlehem.

You see, immediately following the fall of when Adam and Eve yielded to the temptation of the serpent, God made a promise to send the Savior.

In Genesis 3:15 God said to Satan: 15 I will put enmity between you and the woman, and between your offspring and her offspring; he shall bruise your head, and you shall bruise his heel."

Theologians and students of the Scripture identify verse 15 as the protoeuangelium—which means, "the first gospel, or the first announcement of the gospel."

Therefore, even in the lifetime of Adam and Eve there are some words of God that point toward a future salvation: in Genesis 3:15 the curse on the serpent includes a promise that the seed of the woman (one of her descendants) would bruise the head of the serpent, but would himself be hurt in the process—a promise ultimately fulfilled in Christ.[150] Already, God was revealing His plan to defeat Satan and offer salvation to the world through His Son, Jesus Christ.

Transition: The origin of Christmas, God's promise of the Savior, is in Eden.

---

150 Wayne Grudem. *Systematic Theology: An Introduction to Biblical Doctrine*, p. 118.

The Characters of Christmas (v. 1-6)

Essentially in these six verses you have three significant characters:

1. The woman (v. 1).
2. The dragon (v. 3).
3. The male child (v. 5).

We are told in verse 1 that " a great sign appeared in heaven—a woman…"

This is the first of seven signs that appear in the remainder of the Revelation.

Who is this WOMAN (v. 1)? To begin with, the text is clear regarding a few details related to this woman:

- She is clothed with the sun
- The moon is under her feet
- A crown of 12 stars is upon her head
- She is pregnant and in the agony of giving birth

There are FOUR symbolic women in Revelation.

1. The Jezebel in 2:20- symbolizing paganism
2. The prostitute of Chapter 17-symbolizing apostasy
3. The bride of the Lamb in chapter 19[151]-symbolizing the true church

The identity of this woman has been variously understood. For instance…

151 Akin, Kindle Edition, location 4353. Primary Source: MacArthur, *Revelation 1-11*, 3-4.

- The Catholic Church has identified her as Mary.
- Others have said she is Israel
- Some have said she is the church
- Others have said she is the "messianic community"
- Or, the ideal, true Israel (Mounce, Beale, Ladd)

I looked at this issue from virtually every angle--gave me a bit of a headache! However, it was a commentator by the name of Ray Frank Robbins[152] who helped me come to some conclusion on the identity of this woman. What's interesting is that his treatment on the subject was a like an echo chamber among numerous other Bible scholars.

In short, it would seem that the woman symbolizes the messianic community. In other words, it is out of faithful Israel that the Messiah will come. Later within the same chapter the woman will come to signify the church (v. 17).[153]

Secondly, we have the character of the DRAGON (v. 3-4).

> *Rev 12:3 And another sign appeared in heaven: behold, a great red dragon, with seven heads and ten horns, and on his heads seven diadems. Rev 12:4 His tail swept down a third of the stars of heaven and cast them to the earth. And the dragon stood before the woman who was about to give birth, so that when she bore her child he might devour it.*

A second sign appears in the sky—an enormous red dragon with seven heads, ten horns, and seven diadems! The identity of the dragon is much less complicated. His identity is "the ancient serpent called the devil, or Satan" (12:9).

---

152 Ray Frank Robbins. *The Revelation of Jesus Christ: A Commentary on the Book of Revelation*, p. 147.

153 Robert H. Mounce. *NICNT: The Book of Revelation*, p. 232.

Look at verse 9:

> *"And the great dragon was thrown down, that ancient serpent, who is called the devil and Satan, the deceiver of the whole world—he was thrown down to the earth, and his angels were thrown down with him."*

Satan appears as a dragon 13 times in this book. In this vision he is fierce and murderous.

Satan is the sworn, relentless, archenemy of God and God's people. The color red represents his murderous character. Remember that Jesus had once said to the Jews, "You belong to your father, the devil...He was a murderer from the beginning" (John 8:44). Wherever he goes, he wages war. One commentator noted, "The dragon dominates the world by governing global empires, principal authorities, political movements, and philosophical ideas."[154] Yet, it should be articulated that Satan's crowns represent nothing but pretended royalty.

Furthermore, the text says in verse 4 that with his tail he swept away a third of the stars and cast them to earth. Again, here, we have an interpretive difficulty—are these stars literal stars or are the stars a reference to fallen, rebellious angels? Bible interpreters are divided.

On the one hand, John MacArthur, for example, indicates that this is a reference to Satan's original (Ezek. 28:11; Is. 14:12-15) rebellion which resulted in one-third of the angelic host joining his insurrection and becoming demons.[155]

On the other hand, Robert Mounce writes, "The cataclysmic action emphasizes the tremendous size and awesome power of the dragon. That he hurls down a third of the stars indicates no more than

154 Simon Kistemaker. *New Testament Commentary: Revelation*, p. 356.

155 John MacArthur. *MacArthur New Testament Commentary*, p. 925.

that he does so to a very great number. John is not teaching a theology of fallen angels but reporting a great pageant enacted in the sky."[156]

Which is it? I cannot say for certain, but I tend to lean in the direction of what the text says literally.

The emphasis in verse 4 however is to be placed on his posture. The dragon stands before the woman who is about to give birth so that when she does, he can devour the child! That's the critical focus here.

Throughout the ages, Satan's intent and critical mission has been to destroy Christ and the church's testimony regarding the Savior. The hostility toward this child of the redeemed explains, at least on some level, the determination of King Herod to murder the Christ-child (Matt. 2), and continued through the dangers, snares, temptations of the Lord's earthly life, and peaked in the crucifixion.[157]

Transition: By way of review, we have considered the origins of Christmas from Genesis 3:15, and two key characters in Revelation 12. In verses 5-6, we have the final character in this salvation drama.

Lastly, we have the character of the MALE CHILD (v. 5-6).

> *Rev 12:5 She gave birth to a male child, one who is to rule all the nations with a rod of iron, but her child was caught up to God and to his throne, Rev 12:6 and the woman fled into the wilderness, where she has a place prepared by God, in which she is to be nourished for 1,260 days.*

Here is the fulfillment of the messianic prophecies that foretell the coming of the Christ (Isa. 7:14; 66:7). The woman gives birth to a son who will rule all the nations with a rod of iron. He rules, He reigns, He protects, and He shepherds His church. He reigns supreme

---

156 Mounce, p. 233.

157 Ibid., p. 233.

with justice and love. Then, like that, the child is ushered up to God and to His throne. John moves with lightning speed from the Lord's birth to the Lord's ascension. The point seems to be that Satan lost. His attempts to foil Christ's messianic, redemptive ministry failed. Satan's defeat was culminated in the Lord's ascension and exaltation!! Hallelujah! Oh, victory in Jesus! God is in perfect, complete control.

Remember: In Eden, God put enmity between the serpent and the woman and between his offspring and hers. God said that the woman's offspring would crush the serpent's head (Gen. 3:15). This divine prophecy was fulfilled in the birth, life, and ascension of Jesus.

Verse 6 informs the reader that the woman fled into the wilderness and is cared for there by God for 42 months. God provides for His people. He provides for them a place of spiritual refuge. What an assurance this is for the follower of Christ.

When you stop and think about it, we are still in this world, but not a part of it. I have no doubt God will provide for and protect His church.

Christmas in Revelation…who would have thought? Yet, God fulfilled His promise to provide the Savior and to defeat the enemies of sin and death.

25

"THE DEVIL - DANGEROUS, DESPERATE, DEFEATED"

Revelation 12:7-17, ESV

I never cease to be astonished at how desperation can motivate us to act in ways that can be destructive to ourselves and others. Desperation is dangerous. Desperation can drive any one of us to do the dreadfully unthinkable, to act in the most depraved ways.

For instance, and this is a shocking illustration of desperation, I read about the arrest of a woman by the name of Antoinette Davis on the charges of child prostitution. She trafficked her own five-year-old daughter in an act of sheer desperation to pay off a drug debt. Tragically, the child was raped and murdered in the process by a man named Mario O'Neill. It's beyond comprehension that the mother chose this way to secure money to pay off her debt.[158]

Desperate situations can lead us to engage in desperate acts. I read recently that a man once said: "There is nothing more dangerous than a desperate man who has nothing to lose. (Rafay Baloch)"[159] In the text for this morning, I want you to observe with me the actions of the dangerous, desperate, defeated devil.

---

158 https://www.badcredit.org/5-shocking-stories-of-debt-and-desperation/

159 http://www.wiseoldsayings.com/desperate-quotes/

Rev 12:7 Now war arose in heaven, Michael and his angels fighting against the dragon. And the dragon and his angels fought back, Rev 12:8 but he was defeated, and there was no longer any place for them in heaven. Rev 12:9 And the great dragon was thrown down, that ancient serpent, who is called the devil and Satan, the deceiver of the whole world—he was thrown down to the earth, and his angels were thrown down with him. Rev12:10 And I heard a loud voice in heaven, saying, "Now the salvation and the power and the kingdom of our God and the authority of his Christ have come, for the accuser of our brothers has been thrown down, who accuses them day and night before our God. Rev 12:11 And they have conquered him by the blood of the Lamb and by the word of their testimony, for they loved not their lives even unto death. Rev 12:12 Therefore, rejoice, O heavens and you who dwell in them! But woe to you, O earth and sea, for the devil has come down to you in great wrath, because he knows that his time is short!" Rev 12:13 And when the dragon saw that he had been thrown down to the earth, he pursued the woman who had given birth to the male child. Rev 12:14 But the woman was given the two wings of the great eagle so that she might fly from the serpent into the wilderness, to the place where she is to be nourished for a time, and times, and half a time. Rev 12:15 The serpent poured water like a river out of his mouth after the woman, to sweep her away with a flood. Rev 12:16 But the earth came to the help of the woman, and the earth opened its mouth and swallowed the river that the dragon had poured from his mouth. Rev 12:17 Then the dragon became furious with the woman and went off to make war on the rest of her offspring, on those who keep the commandments of God and hold to the testimony of Jesus. And he stood on the sand of the sea.

Before plunging ahead into this text it would seem important and relevant to recount for you a bit of what the Scripture teaches about Satan.

First, Satan is NOT God. You and I are NOT dualists-- meaning that Satan and God are equal in power, but just on opposite sides. The Bible does not suggest this at all.

Satan is a creature. He does not have the power of God. He cannot do the things which ONLY God can do.

However, Satan is more powerful and crafty than human beings. R.C. Sproul writes, "He is stronger than we are, but weaker than God Himself, which is why anyone indwelt by the Holy Spirit does not have to fear being possessed by a demon"[160] (1 John 4:4).

The Scriptures tell us that if we resist Satan, he will flee from us (James 4:7).

Scripture uses different images for Satan: a roaring lion, an accuser, a tempter, an angel of light, and a deceiver. He can morph in that he has the uncanny ability to appear under the auspices of the good. But remember, his goal is to drive people to despair rather than to repentance. He wants to destroy each of us, our families, communities, churches, and nations.

Yet, Christ calls us to forgiveness and redemption.

Now, as this particular text unfolds beginning in verse 7, John's readers are informed of a war.

> *Rev 12:7 Now war arose in heaven, Michael and his angels fighting against the dragon. And the dragon and his angels fought back,*

This war is waged in heaven and is between Michael and his angels and the dragon and his angels.

Michael is named in Scripture as the archangel. He is the guardian and protector of God's people, and he has a specific role with respect to Israel, according to Daniel 12:1.

160 R.C. Sproul. *Everyone's a Theologian*, Kindle Edition, p. 97.

Verse 8 records the result of the war.

> *Rev 12:8 but he was defeated, and there was no longer*
> *any place for them in heaven.*

Satan and his angels are DEFEATED and they are displaced from heaven. In fact verse 9 informs us that the dragon and his angels were thrown down to the earth. John uses some derivative of the phrase "thrown down" some five times. The reason, I think, is to accentuate the significance of the defeat—thrown down from heaven to earth. Displaced. Ousted.

Then, in verse 9, John gives us what might be identified as a descriptive statement clarifying the identity of the dragon.

> *Rev 12:9 And the great dragon was thrown down, that*
> *ancient serpent, who is called the devil and Satan, the*
> *deceiver of the whole world—he was thrown down to*
> *the earth, and his angels were thrown down with him.*

He is the ancient serpent. He is the Devil. He is Satan. He is the deceiver of the whole world. He is defeated. In addition, verse 10 further identifies that Satan is "the accuser of our brothers."

At this defeat notice what John then writes in verse 10:

> *Rev 12:10 And I heard a loud voice in heaven, saying,*
> *"Now the salvation and the power and the kingdom of*
> *our God and the authority of his Christ have come, for*
> *the accuser of our brothers has been thrown down, who*
> *accuses them day and night before our God.*

There is an announcement of Satan's defeat and more to the point, a declaration of the salvation, power, and Kingdom of God and the authority of Christ. Christ is victorious. Satan, the accuser of our brothers, has been conquered.

How was Satan vanquished? The answer is asserted in verse 11:

> *Rev 12:11 And they have conquered him by the blood of the Lamb and by the word of their testimony, for they loved not their lives even unto death.*

Oh, dear church, THERE IS POWER IN THE BLOOD!
Would you be free from the burden of sin?
Would you over evil a victory win?
Would you be free from your passion and pride?
Come for a cleansing to Calvary's tide
Would you do service to Jesus your King?
Would you live daily His praises to sing?
What can wash away my sin?
What can make me whole again?

Nothing but the blood of Jesus

It was the blood of Christ that gained the victory!! And, we as the faithful, and especially those martyred for their testimony of Christ by their lips and lives, take part or share in that victory! Oh, what a great Savior we serve. There is none like Him.

And, notice then in verse 12 the contrast between the occupants of heaven and those who remain on earth. It's haunting…

> *Rev 12:12 Therefore, rejoice, O heavens and you who dwell in them! But woe to you, O earth and sea, for the devil has come down to you in great wrath, because he knows that his time is short!"*

On the one hand, the occupants of heaven are invited to rejoice over the defeat of Satan and his cronies. Yet, on the other hand, those on the earth are warned that the devil is filled with fury, rage, and wrath. Why? Why is this the case? Before we answer that question...

Transition: By way of review, the devil is defeated. He waged war against Michael and lost handily. The enemy is displaced from heaven, thrown down to the earth. Heaven rejoices in the salvation, power, and Kingdom of God and the One who has been granted authority in this realm-King Christ! Satan has been conquered by the blood of Christ and by the word of the testimony of those who loved not their lives even unto death. Satan is outraged. And, it is in this rage that he becomes both desperate and dangerous.

Specifically, why is the devil so infuriated? The answer is found in the text—specifically the latter part of verse 12:

"...because he knows that his time is short!"

Relative to this phrase, Dr. Paige Patterson, in his first-rate commentary makes this insightful distinction: "...that the matter is not simply that time is running short, but that God has set a particular time for the final judgment of Satan."[161]

He is defeated. Satan knows his final judgment is coming. Thus, the devil is dangerous and desperate in his final struggle. This will be a time of extraordinary peril for the church as Satan goes on a vengeful rampage.

Look at verses 13-14:

> *Rev 12:13 And when the dragon saw that he had been thrown down to the earth, he pursued the woman who had given birth to the male child. Rev 12:14 But the woman was given the two wings of the great eagle so that she might fly from the serpent into the wilderness,*

161 Paige Patterson. *The New American Commentary: Revelation*, p. 269.

to the place where she is to be nourished for a time, and times, and half a time.

Satan now affixes his attention on his pursuit of the mother of the male child. The woman is the true Israel, the messianic community of Israel and she now shares with her son the hostility of the dragon.

The dragon is intent on persecuting the woman and her seed. Folks, don't be fooled, Satan despises the church which is rooted in his hatred for Christ.

We can expect the same hostile treatment that Christ received while He was here on earth (John 15:21).

We know that to persecute those who belong to God is to persecute the Savior. We know this from what Paul experienced in Acts 9:4-5, which reads: "…and he fell to the ground and heard a voice saying to him, "Saul, Saul, why are you persecuting Me?" And he said, "Who are You, Lord?" And He said, "I am Jesus whom you are persecuting…" (NASB).

In verse 14 we read that the woman was given two wings of the great eagle that she might evade the serpent as she makes her way into the wilderness.

As you might suspect, this symbolizes divine deliverance and enablement. She is located to a place of spiritual refuge. She nourished in this place for three and a half years.

What follows next? Read with me verses 15-16:

> *12:15 The serpent poured water like a river out of his mouth after the woman, to sweep her away with a flood. Rev 12:16 But the earth came to the help of the woman, and the earth opened its mouth and swallowed the river that the dragon had poured from his mouth.*

The serpent opens its mouth and sends forth a great flood of water to sweep her away. [By the way, the flood is a common metaphor in the OT for overwhelming evil.]

The earth comes to her rescue by opening up and swallowing the torrential waters.

I'm reminded of what Jesus said in Matthew 16:18, "…and upon this rock I will build My church; and the gates of Hades will not overpower it" (NASB).

There can be no question that God provides the means by which the woman is protected.

Again, the dragon fails and is utterly defeated, which brings us to the concluding verse of chapter 12.

Verse 17 reads, Rev 12:17 Then the dragon became furious with the woman and went off to make war on the rest of her offspring, on those who keep the commandments of God and hold to the testimony of Jesus. And he stood on the sand of the sea.

The dragon is furious with the woman. He loses against Michael. He loses against the Messiah. He loses against the woman.

He is the deadly, dangerous enemy of her offspring.

Who are those offspring specifically? The answer to that question is clearly articulated in verse 17. They are "those who keep the commandments of God and hold to the testimony of Jesus."

Listen carefully, dear brothers and sisters in Christ—EVERY follower of Jesus who bears his testimony—will become the final object of satanic hatred.

You can be assured Satan is going to go after the church and Israel with a passion and vengeance.

The devil cannot pour his wrath and fury on God. God is well beyond his dangerous, desperate reach. But, the enemy can, does, and will go after God's people.

With grief in my heart, I believe you can make a case that we are living in the days when you cannot distinguish the church from the culture. A simple case in point is look at modern church architecture. It's as if church leadership almost goes out of its way not to look like a traditional church. But, it's much more than that.

Paul warned: "For the time will come when they will not endure sound doctrine; but wanting to have their ears tickled, they will accumulate for themselves teachers in accordance to their own desires, and will turn away their ears from the truth and will turn aside to myths" (2 Tim. 4:3-4).

I see this as a clever strategy by the deceiver. In my view, the church has sold her soul in order to entertain the masses. I listened with shock recently when a pop culture Christian essentially suggested that "Jesus loves me still" and it doesn't necessarily matter what I do or don't do because that's what grace is for.

Many people in the culture and regrettably the church would stand and applaud that statement. But, it's not biblical. It absolutely matters how you live. Grace is not a license to conduct yourself however you want, but an invitation, a demand really to live holy and obedient lives in the pattern of Christ.

The church in many cases has abandoned her commitment to TRUTH and many who profess faith in Christ now flock to the most "relevant" "hip" "trendy" church that will tickle their ears with half-truths.

Oh church, we must not capitulate or surrender convictions informed by Holy Scripture. We must REMAIN FAITHFUL—to Christ, to His Word, to His Kingdom, to His values by which He perfectly lived.

One of my preaching heroes, the late Dr. Adrian Rogers, has been quoted as saying, "It is better to be divided by truth than to be united in error. It is better to speak the truth that hurts and then heals, than falsehood that comforts and then kills."

Friend, are you saved? Are you sure? Don't be deceived. Have you repented of your sin and sought the forgiveness of God? Have you put your trust, your faith in Christ to save you from sin?

If not, will you right now, this very moment give your heart to Christ?

Believer…PRAY! We, too, are followers of Christ whose spirits are willing, but our flesh is weak. We must keep watch and pray that we will not be deceived to give into temptation. Most of all, we rejoice that the enemy is defeated by the same blood of the Lamb that brought us salvation and forgiveness of sin.

26

"SATAN'S HENCHMEN"

Revelation 13:1-10, ESV

Chapter 13 introduces us to Satan's diabolical henchmen:

- The beast out of the sea (v. 1-10)
- The beast out of the earth (v. 11-18)

In chapter 12, the reader was informed of Satan's relentless perse-cution of the church, and here in chapter 13, we receive a description of his heartless helpers, his lackeys, his minions, his flunkeys, his acolytes.

By strict definition, the word "henchmen" is a derogatory plural pronoun which means, "a faithful follower or political supporter, espe-cially one prepared to engage in crime or dishonest practices by way of service."

This chapter reveals Satan's plan for disrupting the worship and work of God. Furthermore, this chapter reveals the activity of the followers of Satan inflicting on God's people enormous hardship and sorrow.

Let's read about the beast out of the sea: the Antichrist.

> *Rev 13:1 And I saw a beast rising out of the sea, with ten horns and seven heads, with ten diadems on its horns and blasphemous names on its heads.*

Rev 13:2 And the beast that I saw was like a leopard; its feet were like a bear's, and its mouth was like a lion's mouth. And to it the dragon gave his power and his throne and great authority.

Rev 13:3 One of its heads seemed to have a mortal wound, but its mortal wound was healed, and the whole earth marveled as they followed the beast.

Rev 13:4 And they worshiped the dragon, for he had given his authority to the beast, and they worshiped the beast, saying, "Who is like the beast, and who can fight against it?"

Rev 13:5 And the beast was given a mouth uttering haughty and blasphemous words, and it was allowed to exercise authority for forty-two months.

Rev 13:6 It opened its mouth to utter blasphemies against God, blaspheming his name and his dwelling, that is, those who dwell in heaven.

Rev 13:7 Also it was allowed to make war on the saints and to conquer them. And authority was given it over every tribe and people and language and nation,

Rev 13:8 and all who dwell on earth will worship it, everyone whose name has not been written before the foundation of the world in the book of life of the Lamb who was slain.

Rev 13:9 If anyone has an ear, let him hear:

Rev 13:10 If anyone is to be taken captive, to captivity he goes; if anyone is to be slain with the sword, with the sword must he be slain. Here is a call for the endurance and faith of the saints.

What we have in these verses is a description of the Antichrist. What's interesting is that the word antichrist is not mentioned one time in the book of Revelation. Instead, in the Apocalypse, he is called "the beast."

Daniel Akin reminds us that elsewhere in Scripture, he is called:

- The little horn (Dan. 7:8)
- The prince (ruler) who is to come (Dan. 9:26)
- The lawless one or man of sin (2 Thess. 2:3-8)
- The antichrist (1 Jn. 2:18, 22; 4:3; 2 Jn. 7).[162]

Furthermore, the word antichrist means "one who is against Christ" or [and this is critical] "one who is in the place of Christ."

One critical question is essential at this point: how are we to understand the multifaceted uses of the idea or concept of the antichrist?

1. An evil empire or political power (Rev. 13; 17)
2. A past and present impersonal force, presence, or spirit; the evil spirit of this age (1 Jn. 4:3)
3. Literal persons who are forerunners of the final antichrist (1 Jn. 2:18).
4. The final and climactic embodiment of satanic power and opposition to God in a person (2 Thess. 2:3-8; Rev. 13:1-10)[163]

With that said, in chapter 13 we are introduced to two beasts: 1). The beast from the sea which is the focus of verses 1-2, and 2). The beast from the earth, which is the focus of verses 11-18. They are Satan's henchmen. The description of the beast is heavily reminiscent of Daniel's fourth beast in Daniel 7.[164]

To assist us in the making our way through these verses, I want to put on your minds three key thoughts:

1. The Sole Purpose of the Antichrist is to oppose God and Christ (v. 1-7).

162 Daniel Akin. *Exalting Jesus in Revelation: Christ-Centered Exposition Commentary*, Kindle Edition, location 4545.

163 Ibid, Kindle Edition, location 4556.

164 Paige Patterson. *The New American Commentary: Revelation*, p. 274.

2. The Sole Desire of the Antichrist is world domination and worship (v. 3, 8).

3. The Lord's call to His followers is one of patient endurance (v. 10).

Would you please look again at verses 1-7 again?

> *"Rev 13:1 And I saw a beast rising out of the sea, with ten horns and seven heads, with ten diadems on its horns and blasphemous names on its heads.*
>
> *Rev 13:2 And the beast that I saw was like a leopard; its feet were like a bear's, and its mouth was like a lion's mouth. And to it the dragon gave his power and his throne and great authority.*
>
> *Rev 13:3 One of its heads seemed to have a mortal wound, but its mortal wound was healed, and the whole earth marveled as they followed the beast.*
>
> *Rev 13:4 And they worshiped the dragon, for he had given his authority to the beast, and they worshiped the beast, saying, "Who is like the beast, and who can fight against it?"*
>
> *Rev 13:5 And the beast was given a mouth uttering haughty and blasphemous words, and it was allowed to exercise authority for forty-two months.*
>
> *Rev 13:6 It opened its mouth to utter blasphemies against God, blaspheming his name and his dwelling, that is, those who dwell in heaven.*
>
> *Rev 13:7 Also it was allowed to make war on the saints and to conquer them. And authority was given it over every tribe and people and language and nation..."*

It was not uncommon for the ancient world to associate the sea with evil.[165] Some commentators think the sea could represent also

---

165 Robert H. Mounce. *The New International Commentary on the New Testament: Revelation*, p. 244.

the nations of the world with all its ethnic, national, political, and social chaos and wickedness (MacArthur, Revelation 12-22, p. 41).

Nonetheless, the beast is said to come up out of the Abyss as stated in 11:7 and 17:8.

The ten horns speak of GREAT power. The seven heads also speak of GREAT power, but with the added notion of ferocity and intelligence. The ten diadems convey GREAT authority and political influence.

Note, too, that on these heads are BLASPHEMOUS names, mentioned four times in this text: verses 1, 5, 6 [2x].

In verse 5, John records for us that the beast was given a mouth uttering haughty and blasphemous words; and it was allowed to exercise authority for 42 months.

> *Rev 13:5 And the beast was given a mouth uttering haughty and blasphemous words, and it was allowed to exercise authority for forty-two months.*

Filled with arrogance, power, and authority, the beast uses modern means of communication to spread lies, subvert justice, teach false doctrines, and revile the very sacred name of God and Christ. The Antichrist blasphemes God, His name, His dwelling, and His people who dwell in heaven (v. 6).

Additionally, John states in verse 7 that the beast is allowed to make war on the saints, to conquer them, and he was given authority over every tribe, people, language, and nation.

Don't forget, please, church—the SOLE PURPOSE of the Antichrist is to oppose God and Christ.

In addition to his ten horns, the beast is described as having seven heads. One commentator (Akin, Patterson) sets forth that according to Revelation 17 those seven heads represent seven successive world empires: Egypt, Assyria, Babylon, Medo-Persia, Greece, Rome, and Antichrist's final world kingdom.

In other words, these are all world powers hostile to Jesus Christ.[166]

Verse 2 supplies a portrayal of the beast as that of a leopard, with feet like a bear, and its mouth as that of a lion's mouth. This is a depiction of force, speed, and savagery. What you must absolutely see in verse 2 is that the beast receives his power and authority from the dragon.

> *"And to it the dragon gave his power and his throne and great authority."*

And, Satan is empowering the Antichrist to take the place that rightfully belongs to God and His Christ.

Satan, through the beast, rules this world as its supposed head. You recall that Jesus acknowledged that the devil is the prince of this world. Look at verse 3:

> *"Rev 13:3 One of its heads seemed to have a mortal wound, but its mortal wound was healed, and the whole earth marveled as they followed the beast."*

Now, one of Satan's tactics is DECEIT. For, the enemy is a counterfeiter; he is a great imposter. He is a wannabe god who will never be God.

---

166 Simon Kistemaker. *New Testament Commentary: Revelation*, p. 378.

Here in verse 3, we see Satan counterfeiting the RESURRECTION of the Son. In verse 4, we see him counterfeiting the WORSHIP of God.

Apparently, one of the heads of the beast "seemed to have a mortal wound, but its mortal wound was healed," leading the whole world to marvel, be amazed, and be moved to follow the beast.

The word wounded is the same word in Greek translated "slaughtered" in chapter 5:6, 9. Revelation 13:14 adds that the beast "had the sword wound and yet lived."

The word lived is "the very term used for Jesus' resurrection in 2:8"[167]

So, what we have here is nothing less than a counterfeit death and resurrection taking place at the end of the age. What's interesting is that some believe it is the resurrection of a political entity, others of the personal antichrist, and others a combination of both.

May I pause here and remind you at this point, that one of the key thoughts to consider for this text is that the SOLE DESIRE of the Antichrist is world domination and worship.

> *Verse 4 is clear: Rev 13:4 And they worshiped the dragon, for he had given his authority to the beast, and they worshiped the beast, saying, "Who is like the beast, and who can fight against it?"*

> *Look at verse 8: Rev 13:8 and all who dwell on earth will worship it, everyone whose name has not been written before the foundation of the world in the book of life of the Lamb who was slain.*

Who will worship this beast? EVERYONE, except those whose names have been written before the foundation of the world in the

---

167 Akin, Kindle Edition, location 4623. Primary source: Osborne, *Revelation*, p. 495).

book of life of the Lamb who was slain. God's elect will not be deceived by Antichrist, nor will they worship him. Antichrist cannot destroy believers' saving faith. Believers are secure; the atoning work of Christ seals the redemption of believers forever.

The unsaved, unrepentant will worship the Dragon because he gave authority to the beast.

They will worship the beast because they reason, "Who is like the beast?" THIS IS GROSS, DETESTABLE IDOLATRY OF THE WORST NATURE!!

Chuck Swindoll writes, "How like Satan! The one who 'disguises himself as an angel of light' will provide the world with a copycat 'christ' to match all their man-centered ideals of personality, politics, and power. No wonder the whole world will be swept off its feet by this attractive, persuasive figure. It fact, we are told the world will worship the dragon through their worship of the Beast. In this rabid fit of hyper nationalism that will make Hitler's Third Reich look like a high school sporting event, the world will cry out, 'Who is like the beast, and who is able to wage war with him' (13:4). [Insights, p. 181]

It's important to note that Satan's reign of terror will be limited to a period of 42 months. Satan and his henchmen will have an insatiable appetite to oppose God and to command the world's worship, but only for a season. Understand this yet again, God is the ultimate Sovereign and God allots these enemies 42 months to rule on the face of this earth.

Transition: Let me move us along for I want to give some due attention to verses 9 and 10. I say again…

1. The Sole Purpose of the Antichrist is to oppose God and Christ (v. 1-7).

2. The Sole Desire of the Antichrist is world domination and worship (v. 3, 8).

Just one more thought. Look at verses 9 and 10:

Rev 13:9 If anyone has an ear, let him hear:

Rev 13:10 If anyone is to be taken captive, to captivity he goes; if anyone is to be slain with the sword, with the sword must he be slain. Here is a call for the endurance and faith of the saints.

This is the Lord's call. This call is to patient endurance.

These words are not addressed to Satan's henchmen. Oh, no! These words are for the saints and the Lord exhorts to endure hardships and exercise trust in Him.

Verse 9 is simply an exhortation to pay attention and be wise and discerning.

Verse 10 seems to be a statement of destiny, if you will.

You can expect to be captured and imprisoned. Your earthly destiny may very well be to be slaughtered. It is and it will be costly to follow Jesus! Keep following.

You may be ridiculed

You may lose your job

You may lose your wealth

You may be persecuted and oppressed

You may be isolated

You may be imprisoned

You may be slain…nonetheless…follow the Lamb!

We will no doubt be the targets of the Antichrist and his subordinates. Know this, though: God is on our side and He will avenge His adversaries. The Lord calls us to patient endurance!

Satan's antichrist is coming. But, so is God's Christ, the Lord Jesus!

What are you going to do? Will you be pro-Christ? Will you be anti-Christ?

Will you worship God and the Lamb?

Will you worship the dragon and the beast?

The choice is that clear and the choice is yours.

Eternity hangs in the balance. Your eternal home is at stake. There is no neutral ground.

Christ wins in the end. Do you love Christ so much that Satan is defeated by the word of your testimony and by the blood of the Lamb, and thus do you find yourself on the right side of the Lamb when He comes?

I invite you to come to Christ for forgiveness of your sins and to begin a new life in Him.

Let's pray.

27

"THE BEAST OF DECEPTION"

Revelation 13:11–18, ESV

As previously stated last Sunday, chapter 13 introduces us to Satan's two diabolical henchmen:

- The beast out of the sea (v. 1-10)
- The beast out of the earth (v. 11-18)

In chapter 12, the reader was informed of Satan's relentless persecution of the church, and here in chapter 13, we receive a description of his heartless helpers, his lackeys, his minions, his flunkeys, his acolytes.

Chapter 13 records the culmination of Satan's war with God and His people. Satan will strenuously seek to prevent Christ from setting up His earthly kingdom by setting up his own under Antichrist.

Satan has been permanently cast from heaven (12:9). He knows his time remaining is brief (12:12). Therefore, he is urgently intent to lead a last gasp, desperate onslaught against God, thereby employing his henchmen: the beasts of the sea and the earth.

Let's read about the beast out of the earth, accurately labeled as the beast of deception:

> *Rev 13:11 Then I saw another beast rising out of the earth. It had two horns like a lamb and it spoke like a dragon.*

Rev 13:12 It exercises all the authority of the first beast in its presence, and makes the earth and its inhabitants worship the first beast, whose mortal wound was healed.

Rev 13:13 It performs great signs, even making fire come down from heaven to earth in front of people,

Rev 13:14 and by the signs that it is allowed to work in the presence of the beast it deceives those who dwell on earth, telling them to make an image for the beast that was wounded by the sword and yet lived.

Rev 13:15 And it was allowed to give breath to the image of the beast, so that the image of the beast might even speak and might cause those who would not worship the image of the beast to be slain.

Rev 13:16 Also it causes all, both small and great, both rich and poor, both free and slave, to be marked on the right hand or the forehead,

Rev 13:17 so that no one can buy or sell unless he has the mark, that is, the name of the beast or the number of its name.

Rev 13:18 This calls for wisdom: let the one who has understanding calculate the number of the beast, for it is the number of a man, and his number is 666.

There are three central concepts I want to put on your minds this morning:

1. The DECEPTION of the Beast (v. 11-14).
2. The DIVISION of the Beast (v. 15).
3. The DESIGNATION of the Beast (v. 16-18).

First, Note the Deception of the Beast (v. 11-14).

Rev 13:11 Then I saw another beast rising out of the earth. It had two horns like a lamb and it spoke like a dragon.

Rev 13:12 It exercises all the authority of the first beast in its presence, and makes the earth and its inhabitants worship the first beast, whose mortal wound was healed.

Rev 13:13 It performs great signs, even making fire come down from heaven to earth in front of people,

Rev 13:14 and by the signs that it is allowed to work in the presence of the beast it deceives those who dwell on earth, telling them to make an image for the beast that was wounded by the sword and yet lived.

One of the tactics of the enemy is that of deception. This beast rising out of the earth is a clever deceiver. The Bible speaks repeatedly of the enemy as a deceiver (2 Cor. 11:3), a liar (Jn. 8:44), a schemer (Eph. 6:11), a murderer (Jn. 8:44), and an accuser (Rev. 12:10).

So, it makes perfect, logical sense that one of his henchmen will be an accomplished deceiver. First, this beast attempts to deceive by his appearance. Verse 11 states that he LOOKS like a Lamb, but SPEAKS like a Dragon. This beast, this false prophet, will clearly be the mouthpiece for Satan, speaking his words.

His fundamental role and mission is to cause people to worship the first beast. He is going to lead a worldwide effort and religion of Antichrist worship and allegiance.

To do this, to accomplish this mission he must employ every method of deceit imaginable to sway and gain the worship of the masses.

To be clear: with delegated authority given to him by the Antichrist, the beast from the earth will seek to deceive and compel the world to worship Antichrist.

His second deception centers around an event—that event is the apparent healing of the first beast's [Antichrist] mortal wound. This is clear in verse 12. This is satanic mimicry or imitation of Christ's resurrection and of the two witnesses we encountered in chapter 11.[168]

This is all a ruse, a scam, a ploy, and hoax. Yet, the result will be that Antichrist and the false prophet will be lauded and their prestige advanced.

Look again at verse 13. The text says that the beast from the earth will perform great signs. Those signs will imitate those performed by Christ and those of the two witnesses (11:5-6). What's devastating is that the unbelieving, those who reject the true gospel of Jesus Christ, will eagerly go along with this damning false gospel proclaimed by the false prophet since it appears to be legitimate and verified by spectacular supernatural signs. He will even call fire down from heaven to earth in front of people.

Verse 14 again gives emphasis to the result: deception!

> *Rev 13:14 and by the signs that it is allowed to work in the presence of the beast it deceives those who dwell on earth, telling them to make an image for the beast that was wounded by the sword and yet lived.*

Oh, church, the unbelieving world is going to be dreadfully deceived. Satan is going to escalate the false world religion and worship of Antichrist.

Humanity will engage finally in obeying the prophet's command to make an image to the beast. As John MacArthur correctly writes: "The world will engage in the most shocking, blatant idolatry ever seen."[169]

---

168 John MacArthur. *Because the Time is Near: John MacArthur Explains the Book of Revelation*, p. 222.

169 MacArthur, p. 223.

This blasphemous image will probably be set up on the temple grounds in Jerusalem (2 Thess. 2:4) and will be connected with the abomination of desolation (Dan. 9:27; 11:31; 12:11; Matt. 24:15).

Transition: This beast is a deceiver.

Second, Note the Division of the Beast (v. 15)

> *Rev 13:15 And it was allowed to give breath to the image of the beast, so that the image of the beast might even speak and might cause those who would not worship the image of the beast to be slain.*

What a deception! The false prophet will animate the image of Antichrist so that it gives the appearance of being alive. He gives to it the breath of life and the image speaks. The world will be in such a pitiful state, that countless people will flock to the one they believe to be a conqueror of death.

Yet, it will not be long before his true colors are revealed. The false prophet will drop his smokescreen of gentleness and will see to it that those who do not worship the image of the beast will be killed.

Alarmingly, in the last days, there is to be a great division in the human race.[170]

Some will remain true to Christ and His Word even in the face of certain death; others will turn in worship to the Antichrist. It is this crucial decision which accounts for the turning away [apostasy] that is to precede the return of Christ.

Paul wrote in 2 Thessalonians 2:1-3:

> *2Th 2:1 Now concerning the coming of our Lord Jesus Christ and our being gathered together to him, we ask you, brothers,*

---

170 Robert H. Mounce. *NICNT: The Book of Revelation*, p. 258.

2Th 2:2 not to be quickly shaken in mind or alarmed, either by a spirit or a spoken word, or a letter seeming to be from us, to the effect that the day of the Lord has come.

2Th 2:3 Let no one deceive you in any way. For that day will not come, unless the rebellion comes first, and the man of lawlessness is revealed, the son of destruction,

2Th 2:4 who opposes and exalts himself against every so-called god or object of worship, so that he takes his seat in the temple of God, proclaiming himself to be God.

Listen to me: If you are a half-hearted Christian, just going through the motions of being a follower of Jesus, you should worry. If you are simply a fan of Jesus, you should worry. Why?

I cannot imagine a half-hearted Christian being willing to yield his/her life for a cause in which you do not really believe.

Transition: Again, the false prophet, this beast from the earth, is going to act in such a way as to create a division in the human race. You best know what side you are going to take.

Finally, Note the Designation of the Beast (v. 16-18).

Rev 13:16 Also it causes all, both small and great, both rich and poor, both free and slave, to be marked on the right hand or the forehead,

Rev 13:17 so that no one can buy or sell unless he has the mark, that is, the name of the beast or the number of its name.

Rev 13:18 This calls for wisdom: let the one who has understanding calculate the number of the beast, for it is the number of a man, and his number is 666.

As part of his diabolical plan to FORCE the worship of Antichrist, the false prophet will require all people "to be marked on the right hand or the forehead."

All of human society: small and great, rich and poor, free and slave…all must receive this mark.

This mark will signify that the person bearing it is a loyal follower of the Antichrist. In the Ancient world, such marks were commonly given to slaves, soldiers, and devotees of religious cults.

The significance of the "mark" in this present passage is to parody the sealing of God's servants in chapter 7.

As the elect of God are sealed upon their foreheads to escape the destruction about to fall upon the earth, so the followers of the beast are to escape his wrath against the church by bearing his mark.

The long and short of it is: in the final days of Antichrist it will represent the ultimate test of religious loyalty. Only those who would rather die than compromise their faith will resist the mark of Antichrist.[171]

Furthermore, refusing to take the mark of the beast will have extreme practical consequences as well. No one will be able to buy or sell without it.

Antichrist's empire will exercise economic control over the world.

Food, and other necessities of life in demand on a decimated earth, will be very difficult to obtain without the mark. Some suspect this is indicative of a cashless society. There is speculation which suggests that instead of a credit card, people will have a mark of some type on their forehead or hand.

The mark, according to John, will be either the name of the beast or the number of that name.

---

171 Mounce, p. 260.

The bottom line: you will either have the identifying mark or suffer the consequences.

Now, that brings us to Revelation 13:8. Robert Mounce writes of this verse: "No verse in Revelation has received more attention than this one with its cryptic reference to the number of the beast."[172]

> Rev 13:18 This calls for wisdom: let the one who has understanding calculate the number of the beast, for it is the number of a man, and his number is 666.

What do we make of this intriguing verse? Clearly, wisdom is needed. It would be a significant challenge to find any kind of consensus among Bible scholars as to exactly what John meant in reference to verse 18.

The text is clear in that the number of the beast is a number of a certain man. The beast's number is 666.

Paige Patterson writes, "But just as six falls short of the ideal number "seven," this false prophet who deceives the whole earth in this way is hopelessly compromised; and the repetition of the "six" in its trifold from 666 is clearly intended to underscore the intrinsic evil bound up in this individual."[173]

Simon Kistemaker [174]observes: "John puts the entire chapter in the framework of symbolism, so the reader may expect that the number in verse 18 must also be taken figuratively. The number seven signifies completeness; six, incompleteness. Satan, the great imitator, strives to achieve the sum total of seven but always falls short and

---

172 Mounce, p. 261.

173 Paige Patterson. *NAC: An Exegetical and Theological Exposition of Holy Scripture*: Revelation, p. 282.

174 Simon Kistemaker. *New Testament Commentary: Revelation*, p. 395-96.

ends up with six…In Revelation the number six points to judgment: at the end of the sixth seal, the sixth trumpet, and the sixth bowl. Satan's works always results in failure."

Suffice it to say—the opinions and perspectives vary.

Transition: The beast will have his designation and so will those who follow him.

What do you need to do this morning?

What prayer might you need to pray right now?

What changes in your thinking need to be made?

Are you securely grounded in the truth or will you be easily duped by the deceptions of evil?

Have you turned from your sin and turned to Christ by faith inviting Him into your life to be your Savior?

Do you have a church home?

Are you reading your Bible regularly?

Do you have a regular time alone to be with God?

Are you aware of what is happening all around us as we anticipate the return of Christ?

Don't be deceived. Be ready. Be armed with truth.

Be in Christ.

28

"STANDING WITH THE LAMB"

Revelation 14:1–5, ESV

Whether we realize it or not, our lives are often the results of the stands we take. Really, who we stand with and what we stand for defines us.

Think about it. Frequently, you take a stand for some person, some cause, some value, some priority, some issue which contributes to defining who you are and who you will be. It's kind of a line in the sand moment.

Over the course of a lifetime, something inside of you will compel you to take at least one public stand, or maybe two or three.

However, most of the stands we take are done in the recesses of our hearts and are not known to a wider audience.

For example, the man who says, upon becoming a father, "I'm going to be home most nights and be involved in the life of my child. I'll choose to make less money if it means I can be home more with my family."

The young adult who refuses to go out and drink with fellow employees and employers as a means to climb the corporate ladder—take a moral stand.

The couple who says, "We are going to manage our money responsibly and not live beyond our financial means."

The person who resists letting others do his thinking for him. The person who says, "I am going to let the Bible define my morals, my values, viewpoints, my actions, and worldview."

One of my favorite, "public" stands in the Scripture is found in Joshua 24. A character in Scripture by the name of Joshua stood before the Israelites and took a bold stand. He drew a line in the sand. In essence Joshua told the people to put away their false gods and serve the Lord. And, if you don't want to lay aside your false gods, heartless idols, and empty religion, if you want to serve the impotent gods of your fathers in Egypt, then make your choice. Get off the fence! Then, Joshua went on to say, "…but as for me and my house, we will serve the Lord" (Josh. 24:15).

In other words, regardless of what his contemporaries, peers, or friends chose to do, it was a foregone conclusion in his heart and conviction that Joshua was going to stand with the Lord—he and his family!

Our hearts will be inclined toward the Lord. How about you? Decide for yourselves. Take your stand!

> *Rev 14:1 Then I looked, and behold, on Mount Zion stood the Lamb, and with him 144,000 who had his name and his Father's name written on their foreheads.*
>
> *Rev 14:2 And I heard a voice from heaven like the roar of many waters and like the sound of loud thunder. The voice I heard was like the sound of harpists playing on their harps,*
>
> *Rev 14:3 and they were singing a new song before the throne and before the four living creatures and before the elders. No one could learn that song except the 144,000 who had been redeemed from the earth.*

Rev 14:4 It is these who have not defiled themselves with women, for they are virgins. It is these who follow the Lamb wherever he goes. These have been redeemed from mankind as firstfruits for God and the Lamb,

Rev 14:5 and in their mouth no lie was found, for they are blameless.

Three ideas seem to leap out of this text of Holy Scripture. They are:

1. We will STAND with the Lamb (v. 1).
2. We will SING with the Lamb (v. 2-3).
3. We will be SANCTIFIED through the Lamb (v. 4-5).

First, We Will Stand with the Lamb (v. 1).

Rev 14:1 Then I looked, and behold, on Mount Zion stood the Lamb, and with him 144,000 who had his name and his Father's name written on their foreheads.

Chapter 14 is such a contrast to chapter 13 of Revelation. It would seem that chapter 14 is a word of encouragement to John's audience after the frightful, unsettling description of the beast and the false prophet in the preceding chapter.

What realities await the saints? Persecution, suffering, difficulty, ridicule, hardship, death, mixed in with a call to remain loyal and faithful to Christ. So, chapter 14 rings a bit like a much needed word of encouragement and a reminder of the ultimate reward for those who endure!

You may remember that in chapter 7 the servants of God were sealed on the forehead to protect them from the coming judgments in verses 2-4.

In chapter 13, we were exposed to yet another kind of mark—that of the beast in verse 16.

You might also remember that without this mark on the right hand or forehead no one would be able to buy or sell (v. 17).

And, here's the point: in each case the "mark" is the name of the one to whom ultimate loyalty is given (13:17; 14:1). Robert Mounce insightfully remarks, "The destiny of every person is determined by the mark the person bears. When judgment comes there will be no room for ambiguity; people will have by their "mark" declared their master."[175]

In verse 1 John sees the Lamb standing on Mount Zion and with Him is 144,000 who had his name and His Father's name written on their foreheads.

The Lamb, the Lord Jesus Christ, counted worthy to unloose the seals of the scroll of destiny, and who receives the adoration and worship of the innumerable multitude of heaven, now stands victorious with his followers.

The identity of the 144,000 has been variously understood. Some commentators set forth that it is reasonable to conclude that this is the same group mentioned in 7:4-8.[176] Whereas Mounce adds a thought which is astute: "the repetition of the number is not to ensure an exact identification between the two groups but to point out that not one has been lost. John's symbols are fluid, and, in fact, the number 144,000 of chapter 14 corresponds with the innumerable multitude found in the second vision of chapter 7. Both portray the full complement of the redeemed throughout history."[177]

Transition: Those who bear the mark of Christ and His Father, they are the overcomers who stand with the Lamb on Mount Zion. What a scene!

175 Robert Mounce. *NICNT: Revelation*, p. 264.

176 Walvoord and Zuck. *The Bible Knowledge Commentary: New Testament,* p. 964.

177 Mounce, p. 265.

Second, We Will Sing with the Lamb (v. 2-3).

Rev 14:2 And I heard a voice from heaven like the roar of many waters and like the sound of loud thunder. The voice I heard was like the sound of harpists playing on their harps,

Rev 14:3 and they were singing a new song before the throne and before the four living creatures and before the elders. No one could learn that song except the 144,000 who had been redeemed from the earth.

Right away you may notice the numerous similes. By definition a simile is:

"a figure of speech likening one thing to another by the use of like or as..."

In verse 2, John hears a voice from heaven LIKE the roar of many waters and LIKE the sound of loud thunder. The voice I heard was LIKE the sound of harpists playing on their harps.

The sound heard is nothing short of impressive—the roar of many waters, the sound of loud thunder, and the sound of harpists playing their harps. This, ladies and gentlemen, is not the sound of an angelic choir; rather, it is the anthem of redemption sung by the 144,000, representative of the redeemed. They sing of what they have experienced—redemption, salvation from sin. It is a new song. The new song is found in Revelation 5:9, "And they sang a new song, saying, "Worthy are you to take the scroll and to open its seals, for you were slain, and by your blood you ransomed people for God from every tribe and language and people and nation, Rev 5:10 and you have made them a kingdom and priests to our God, and they shall reign on the earth."

They have been delivered and so they sing. Angels cannot sing of what they have not experienced.

If you are saved, born again, regenerated by the Holy Spirit, if you have experienced genuine conversion, if Jesus is your Savior, you are blessed beyond what you can possibly comprehend.

Listen to 1 Peter 1:10-12: "As to this salvation, the prophets who prophesied of the grace that would come to you made careful searches and inquiries, seeking to know what person or time the Spirit of Christ within them was indicating as He predicted the sufferings of Christ and the glories to follow. It was revealed to them that they were not serving themselves, but you, in these things which now have been announced to you through those who preached the gospel to you by the Holy Spirit sent from heaven—things into which angels long to look."

What does that mean? Peter wants us to burst with gratitude, wonder and joy for our salvation because the prophets of God and even the angels of heaven have longed to see what we have experienced through the gospel of Jesus Christ.

Indeed, we should be amazed by the greatness of our salvation. No wonder they sing! No wonder they sing with the Lamb, the author of salvation. They sing this anthem of victory.

They sing before the throne of God, those who paid the full price of endurance and loyalty, they sing with the living creatures and the elders as the audience.

Do you have goosebumps yet? Wow!

Transition: We will stand with victorious Lamb. We will sing with the victorious Lamb! There is yet one final idea.

Third, We Will Be Sanctified Through the Lamb (v. 4-5).

Rev 14:4 It is these who have not defiled themselves with women, for they are virgins. It is these who follow the Lamb wherever he goes. These have been redeemed from mankind as firstfruits for God and the Lamb,

Rev 14:5 and in their mouth no lie was found, for they are blameless.

Here the 144,000 are described. Look at the descriptions:

1. They are virgins; they have not defiled themselves with women.
2. They are followers of the Lamb.
3. They are firstfruits redeemed from mankind.

Interestingly, the first description has garnered much discussion. Are they "supersaints"?

Are they an elite group of Christ-followers who have attained the utmost in spirituality by renouncing marriage with its sexual relationships?

Are they strict celibates and virgins? It is true that the early church exalted celibacy. Paul wished that all people possessed the gift of self-restraint so as to serve Christ without hindrance and distraction.

However, it should be noted that the Bible holds marriage in high esteem. Paul used the marriage relationship as an illustration of the intimate relationship between Christ and His church (Eph. 5:31-32).

From the beginning, God made male and female for one another, and what He has joined together in wedlock no one is to separate.

Another interpretation, which is more plausible, is that this description is symbolic of their fidelity and allegiance to the Lamb whom they follow wherever He goes.[178]

---

178 Daniel Akin. *Exalting Jesus in Revelation: Christ-Centered Exposition*, Kindle Edition, location 4976.

These words may be more apt to take them in a more figurative sense and understand the 144,000 to be those who have kept themselves free from adultery and fornication.[179]

In other words, and this is the point: these have been spiritually faithful in a world steeped in idolatry and immorality.

They have remained faithful, morally pure, and devoted in their love for the Lamb; they follow Christ. He redeemed them and set them free from the enslavement of sin.

Verse 5 makes clear that as they follow Christ, there is no lie in their mouth, and they are blameless.

They follow Christ—His life and teachings. Their desire is to imitate Jesus; to live lives worthy of the Savior.

They are ethically blameless. They are above reproach. They strive to live holy lives, evidence that Christ is at work in and through them causing them to live sanctified lives before Him.

Aren't these verses a breath of fresh air? What an encouragement.

We will stand with the Lord.

We will sing with the Lord.

We will be sanctified through the Lord.

May God be pleased to use this vision to strengthen and inspire believers to endure the reality of what must be before we stand with the Lord with the multitude of the redeemed.

Where are you standing right now?

-Are you right with God?

-Do you know for certain that you will spend your eternity with Christ?

If so, who are you praying for to be saved?

What conversations do you need to have with others on matters of eternity?

179 Mounce, p. 267.

29

"THE PROFOUND FOOLISHNESS OF REJECTING GOD"

Revelation 14:6-13, ESV

It is a choice of profound foolishness to reject God.

At one time or another, every last one of us has done something foolish. I offer a few broad examples...

- Some people foolishly put themselves in harm's way physically-thinking they are invincible.
- Some people foolishly invite danger into their lives by drinking and abusing various substances.
- Some people foolishly get behind the wheel of a car while they are impaired and under the influence of a precarious substance.
- Some people foolishly rush into marriage. Some people foolishly quit a job before they have secured another job—and then put themselves in a very difficult spot financially.
- Some people foolishly take on too much financial debt and live way beyond their means.
- YET, none of these examples compares to the profound foolishness of rejecting God!!

Rev 14:6 Then I saw another angel flying directly overhead, with an eternal gospel to proclaim to those who dwell on earth, to every nation and tribe and language and people.

Rev 14:7 And he said with a loud voice, "Fear God and give him glory, because the hour of his judgment has come, and worship him who made heaven and earth, the sea and the springs of water."

Rev 14:8 Another angel, a second, followed, saying, "Fallen, fallen is Babylon the great, she who made all nations drink the wine of the passion of her sexual immorality."

Rev 14:9 And another angel, a third, followed them, saying with a loud voice, "If anyone worships the beast and its image and receives a mark on his forehead or on his hand,

Rev 14:10 he also will drink the wine of God's wrath, poured full strength into the cup of his anger, and he will be tormented with fire and sulfur in the presence of the holy angels and in the presence of the Lamb.

Rev 14:11 And the smoke of their torment goes up forever and ever, and they have no rest, day or night, these worshipers of the beast and its image, and whoever receives the mark of its name."

Rev 14:12 Here is a call for the endurance of the saints, those who keep the commandments of God and their faith in Jesus.

Rev 14:13 And I heard a voice from heaven saying, "Write this: Blessed are the dead who die in the Lord from now on." "Blessed indeed," says the Spirit, "that they may rest from their labors, for their deeds follow them!"

From this text, I want you to observe three essential thoughts relative to the profound foolishness of rejecting God. It is foolish, profoundly reckless, to reject God because:

1. Judgment is Near (v. 7).
2. God's Wrath is Severe (v. 10-11).
3. Blessed Are Those Who Die in the Lord (v. 12-13).

First, It is Foolish to Reject God Because Judgment is Near (v. 7).

> *Rev 14:7 And he said with a loud voice, "Fear God and give him glory, because the hour of his judgment has come, and worship him who made heaven and earth, the sea and the springs of water."*

In verse 6, we are told of another angel flying overhead with an "eternal gospel to proclaim to those who dwell on earth—every nation and tribe and language and people."

What is meant by the term, "eternal gospel"? The word "gospel" is a noun, which is preceded by an adjective "eternal."

The adjective [eternal] speaks of the timeless and permanent nature of the Word of God, which by the way, you may choose to ignore at YOUR OWN PERIL!

What's interesting is that the emphasis here is not upon the gospel as good news, but rather as a potent reminder of God's unchanging truth.

The angel calls men and women to respond to God's message BEFORE judgment comes.

Regrettably, too many people are content to live their lives without any thought of God's imminent judgment.

In short, this is really a summons…[loud and abundantly clear], as Robert Mounce states it, "to fear, honor, and worship the Creator."[180]

---

180 Robert Mounce. *The New International Commentary on the New Testament: The Book of Revelation*, p. 270.

In other words…

- Fear God
- Give Him Glory
- Pay Him the respect He is rightfully due.
- Repent. Fall on your knees before God.
- Worship Him
- The hour of His judgment has come.

Transition: Ignore this summons at your own peril. Be tone deaf at your own risk. Pay no heed to the clear call of the eternal gospel and you will put yourself in grave jeopardy.

It is a choice of profound foolishness to reject God.

Secondly, It is Foolish to Reject God Because His Wrath is Severe (v. 10-11).

> *Rev 14:10 he also will drink the wine of God's wrath, poured full strength into the cup of his anger, and he will be tormented with fire and sulfur in the presence of the holy angels and in the presence of the Lamb.*
>
> *Rev 14:11 And the smoke of their torment goes up forever and ever, and they have no rest, day or night, these worshipers of the beast and its image, and whoever receives the mark of its name."*

In verse 8, another angel, a second, speaks. Verse 8 reads, "Fallen, fallen is Babylon the great, she who made all nations drink the wine of the passion of her sexual immorality."

Notice also that no explanation is provided by John in respect to this "Babylon" reference.

However, this cry is taken from Isaiah 21:9 and Daniel 4:30, which means successively the fall and the greatness of Babylon.[181]

---

181 Simon Kistemaker. *New Testament Commentary: Revelation*, p. 409.

With that said, what is the meaning of Babylon? John writes this name six times in Revelation.

There are at least three interpretations for this name:

1. Literal Babylon, because the name of the Euphrates River also appears in 9:14 and 16:12.
2. A code name for Rome, which Peter apparently used (1 Peter 5:13).
3. A reference to the converging of evil in particular places throughout history.[182]

Perhaps Robert Mounce expresses it best: "It is a symbol of the spirit of godlessness that in every age lures people away from the worship of the Creator."[183]

Put simply, Babylon is God's enemy that as a world power oppresses the saints.

Furthermore, John is drawing from Jeremiah 51:7 in describing the doomed city. She made all the nations drink the wine of depraved drunkenness and sexual sin.

Think about it: the world is seduced by the intoxicating influences of depraved practices which lead to the rejection of God and His truth.

In verse 9 a third angel speaks. This verse escorts us to the idea present in verses 10-11.

Verse 9 reads: Rev 14:9 And another angel, a third, followed them, saying with a loud voice, "If anyone worships the beast and its image and receives a mark on his forehead or on his hand.

The imagery here is that if anyone worships the beast and its image, and receives a mark on his forehead or on his hand, then he will drink of the wine of the severity of God's wrath.

---

182 Kistemaker, p. 409.

183 Mounce, p. 271.

These verses are kind of a "counter-proclamation" to that of the image in chapter 13. You recall in that text that there it was decreed that those who would not worship the image of the beast would be killed and those without the mark of the beast would not be able to buy nor to sell (13:15, 17).

Here, those who worship the beast will suffer the wrath of God. The wine of God's fury is written to be "poured full strength into the cup of his anger."

This is not a diluted, watered-down wrath, but is "poured full strength into the cup of his anger."

This is not just some out-of-control, coming off the rails, coming apart at the seams fit of rage; rather, this is the response of a holy, righteous God to people's foolish, adamant, willful refusal to accept His love and grace.

Notice that: the torment of those who worship the beast will be with fire and sulfur—a figure taken from God's judgment upon Sodom and Gomorrah.

What's weird is that the suffering of the damned takes place not in the presence of martyred believers who rejoice to see their oppressors burning in hell. RATHER, it is the holy angels and even the Lord (v. 10) who witness divine retribution upon the unrepentant wicked.[184]

Furthermore, verse 11 informs us that the smoke of their torment is eternal—they have no rest—day or night. It is unrelenting. It is never ceasing.

This is a terrifying reality. Yet, people go on living their lives without an awareness of what their refusal of God is going to one day cost them.

---

184 Mounce, p. 274.

Transition: I ask you—why is it foolish to reject God and His truth? First, because judgment is near. Second, because God's wrath is severe.

It is a choice of profound foolishness to reject God.

Finally, It is Foolish to Reject God Because Blessed Are Those Who Die in the Lord (v. 12-13).

Rev 14:12 Here is a call for the endurance of the saints, those who keep the commandments of God and their faith in Jesus.

Rev 14:13 And I heard a voice from heaven saying, "Write this: Blessed are the dead who die in the Lord from now on." "Blessed indeed," says the Spirit, "that they may rest from their labors, for their deeds follow them!"

John has not forgotten the people of God, and more importantly, God has not forgotten His people.

What we have here is a call to remain unswervingly resolute in our commitment to the faith. Hold on to Jesus. Do not let go. Patiently endure.

In the midst of rampant evil, be faithful, steadfast.

In the face of certain persecution and even martyrdom for not worshiping the beast and receiving his mark, play the long game here and endure. Persist.

The days are going to be evil, dreadful, even terrifying.

How do followers of Christ live in a hostile, secular, pagan world and culture? The answer is…

Keep the commandments of God.

Live out your faith.

Keep your faith in Christ. Don't bail. Hold fast.

No matter what may come against you—persevere!

When the world views Christianity as archaic, outdated, and obsolete, you, dear people of God, are called and commanded to keep the commands of Holy Scripture.

Kistemaker says it well: "God's law endures throughout the ages, need not be amended, is relevant in all cultures, and will never be repealed."[185]

Verse 13 is one of seven beatitudes within the book of Revelation.

The first of the beatitudes in Revelation is found in chapter 1:3, which reads…

> *"Blessed is the one who reads the words of this prophecy, and blessed are those who hear it and take to heart what is written in it, because the time is near."*

John does not identify the speaker in verse 13, which is often the case in Revelation.

This voice utters the second beatitude in the Apocalypse. We do know that the voice instructs John to write.

This beatitude is aimed at those who die in the Lord. What's peculiar is the phrase, "from now on." Does this mean that only saints who die a martyr's death are called blessed? Or, are all believers blessed?

Robert Mounce's explanation is helpful:

> *"To assure those facing the prospect of martyrdom that to die in the Lord is to enter into eternal blessedness is not to deny the same reward to those saints who previously died in less trying circumstances. 'From now*

---

185 Kistemaker, p. 413.

on' marks the transition into the more active persecution of those who hold unswervingly to their faith. "[186]

To this declaration of blessedness the Spirit adds an emphatic affirmation. Yes indeed!

What is the promised blessing? Oh, this is great. It is the cessation of all the trials and sufferings brought upon the faithful by the demands of corrupt, misguided worship. It is a rest from the troubles that have entered into their lives because of the steadfastness of faith.

God will not forget what has been endured in loyalty to Christ. Their deeds are acts of steadfast resistance to the demands of Antichrist.

As always one's deeds do not merit favor with God but reveal one's devotion to Christ.

What a text, ladies and gentlemen. Every person in this room and listening via the live feed has a choice to make this morning.

The wise choice—to trust Christ to be your Savior and follow Him as Lord. Stand with Christ.

The profoundly foolish choice is to reject God. Why?

- Judgment is near.
- God's wrath is severe.
- Blessed are those who die in the Lord.

To the saved I echo what John relayed to his audience, "Persevere. Remain resolute in your faith. Endure. Keep a long-haul perspective. Remain loyal to King Christ."

To the one who is not yet a follower of Jesus I appeal to you this morning to be reconciled to God by faith in Christ. Resist the

---

186 Mounce, p. 276.

seduction and lure of this dangerous, corrupt, Babylonian type of world system and philosophy and come to Jesus!

Let's pray about it.

30

"THE GREAT WINEPRESS OF GOD'S WRATH"

Revelation 14:14-20, ESV

As we begin, it would seem beneficial to define three concepts, each we will encounter in this extraordinary text.

1. The sickle
2. The winepress
3. The wrath of God

According to the Holman Bible Dictionary, a sickle is a curved blade of flint or metal used to cut stalks of grain. Biblical texts often use the sickle symbolically to speak of coming judgment. "Revelation 14 uses the analogy of Christ reaping the harvest of humankind at the great judgment."[187]

Again, according to the Holman Bible Dictionary, a winepress is a machine used for making wine from grapes. The juice is squeezed from the grapes by treading over them with the feet.[188]

---

187 Holman Bible Dictionary, 1991 edition, p. 1277.

188 Holman Bible Dictionary, 1991 edition, p. 1410-1411.

Wayne Grudem in his voluminous work entitled, Systematic Theology, defines God's wrath as follows: "God's wrath means that he intensely hates all sin."[189]

We cannot possibly forge t that God DOES NOT delight in sin. What would God be like if He did not HATE sin? What would God be like if He wasn't too troubled by sin?

The Almighty has a righteous, holy hatred toward gross injustice, evil, and sin.

Gratefully, God's people are not the objects of His wrath. While it is true that we are by nature children of wrath, we are as a result of our trust in Jesus, delivered from the wrath to come (1 Thess. 1:10).

Oh, praise God, Jesus Christ bore the wrath of God that was due to our sin, in order that we might be saved, rescued (Rom. 3:25-26).

Furthermore, we should thank God for His great patience. God delays the pouring out of His wrath upon evil for the express purpose that people might repent and turn to Christ for salvation (Rom. 2:4).

I ask you to please hold these few thoughts as we now read the sermon text for this morning.

> *Rev 14:14 Then I looked, and behold, a white cloud, and seated on the cloud one like a son of man, with a golden crown on his head, and a sharp sickle in his hand. Rev 14:15 And another angel came out of the temple, calling with a loud voice to him who sat on the cloud, "Put in your sickle, and reap, for the hour to reap has come, for the harvest of the earth is fully ripe." Rev 14:16 So he who sat on the cloud swung his sickle across the earth, and the earth was reaped. Rev 14:17 Then another angel came out of the temple in heaven, and he too had a sharp sickle.*

---

189 Wayne Grudem. *Systematic Theology: An Introduction to Biblical Doctrine*, p. 206.

> *Rev 14:18 And another angel came out from the altar, the angel who has authority over the fire, and he called with a loud voice to the one who had the sharp sickle, "Put in your sickle and gather the clusters from the vine of the earth, for its grapes are ripe." Rev 14:19 So the angel swung his sickle across the earth and gathered the grape harvest of the earth and threw it into the great winepress of the wrath of God. Rev 14:20 And the winepress was trodden outside the city, and blood flowed from the winepress, as high as a horse's bridle, for 1,600 stadia.*

As we labor to unpack this text of Holy Scripture, I want you to notice two characters, two sickles, two harvests.

First, We Have Jesus Christ and His Sickle (v. 14-16).

> *Rev 14:14 Then I looked, and behold, a white cloud, and seated on the cloud one like a son of man, with a golden crown on his head, and a sharp sickle in his hand. Rev 14:15 And another angel came out of the temple, calling with a loud voice to him who sat on the cloud, "Put in your sickle, and reap, for the hour to reap has come, for the harvest of the earth is fully ripe." Rev 14:16 So he who sat on the cloud swung his sickle across the earth, and the earth was reaped.*

John notes that he looked and saw a [white cloud], and seated on the cloud was "one like a son of man." This is unquestionably a reference to Christ.

In fact, this is the title Christ used most frequently for Himself. He used this title a total of 81 times in the Gospel accounts. It is an implied claim to deity. The imagery here of the Lord on a cloud is taken from Daniel 7:13. Dr. John MacArthur notes that it indicates magnificent majesty.[190]

---

190 John MacArthur. *MacArthur New Testament Commentary*, p. 932.

Furthermore, John notes that this "son of man" had "a golden crown on his head, and a sharp sickle in his hand."

This is, ladies and gentlemen, the victor's crown. Christ now wears this gold crown as the triumphant, victorious conqueror over His enemies! Praise God.

And, with this sickle in His hand, Christ is prepared to reap the harvest. Rightfully, this escorts us to an important question. Which harvest? What/who is Christ going to reap in His harvest?

The answer to that question is somewhat embedded in verses 15 and 16.

In verse 15 we are told of another angel. So, if you are keeping count, it should be noted that this is the fourth angel, with two more to come. We have already encountered different angels in verses 6, 8, and 9.

The angel simply communicates that the time for harvest has come—a message no doubt which comes from the Father.

The angel appears from the Temple, from the very presence of God. The time for harvesting is a clear reference to the Day of Judgment (Jer. 51:33; Joel 3:13; Matt. 13:30, 40-42).

Yet, who is Christ harvesting? There is a difference of opinion about the identity of those who will be harvested. For instance, Robert Mounce writes, "Some understand this scene (v. 14-16) as the gathering of the righteous at the return of Christ and interpret the next unit (v. 17-20) as the judgment of the wicked."[191]

To be sure, this is not an unscriptural position. Supporting texts would include: Matt. 9:37-38; Mark 4:29; Luke 10:2; John 4:35-38).

Matthew 9:37-38 says, "He said to his disciples, "The harvest is so great, but the workers are so few. So pray to the Lord who is in charge of the harvest; ask Him to send out more workers for his fields."

---

191 Robert Mounce. *NICNT: Revelation*, p. 278.

Mark 4:29 reads: "And as soon as the grain is ready, the farmer comes and harvests it with a sickle."

Luke 10:2 states, "These were his instructions to them: "The harvest is so great, but the workers are so few. Pray to the Lord who is in charge of the harvest, and ask him to send out more workers for his fields."

Simon Kistemaker [he is one among those who hold to this specific position] points out: "It is the time of gathering the believers into the kingdom, for the sickle goes forth to reap God's people."[192]

Yet, Mounce adds, "The idea of an eschatological harvest, however, is not limited to the gathering of the elect."[193]

It is safe to say, at a minimum, that the harvest of verses 14-16 is likewise a general picture of coming judgment. The precise time to reap the harvest is determined by God.

It's interesting to note that verse 16 is brief. John states on that He Who sat on the cloud swung His sickle across the earth, and the earth was reaped. In a sense, you will just have to imagine the details on your own!

Transition: Thus, in verses 14 through 16 we have a reference to Christ, His sickle, and His harvest of the saints, the elect, those who are believers.

Second, We Have An Unnamed Angel and His Sickle (v. 17-20).

Rev 14:17 Then another angel came out of the temple in heaven, and he too had a sharp sickle.

192 Simon Kistemaker. *New Testament Commentary: Revelation*, p. 417.

193 Ibid., p. 278.

*Rev 14:18 And another angel came out from the altar,
the angel who has authority over the fire, and he called
with a loud voice to the one who had the sharp sickle,
"Put in your sickle and gather the clusters from the vine
of the earth, for its grapes are ripe." Rev 14:19 So the
angel swung his sickle across the earth and gathered
the grape harvest of the earth and threw it into the
great winepress of the wrath of God. Rev 14:20 And
the winepress was trodden outside the city, and blood
flowed from the winepress, as high as a horse's bridle,
for 1,600 stadia.*

Intriguingly, we have here two more angels. One angels appears from out of the temple and he has a sickle (v. 17). He is God's agent for this extraordinary event. Like Christ in one sense, he also has a sharp sickle.

In verse 18 another angel appears "out from the altar." This is the altar of incense and prayer previously discussed. You remember hopefully that here at the altar the prayers of God's people rise up to Him, who answers their petitions by sending forth an angel to announce the judgment.

He is an angel who has been granted a measure of authority—authority over the fire. You recall that fire is often associated with judgment in the New Testament.

This angel (the 6th), who has charge of the fire, instructs/commands the angel with the sickle to gather the harvest (v. 18).

The fifth angel is given instruction to harvest all those who throughout their lives have opposed God, His Word, and His Kingdom.

The unsaved.

The unrepentant.

The willful disobedient.

Those who have persistently rejected God.

Kistemaker points out, "The second sickle is used not for the harvesting of grain (God's people) but for the grapes of wrath (God's enemies)."[194] In other words, this angel is told to reap grapes of God's wrath. As an important side note…

What are we to make of the "wrath of God?"

The word for "wrath" in the New Testament is orge. The word orge has the following meanings: retributive anger, indignation, vengeance, or wrath.

Let's be honest: We are woefully uncomfortable with the biblical concept of God's Wrath, in large part, because of cultural influences. In fact, God, as He is revealed in the Scripture, doesn't match up with our "preferred" vision of God.

For instance, we don't easily warm up to the idea of God being vengeful, angry, indignant, or wrathful. We prefer a tame god, a manageable god, more in the likeness of "Mr. Rogers." We prefer that God take a "boys will be boys" view stance when we sin. As Charles Swindoll writes: "The god of today's making looks more like a henpecked, pathetically passive father than the Almighty Creator who genuinely cares about His creation. A God of love must hate anything that harms those He loves."[195] We don't like the actuality of God reacting negatively to our sin.

Yet, God's wrath is not the "anger" of an emotional, abusive person; God's wrath is the rightful, just reaction of a holy God to sin.[196] God's anger is NOT like ours, nor is it like the wrath of the Greek gods.

---

194 Kistemaker, p. 418.

195 Charles Swindoll, *Romans: New Testament Insights*, p. 38-9.

196 Ibid., p. 60.

God's anger IS motivated by an offense against His divine standards, laws, commands, and decrees…never because of His ego, as if He feels some need to defend His divine dignity.

Nor is God's wrath capricious, for He always acts justly, on the basis of His own immutable standards revealed in His holy Word. Hey folks, sin is grave, serious. God's view of sin and His reaction to sin should strike utter fear in our hearts.

Yet, these grapes are not to be harvested for the sake of human consumption and enjoyment; rather, these harvested cluster of grapes are destined for the great winepress of God's wrath.[197]

John seems to have in mind here Isaiah 63:2, where the word winepress is placed within the context of God trampling the grapes of wrath (Lam. 1:15).

Joel 3:13 reads, "Now let the sickle do its work, for the harvest is ripe. Come, tread the winepress because it is full. The storage vats are overflowing with the wickedness of these people."

Isaiah 63:3-4 states, "I trampled the winepress alone, and no one from the nations was with me. I trampled them in My anger and ground them underfoot in My fury; their blood spattered My garments, and all My clothes stained. For I planned the day of vengeance, and the year of My redemption came."

It is the Day of Judgment when God metes out just punishment on the nations and grants redemption to His people.

Look at verse 20. Blood flows from the winepress and will do so outside Jerusalem. Jerusalem will be battered but not destroyed. The slaughter is evidently quite severe. Blood will flow or be splattered up to a horse's bridle, or about four feet high.

---

197 Kistemaker, p. 419.

It will run for 1,600 stadia—about 184 miles.

Surely this is hyperbole which suggests massive, unimaginable slaughter and destruction. Regardless, it's going to be brutally ugly.

Clearly, it is imperative that each of you understand the gravity of what it means to stand either with Jesus or against Jesus.

I trust you realize what is at stake. I would not want any of you to be thrown into the winepress of God's holy wrath. Don't risk it!

If you will trust your soul to Jesus Christ you will be eternally saved.

If you will trust Him, putting your confidence in Him then one day you will see Him seated on the white cloud, wearing the golden crown, and you shall be gathered.

But, if you reject Him, do not think it is wrong that you should be cast with the grapes into the winepress of the wrath of God...

Take Christ as your Savior.

Lay hold of Jesus.[198]

198 Daniel Akin. *Exalting Jesus in Revelation: Christ-Centered Exposition Commentary*, Kindle Edition, location 5155.

31

"JUDGMENT DAY HAS COME"

Revelation 15-16, ESV

Throughout the Word of God we are warned that judgment day is coming.

The eschatological Day of the Lord is inevitable. It's coming.

- Joel 1
- Zephaniah 1
- Malachi 4
- Matthew 24
- 1 Thessalonians 5
- 2 Thessalonians 2 provide just a mere sampling of the passages that guarantee the arrival of the Day of the Lord.

In Revelation 15-16 THAT DAY HAS ARRIVED!

Chapter 15 serves as a prelude, a statement of preparation if you will, for the BOWL judgments of chapter 16. Let's read chapter 15 at this point.

> *Rev 15:1 Then I saw another sign in heaven, great and amazing, seven angels with seven plagues, which are the last, for with them the wrath of God is finished. 2 And I saw what appeared to be a sea of glass mingled*

with fire—and also those who had conquered the beast and its image and the number of its name, standing beside the sea of glass with harps of God in their hands. 3 And they sing the song of Moses, the servant of God, and the song of the Lamb, saying, "Great and amazing are your deeds, O Lord God the Almighty! Just and true are your ways, O King of the nations! 4 Who will not fear, O Lord, and glorify your name? For you alone are holy. All nations will come and worship you, for your righteous acts have been revealed." 5 After this I looked, and the sanctuary of the tent of witness in heaven was opened, 6 and out of the sanctuary came the seven angels with the seven plagues, clothed in pure, bright linen, with golden sashes around their chests. 7 And one of the four living creatures gave to the seven angels seven golden bowls full of the wrath of God who lives forever and ever, 8 and the sanctuary was filled with smoke from the glory of God and from his power, and no one could enter the sanctuary until the seven plagues of the seven angels were finished.

Briefly, (because I want to move quickly to the content of chapter 16) John begins this section of Scripture by reporting that he saw ANOTHER sign in heaven and it was amazing (v. 1).

What does he see? He sees "seven angels with seven plagues, which are the last, for with them the wrath of God is finished." History is at its finale, and the end is going to be horrific. God's wrath is about to be brought to its climactic, decimating conclusion.

Robert Mounce writes, "These are the last of the plagues in that they complete the warnings of God to an impenitent world. All that remains is final judgment itself."[199]

Standing beside the sea of glass with harps of God in their hands are those who, according to John in verse 2, "had conquered the beast and its image and the number of its name."

---

199 Robert Mounce. *NICNT: The Book of Revelation*, p. 284.

They sing a victory song, what is called the song of Moses and the Lamb (v. 3).

God is rightly and joyfully praised. He is revered in their song of praise for His:

1. Great & Amazing deeds (v. 3)
2. His might (v. 3)
3. His just and true ways (v. 3)
4. His reign/sovereignty over the nations (v. 3)
5. We revere Him and glorify His name (v. 4)
6. He alone is holy (v. 4)
7. The nations will come to worship Him (v. 4)

Every tribe, language, people, and nation will gather to sing and worship this awesome God, for His righteous acts have been revealed (v. 4).

The focus of this worship gathering: GOD…as it should be.

In verse 5, John states what else he sees. This time it is the heavenly sanctuary. This is the place where God displays His presence. According to verse 6, the seven angels with the seven plagues emerge from out of this sanctuary. They are "clothed in pure, bright linen, with golden sashes around their chests."

One of the four living creatures (introduced previously in chapter 4) gives them bowls full of the wrath of the eternal God (v. 7). Immediately, "the sanctuary was filled with smoke from the glory of God and from His power" (v. 8). This display is so significant and great that no one could enter the sanctuary until judgment was finished.

You may recall that after Israel placed the Ark of the Covenant in the tabernacle, God's presence was symbolized with smoke and fire (Ex. 40:34-35). In Solomon's temple the glory of the Lord filled the holy place in the form of a cloud (1 Ki. 8:10-11).[200]

---

200 Daniel Akin. *Exalting Jesus in Revelation: Christ-Centered Exposition Commen-*

Transition: That brings us then to chapter 16. Let's read this text in full.

> *Rev 16:1 Then I heard a loud voice from the temple telling the seven angels, "Go and pour out on the earth the seven bowls of the wrath of God."*
>
> *Rev 16:2 So the first angel went and poured out his bowl on the earth, and harmful and painful sores came upon the people who bore the mark of the beast and worshiped its image.*
>
> *Rev 16:3 The second angel poured out his bowl into the sea, and it became like the blood of a corpse, and every living thing died that was in the sea.*
>
> *Rev 16:4 The third angel poured out his bowl into the rivers and the springs of water, and they became blood.*
>
> *Rev 16:5 And I heard the angel in charge of the waters say, "Just are you, O Holy One, who is and who was, for you brought these judgments.*
>
> *Rev 16:6 For they have shed the blood of saints and prophets, and you have given them blood to drink. It is what they deserve!"*
>
> *Rev 16:7 And I heard the altar saying, "Yes, Lord God the Almighty, true and just are your judgments!"*
>
> *Rev 16:8 The fourth angel poured out his bowl on the sun, and it was allowed to scorch people with fire.*
>
> *Rev 16:9 They were scorched by the fierce heat, and they cursed the name of God who had power over these plagues. They did not repent and give him glory.*
>
> *Rev 16:10 The fifth angel poured out his bowl on the throne of the beast, and its kingdom was plunged into darkness. People gnawed their tongues in anguish*
>
> *Rev 16:11 and cursed the God of heaven for their pain and sores. They did not repent of their deeds.*

tary, Kindle Edition, location 5252.

Rev 16:12 The sixth angel poured out his bowl on the great river Euphrates, and its water was dried up, to prepare the way for the kings from the east.

Rev 16:13 And I saw, coming out of the mouth of the dragon and out of the mouth of the beast and out of the mouth of the false prophet, three unclean spirits like frogs.

Rev 16:14 For they are demonic spirits, performing signs, who go abroad to the kings of the whole world, to assemble them for battle on the great day of God the Almighty.

Rev 16:15 ("Behold, I am coming like a thief! Blessed is the one who stays awake, keeping his garments on, that he may not go about naked and be seen exposed!")

Rev 16:16 And they assembled them at the place that in Hebrew is called Armageddon.

Rev 16:17 The seventh angel poured out his bowl into the air, and a loud voice came out of the temple, from the throne, saying, "It is done!"

Rev 16:18 And there were flashes of lightning, rumblings, peals of thunder, and a great earthquake such as there had never been since man was on the earth, so great was that earthquake.

Rev 16:19 The great city was split into three parts, and the cities of the nations fell, and God remembered Babylon the great, to make her drain the cup of the wine of the fury of his wrath.

Rev 16:20 And every island fled away, and no mountains were to be found. Rev 16:21 And great hailstones, about one hundred pounds each, fell from heaven on people; and they cursed God for the plague of the hail, because the plague was so severe.

As we break this chapter down into manageable bites, I want us to look first at the SEVEN BOWLS (notice also that each bowl is "poured out" by an angel):

A voice from the temple, that is God's voice, commands the angels to "go and pour out on the earth the seven bowls of the wrath of God" (v. 1).

- First bowl-harmful and painful sores come upon those people who bore the mark of the beast and worshiped its image (v. 2).
- Second bowl-the sea becomes as blood, like that of a corpse and every living thing died that was in the sea (v. 3).
- Third bowl-the rivers and springs of water became blood (v. 4).
- Fourth bowl-the scorching heat of the sun upon people (v. 8).
- Fifth bowl-the beast of the kingdom was plunged into darkness and people gnawed their tongues in anguish (v. 10).
- Sixth bowl-the water of the great river, Euphrates was dried up, preparing the way for the kings from the east (v. 12).
- Seventh bowl-poured out into the air-natural disastrous phenomena takes place: flashes of lightning, rumblings, peals of thunders, and a great earthquake such as never before. The great city is split into three parts, the islands fled away, the mountains disappear, and great, 100 lb. hailstones fell from heaven on people (v. 17-21).

Transition: The bowls of God's fury, God's righteous wrath are devastating.

Yet, there is something else you must give attention to in this chapter. That is the RESPONSES of the people who are on earth at this time.

> *Look at verse 9: Rev 16:9 They were scorched by the fierce heat, and they cursed the name of God who had power over these plagues. They did not repent and give him glory.*

> *Look at verse 11: Rev 16:11 and cursed the God of heaven for their pain and sores. They did not repent of their deeds.*

Look at verse 21: Rev 16:21 And great hailstones, about one hundred pounds each, fell from heaven on people; and they cursed God for the plague of the hail, because the plague was so severe.

Remarkably, the godless world does not respond with brokenness over sin, but with a willful refusal to repent. They curse the name of God.

Remarkably, the followers of the beast curse God for their pain and resist the need to repent of their deeds. They blaspheme God. They persevere in evil.

Remarkably, they continue to curse God. No repentance. No remorse. No cries for mercy…just curses and blasphemies.

Now, lest you think God is being unfair, unreasonable, or throwing a temper tantrum at the unrepentant, you must re-consider.

Look at verse 5: Rev 16:5 And I heard the angel in charge of the waters say, "Just are you, O Holy One, who is and who was, for you brought these judgments.

The testimony of this angel is that

- God is just
- God is holy
- God is eternal
- God is righteous in bringing these judgments.

Verse 6 reads: Rev 16:6 For they have shed the blood of saints and prophets, and you have given them blood to drink. It is what they deserve!"

These folks are getting exactly, judiciously what their evil, murderous deeds deserve. They slaughtered the saints and prophets.

Verse 7 comments further: Rev 16:7 And I heard the altar saying, "Yes, Lord God the Almighty, true and just are your judgments!"

This is significant. The altar speaks, which clearly is a statement of personification.[201] This represents the testimony of the martyrs in 6:9 and the prayers of the saints in 8:3-5. Furthermore, the altar in Revelation is always connected with judgment (6:9; 8:3-5; 9:13; 14:18; 16:7).

The altar affirms, "Yes, Lord God the Almighty, true and just are your judgment!" That's right. There is nothing unfair, unjust, or corrupt about the judgments of Holy God.

Transition: Thus far, by way of review, we have the seven bowls of God's wrath and we have the remarkable responses of the unrepentant.

One final item to consider—that is the identified place of an intense battle-ARMAGEDDON.

Specifically, this location is mentioned in verse 16, which says, "Rev 16:16 And they assembled them at the place that in Hebrew is called Armageddon."

Verse 14 speaks of a battle on the "great day of God the Almighty." This is the battle of Armageddon.

Who will be at this battle? To answer this question, you must look at verse 12 and verse 14.

In verse 12 we have mention of kings from the east; these are they who will lay siege to Rome.

In verse 14 we have mention of the kings of the whole world who will wage the final war against Christ and the armies of heaven.

Verses 13-16 expand on what we read in verse 12. Essentially, three unclean spirits like frogs come out of the mouths of the dragon, the beast, and the false prophet.

These unclean spirits are demonic, they perform signs, and they rally the kings of the world to assemble for battle (v. 14).

---

201 Robert H. Mounce. *NICNT: Revelation*, p. 295.

Perhaps they think they are gathering to battle earthly powers, perhaps Israel (Ezek. 38-39; Zech 14), or the people of God as a whole.

Actually, you read Revelation 19:11-21, and it is God who is the One who brought them there to do battle with Him!

One commentator has claimed that "Armageddon has taken on the idea of the place and time of the war that ends all wars as history draws to a close." He believes history will end in cataclysmic world war.[202]

Robert Mounce writes, "Armageddon is symbolic of the final overthrow of all the forces of evil by the might and power of God. The great conflict between God and Satan, Christ and Antichrist, good and evil, that lies behind the perplexing course of history will in the end issue in a final struggle in which God will emerge victorious and take with Him all who have placed their faith in Him. This is Har-Magedon."[203]

Verse 19 speaks of a great city being split into three parts. What is the identity of the city? Some say Jerusalem. Some say spiritual Babylon. Others say Rome.

By the way, Babylon in Revelation is the city of man that stands in opposition to the city of God, the new Jerusalem (Rev. 21-22).

At any rate "the cities of the nations fell, and God remembered Babylon the great." She will drink the full cup of the wine of the fury of God's wrath!

Verse 20 is simply a statement of cosmic upheaval.

This is the world experiencing the full wrath of a Holy God… culminating with great hailstones weighing 100 pounds each falling to earth and on people.

202 Akin. Kindle Edition, location 5331.

203 Mounce, p. 302.

What little of earth remains will now be pummeled and pulverized with hailstones…even then…men curse God for His righteous judgment. Beaten, they blaspheme.

As I close, look at verse 15. Rev 16:15 ("Behold, I am coming like a thief! Blessed is the one who stays awake, keeping his garments on, that he may not go about naked and be seen exposed!")

Christ is coming again. Soon. He will come like a thief.

Many will be caught by surprise, unprepared, and not ready. Do not find yourself in this camp.

Be alert; "stay awake." There is a blessing for those who do. Have your spiritual clothes on at all times.

At the cross, God demonstrated His wrath and poured it out on His beloved Son. His great love for sinners was on full display. In the great tribulation He will pour out His wrath on rebellious and unrepentant sinners who curse His name. There is really no middle ground.

32

"JUDGMENT OF THE GREAT HARLOT"

Revelation 17, ESV

Open your Bibles to Revelation 17. Let's begin this morning with the "setting of the table" by reading the biblical text.

> *Rev 17:1 Then one of the seven angels who had the seven bowls came and said to me, "Come, I will show you the judgment of the great prostitute who is seated on many waters,*
>
> *Rev 17:2 with whom the kings of the earth have committed sexual immorality, and with the wine of whose sexual immorality the dwellers on earth have become drunk."*
>
> *Rev 17:3 And he carried me away in the Spirit into a wilderness, and I saw a woman sitting on a scarlet beast that was full of blasphemous names, and it had seven heads and ten horns.*
>
> *Rev 17:4 The woman was arrayed in purple and scarlet, and adorned with gold and jewels and pearls, holding in her hand a golden cup full of abominations and the impurities of her sexual immorality.*
>
> *Rev 17:5 And on her forehead was written a name of mystery: "Babylon the great, mother of prostitutes and of earth's abominations."*

Rev 17:6 And I saw the woman, drunk with the blood of the saints, the blood of the martyrs of Jesus. When I saw her, I marveled greatly.

Rev 17:7 But the angel said to me, "Why do you marvel? I will tell you the mystery of the woman, and of the beast with seven heads and ten horns that carries her.

Rev 17:8 The beast that you saw was, and is not, and is about to rise from the bottomless pit and go to destruction. And the dwellers on earth whose names have not been written in the book of life from the foundation of the world will marvel to see the beast, because it was and is not and is to come.

Rev 17:9 This calls for a mind with wisdom: the seven heads are seven mountains on which the woman is seated;

Rev 17:10 they are also seven kings, five of whom have fallen, one is, the other has not yet come, and when he does come he must remain only a little while.

Rev 17:11 As for the beast that was and is not, it is an eighth but it belongs to the seven, and it goes to destruction.

Rev 17:12 And the ten horns that you saw are ten kings who have not yet received royal power, but they are to receive authority as kings for one hour, together with the beast.

Rev 17:13 These are of one mind, and they hand over their power and authority to the beast.

Rev 17:14 They will make war on the Lamb, and the Lamb will conquer them, for he is Lord of lords and King of kings, and those with him are called and chosen and faithful."

Rev 17:15 And the angel said to me, "The waters that you saw, where the prostitute is seated, are peoples and multitudes and nations and languages.

Rev 17:16 And the ten horns that you saw, they and the beast will hate the prostitute. They will make her desolate and naked, and devour her flesh and burn her up with fire,

Rev 17:17 for God has put it into their hearts to carry out his purpose by being of one mind and handing over their royal power to the beast, until the words of God are fulfilled.

Rev 17:18 And the woman that you saw is the great city that has dominion over the kings of the earth."

WOW! What a text. There's much to consider in this chapter: you have the scarlet woman, the beast, the great city, seven hills, seven mountains, seven heads, seven kings, ten horns, and ten kings. The first question which likely enters your mind is: "Who is the great prostitute?"

Chapter 17 records for us the judgment of God on the great prostitute, which is of course, ROME.

One of the key interpretive principles that we should not soon forget when seeking to understand Revelation is to ask periodically the question: "How would first-century readers have understood the text?" Paige Patterson writes, "There can be little doubt that they would have understood it to be Rome."[204]

Robert Mounce pens, "Chapter 17 and 18 portray the judgment of God on the great prostitute, Rome, that citadel of pagan opposition to the cause of Christ."[205]

With that said, you can identify ten observations regarding the woman sitting on a scarlet beast (v. 3).

1. She is a prostitute (v. 1)
2. She sits on many waters (v. 1)
3. The kings of the earth are her paramours (v. 2)
4. She rides a seven-headed, 10-horned scarlet beast (v. 3)
5. She carries a golden cup filled with abominations (v. 4)

---

204 Paige Patterson. *The New American Commentary: Revelation*, p. 326.

205 Robert Mounce. *NICNT: Revelation*, p. 306.

6. She has the title "mystery" (v. 5)
7. She bears an identity with Babylon (v. 5)
8. She is dressed in purple and scarlet and is filthy rich (v. 4)
9. She is drunk, having imbibed extensively the blood of the saints (v. 6)
10. She is identified with the city that rules over all the kings of the earth (v. 18)

Not a particularly flattering resume'. For instance, in verse 2, she has entered into illicit, corrupt relations with the kings of the earth. They represent apostate nations which Rome has seduced into idolatrous worship of herself and the beast.

Her immoral influence has spread to the all-encompassing pagan populace. These people on earth are further identified in verse 8 as those "whose names have not been written in the book of life from the foundation of the world."

According to verse 4, she is arrayed in purple and scarlet (signifying luxury and splendor), lavishly adorned with gold, jewels, and pearls, and shockingly, she holds in her hand a "golden cup full of abominations and the impurities of sexual immorality."

Look again at verse 5: "And on her forehead was written a name of mystery: 'Babylon the great, mother of prostitutes and of earth's abominations.'"

Again, Mounce proves insightful here: "The prostitute is Babylon the Great, that great system of godlessness that leads people away from the worship of God and to their own destruction. Specifically she is Rome, who, like Babylon of old, has gained a worldwide reputation for luxury, corruption, and power."[206]

---

206 Mounce, p. 311.

Tacitus once described Rome as the place "where all the horrible and shameful things in the world congregate and find a home."[207]

What's most striking about these observations is found in verse 6:

> *"And I saw a woman, drunk with the blood of the saints, the blood of the martyrs of Jesus. When I saw her, I marveled greatly."*

Rome took this twisted delight in the wanton aggravation and slaughter of believers historically, but John must surely have in mind here the drunken prostitute in the final days of persecution of God's people at the end of the age.

The woman is said to be drunk with the blood of the faithful, God's people--the martyrs of Christ. For John this is revolting and causes within him an unusual marvel. I suspect his stomach turned.

Furthermore, the harlot is pictured sitting upon many waters. According to verse 15, the waters are peoples, multitudes, nations, and languages, symbolic of Rome's vast influence and power.

Transition: The text says (v. 3) John was carried away into a desert to watch the coming judgment of the prostitute. Thus, this vision of the great prostitute in verses 1-6 is simply vile, unsettling, disturbing, and repulsive. What a contrast she will prove to be with the Bride of Christ.

Now, we consider the next section of Scripture which provides additional details and explanations, verses 7-18. In these verses we appear to have an explanation from the angel to John regarding the mystery of the woman and the beast she rides.

The beast mentioned in verse 8 is, as you might guess, the beast of chapter 13. Again, he rises up from the Abyss and goes to work to attempt to destroy God's people. The beast arrives on the scene

---

207 Mounce, p. 311 (secondary source). See footnote 20 on p. 311.

again but for the last time. Apparently, he has appeared multiple times throughout history. Some scholars suggest he is Antiochus Epiphanes, or Nero, who instigated an intense persecution of Christians to avert suspicion that he was responsible for the burning of Rome.

Robert Mounce suggests, "John understood the persecution that lay in the immediate future to be the return of the beast expressed in the ruthless tyranny of the imperial government."[208]

Those whose names are not found in the book of life marvel to see the beast. Oh, what a distinction between those who follow Christ and those whose allegiance is to the beast.

Look at verses 9-10:

> Rev 17:9 This calls for a mind with wisdom: the seven heads are seven mountains on which the woman is seated;

> Rev 17:10 they are also seven kings, five of whom have fallen, one is, the other has not yet come, and when he does come he must remain only a little while.

Verse 9 is largely accepted as a reference to Rome, the city built upon seven hills. Again, keep in mind that in John's day Rome epitomized all the antagonism and opposition to the Christian faith.

In verse 10 we have seven kings representative of the seven great world empires: Egypt, Assyria, Babylon, Medo-Persia, Greece, Rome, and that of the Antichrist.[209]

These kingdoms were radically oppressive and opposed to Christians and constantly subjected the people of God to severe persecution.

When John wrote Revelation, Egyptian, Assyrian, Babylonian, Medo-Persian, and Greek empires had gone out of existence; Rome

208 Mounce, p. 314.

209 John MacArthur. *MacArthur New Testament Commentary*, p. 938.

still existed, and Antichrist's empire had not yet come.[210] When it does, it will be brief, and he will end in destruction as stated in verse 11, which says, "As for the beast that was and is not, it is an eighth but it belongs to the seven, and it goes to destruction."

The important point in all of this is: the end is drawing near. That's helpful. Why? Because there are a variety of approaches to understanding what is being set forth in these verses.

What's interesting in verse 11 is that the Antichrist is an eighth king who is at the same time one of the seven.

He is Antichrist. He is different from the other kings. He is part of the cosmic struggle between God and Satan.

Look at verse 12: Rev 17:12 And the ten horns that you saw are ten kings who have not yet received royal power, but they are to receive authority as kings for one hour, together with the beast.

Here we have the identity of 10 kings who have not yet received power but soon will for a period of one hour. Thus, for this brief duration they will receive authority as kings along with the beast.

A noted Bible scholar makes this astute observation: "Ultimately the ten kings are 'purely eschatological figures representing the totality of the powers of all nations on the earth which are to be made subservient to Antichrist.'"[211]

They will have only a short reign. Why? The reason is found in verse 13: Rev 17:13 These are of one mind, and they hand over their power and authority to the beast.

They exist for one purpose—to give their authority to the beast.

Verse 14 says, "They will make war on the Lamb, and the Lamb

210 MacArthur, p. 938.

211 Mounce, p. 319. Primary source: Beckwith, 700. See footnote #54.

will conquer them, for HE IS LORD OF LORDS AND KING OF KINGS...and those with Him are called, chosen, and faithful."

They go to war with Christ...and lose, for He is Lord of lords and King of kings. This is the victory for the Lamb in the battle of Armageddon (16:14-16).

And, you have to love the idea of the righteous taking part in the destruction of the wicked. This is a recurring apocalyptic theme. Those who accompany the Lamb in battle are identified in the text as the called, chose, and faithful.

Finally, in verses 16-18, we have the fate of the great prostitute:

> *Rev 17:16 And the ten horns that you saw, they and the beast will hate the prostitute. They will make her desolate and naked, and devour her flesh and burn her up with fire,*
>
> *Rev 17:17 for God has put it into their hearts to carry out his purpose by being of one mind and handing over their royal power to the beast, until the words of God are fulfilled.*
>
> *Rev 17:18 And the woman that you saw is the great city that has dominion over the kings of the earth."*

Notice that the beast and the ten kings turn in utter hatred upon the prostitute. They are wicked. And, as one man put it, "The wicked are not a happy band of brothers."[212]

She is stripped bare, naked and exposed. She is fiercely and savagely attacked.

After using a false religious system of worship to unify the world kingdoms and gain control, the Antichrist with the help of his ten subordinates turns against that system, and seizes all power and worship for himself.

---

212 Mounce, p. 320.

Ironically, in doing so, they carry out the very will of God.

The angel explains in verse 17 that it was God who brought about the slaughter of the prostitute by putting it into the hearts of the ten kings to do his will.

PLEASE HEAR THIS DEAR CHURCH—in the final analysis the powers of evil serve the sovereign purposes of God.

Our God reigns supremely. There is no higher authority. His authority transcends any and all other kingdoms.

Verse 18 is clear in its designation and interpretation. The angel clarifies that "the woman John saw is the great city that has dominion over the kings of the earth."

For John, that city is Rome.

As Mounce so aptly puts it, "John's words extend beyond his immediate setting in history and sketch the portrait of an eschatological Babylon, which will provide the social, religious, and political base for the last attempt of Antichrist to establish his kingdom.[213]

One day Jesus will return. I'm ready. How about you?

You need to be. There is no middle ground. And, your only and best hope is to put your faith in Christ to be your Savior and follow Him as Lord.

Tough times are upon us. Who will you follow? The empty, godless systems of this world, or King Christ?

In the end, only one King will be victorious, and it is not the false Christ, it is the One Who the Scriptures declare to be the King of kings and Lord of lords! Don't be seduced by this world. Give your heart to Jesus!

---

213 Mounce, p. 321.

33

"THE WRATH OF A RIGHTEOUS GOD"

Revelation 18:1–8, ESV

This morning we wade into the opening verses of chapter 18. Essentially, what we encounter here is the Apostle John at his prophetic best as he foretells of Rome's demise—all told, interestingly enough, in the past tense.

To appreciate this chapter it is crucial to understand that in historical context:

- Rome is at the apex of her glory.
- She rules the world.
- The nations serve her interests.
- Her power is unparalleled and unchallenged.

Against this backdrop stands a lonely exiled prophet on the island of Patmos. As Rome continues in her indulgent, opulent lifestyle unaware of impending judgment, wrath, and danger, "John sings her funeral dirge—in the past tense!"[214] Rome has fallen.

The mighty city has met its destruction and demise.

---

214 Robert H. Mounce. *NICNT: Revelation*, p. 323,

You can imagine how this message would have fallen on the ears and hearts of the believers of the seven churches.

Facing persecution and great personal loss, they are led by the Spirit to understand that their relentless oppressor will soon be destroyed. Their faith in Christ will be vindicated by the wrath of a righteous God.

> *Rev 18:1 After this I saw another angel coming down from heaven, having great authority, and the earth was made bright with his glory.*
>
> *Rev 18:2 And he called out with a mighty voice, "Fallen, fallen is Babylon the great! She has become a dwelling place for demons, a haunt for every unclean spirit, a haunt for every unclean bird, a haunt for every unclean and detestable beast.*
>
> *Rev 18:3 For all nations have drunk the wine of the passion of her sexual immorality, and the kings of the earth have committed immorality with her, and the merchants of the earth have grown rich from the power of her luxurious living."*
>
> *Rev 18:4 Then I heard another voice from heaven saying, "Come out of her, my people, lest you take part in her sins, lest you share in her plagues;*
>
> *Rev 18:5 for her sins are heaped high as heaven, and God has remembered her iniquities.*
>
> *Rev 18:6 Pay her back as she herself has paid back others, and repay her double for her deeds; mix a double portion for her in the cup she mixed.*
>
> *Rev 18:7 As she glorified herself and lived in luxury, so give her a like measure of torment and mourning, since in her heart she says, 'I sit as a queen, I am no widow, and mourning I shall never see.'*
>
> *Rev 18:8 For this reason her plagues will come in a single day, death and mourning and famine, and she will be burned up with fire; for mighty is the Lord God who has judged her."*

What do you know about ancient Imperial Rome?

If you might indulge me for a few moments, I would like to share some historical background information on the Roman Empire that is quite difficult to hear and even offensive to consider. It's truly nauseating. Brace yourself. Yet, it is helpful and valuable in understanding the paramount significance of Revelation 18.

Imagine a time when to be a Christian, and to hold to a Christian ethic, is to be considered an outsider, a traitor, and even a danger to the accepted norms of a society.

When the day comes that a distinctively Christian brand of ethics and morality threatens to destabilize all of society, then it should come as no surprise that Christians will be scorned and persecuted.

The New Testament church was birthed into a culture and world utterly opposed to Christian morality, especially as applied to sexual ethics.

Tim Challies correctly identifies, "Almost all of the New Testament texts dealing with sexuality were written to Christians living in predominantly Roman cities."[215]

The Christian sexual ethic clashed bitterly with Roman sexual morality. Let me offer several depraved distinctions.

1. Roman Sexuality Was about Dominance.

According to Matthew Rueger, Romans did not think in terms of sexual orientation. Rather, sexuality was tied to ideas of masculinity, male domination, and the adoption of the Greek pursuit of beauty.[216]

---

215 https://www.challies.com/articles/3-awful-features-of-roman-sexual-morality/

216 Matthew Rueger. *Sexual Morality in a Christless World* as identified in Tim Challies article entitled, "Three Awful Features of Roman Sexual Morality."

In the depraved Roman way of thinking, the strong took what they wanted. It was socially acceptable for a strong Roman male to have intercourse with men or women alike, provided he was the aggressor.

He would have sex with his slaves whether they were male or female; he would visit prostitutes; he would have homosexual encounters even while married; he would engage in pederasty, which I will explain in a moment. Even rape was generally acceptable as long as he only raped people of a lower status. Romans did not think of people as being oriented toward homosexuality or heterosexuality. They simply understood that a respectable man would express his dominance by having sex—consensual or forced, with men, women, and even children.

2. Roman Sexuality Accepted Pedophilia.

The pursuit of beauty and the obsession with the masculine ideal led to the widespread practice of pederasty—a sexual relationship between an adult man and an adolescent boy.

This had been a common feature of the Greek world and was adapted by the Romans who saw it as a natural expression of male privilege and domination.

These relationships were seen as an acceptable and even idealized form of love. In the Roman world a sexual relationship with another male, boy or man, represented a higher form of intellectual love and engagement.

It was a man joining with that which was his equal and who could therefore share experiences and ideas with him in a way he could not with a woman.

3. Roman Sexuality Had a Low View of Womanhood.

Women were not generally held in high regard in Roman culture. "Women were often seen as weak physically and mentally. They were inferior to men and existed to serve men as little more than slaves at times."

A woman's value was largely in her ability to bear children and if she could not do so, she was quickly cast off. When it came to sexual norms, women were held to a very different standard than men.

Whereas a man was free to carry on homosexual affairs to commit adultery with slaves, prostitutes, and concubines, a woman caught in adultery could be charged with a crime. "The legal penalty for adultery allowed the husband to rape the male offender and then, if he desired, to kill his wife." Under Augustus Caesar it even became illegal for a man to forgive his wife—he was forced to divorce her.

Clearly, Rome was a culture of extreme promiscuity and inequality. This system was evil, but accepted and even celebrated by Rome. To be a good Roman citizen a man needed to participate in it, or at least not protest against it. To be loyal to Rome, one had to be loyal to the morality of Rome.

To the Romans, the biblical view of sexuality would have been viewed as woefully disruptive to the social fabric and especially demeaning of the Roman ideal of masculinity.

Christianity condemned the Roman system in its every part.

A Christian man was not measured by his dominance, but rather by chastity, self-sacrifice, deference to others, joyfully refraining from all sexual activity except with his wife.

The Christian sexual ethic limits sexual expression to a married man to his wife. The Christian sexual ethic protected children and gave them dignity.

The Christian ethic elevated women to be as important as any man in the eyes of God.

Christianity wasn't just an alternative system, it condemned the existing system, one that was foundational to Roman identity and stability.

Is it any wonder, then, that Christians were scorned and persecuted? This was not a safe culture in which to express Christian conviction and morals.

Transition: With that said, let's unpack the meaning of verses 1-8 of Revelation 18.

First, Note the Declaration of Babylon's Desolation (v. 1-3).

Rev 18:1 After this I saw another angel coming down from heaven, having great authority, and the earth was made bright with his glory.

Rev 18:2 And he called out with a mighty voice, "Fallen, fallen is Babylon the great! She has become a dwelling place for demons, a haunt for every unclean spirit, a haunt for every unclean bird, a haunt for every unclean and detestable beast.

Rev 18:3 For all nations have drunk the wine of the passion of her sexual immorality, and the kings of the earth have committed immorality with her, and the merchants of the earth have grown rich from the power of her luxurious living."

In these verses an angel descends from heaven to declare, to herald the announcement of the fate of Babylon, or to be understood as Rome.

The angel comes from the very presence of God, empowered with great authority and reflecting the glory and radiance of God.

With GREAT AUTHORITY, the angel prophesies the downfall of Babylon. Of course, Babylon has always symbolized that which is in wholesale opposition to the kingdom of God.

Robert Mounce notes that "part of the reason for using "Babylon" is that the readers will know what God did to the first Babylon and be quick to recognize that in giving Rome that title He will once again carry out his judgment on the city."[217]

The once proud city will lie utterly desolate, a dwelling place for demons, a haunt for every unclean spirit, a haunt for every unclean bird, a haunt for every unclean and detestable beast (v. 2).

This declaration occurs in the prophetic aorist tense which indicates that the fall of the city is so certain and imminent that it is described as if it has already been accomplished.

As you may know a "haunt" is a place frequented by a specified person or a group of people.

Babylon will become a dwelling place for demons, every unclean spirit, every unclean bird, and every unclean and detestable beast. This is the idea that they will dwell there; they are at home there.

When this great city falls all that will remain will be the evil spirits and ceremonially unclean creatures.

Why this great fall? The answer is clearly laid out in verse 3:

- Nations intoxicated with her sexual immorality
- Kings of the earth who committed adultery with her
- Merchants who grew from her desire for opulence and luxury.

Babylon has fallen because she has seduced the nations with her intoxicating wine of debauchery.

---

217 Mounce, p. 325.

Adultery is a well-known expression in the Old Testament for apostasy from God (Hos. 4:10; Jer. 3:2).

And, in the last days this apostasy will be epitomized by the worship of the beast.

Second, Note the Address to the People of God (v. 4-5) and Then the Voice to Those Who Execute God's Wrath (v. 6ff).

Rev 18:4 Then I heard another voice from heaven saying, "Come out of her, my people, lest you take part in her sins, lest you share in her plagues;

Rev 18:5 for her sins are heaped high as heaven, and God has remembered her iniquities.

The people of God are called upon to get out of the doomed city. This call to separation is nothing new for God's people.

We are strangers and exiles here.

We are a "set apart" people.

We are sojourners on our way home.

We are aliens in this world.

Our citizenship is ultimately in heaven.

We live with this constant tension between being in this world but not of it.

We are counter-culture people.

We are people swimming upstream.

We will always face the temptation to compromise and go the way of the Romans. You know the old saying, "When in Rome, do as the Romans." That doesn't work for the Christian.

The saying should instead be, "When in Cleburne, do as Christ would do. When in Rome, do as Christ would do. Wherever you find yourself, apply the ethic of Scripture to life and circumstance."

Two reasons are given for getting out of Babylon in verse 4:

1. So as not to share in her sins
2. So as not to receive any of her plagues

Her sins are piled high as heaven, God remembers, and He is going to pour out His righteous wrath (v. 5).

God remembers the iniquities of Babylon and He will make her drink the cup of His wrath (Rev. 16:19).

The Scriptures remind us that "It is a dreadful thing to fall into the hands of the living God" (Heb. 10:31).

Finally, look now at verses 6-8:

Rev 18:6 Pay her back as she herself has paid back others, and repay her double for her deeds; mix a double portion for her in the cup she mixed.

Rev 18:7 As she glorified herself and lived in luxury, so give her a like measure of torment and mourning, since in her heart she says, 'I sit as a queen, I am no widow, and mourning I shall never see.'

Rev 18:8 For this reason her plagues will come in a single day, death and mourning and famine, and she will be burned up with fire; for mighty is the Lord God who has judged her."

The voice from heaven continues, but now addresses some undesignated agents of divine vengeance.

Judgment is going to be repaid. Give back to her as she has given, yet double. This is the wrath of a righteous God.

From the very cup from which she made the nations drink the maddening wine of her adulteries, she must now drink the wrath of God.

As she glorified herself in over-the-top luxury and self-glorification, Rome is going to receive misery, torment, and mourning in exact proportion. She will be humbled.

Remember again the Scripture says, "For everyone who exalts himself will be humbled..." (Luke 14:11).

Note, too, the reasons for this humbling:

- Rome sees herself as a queen beyond any possibility of sorrow or loss. Rome's soldiers were victorious. They did not die on battlefields. There is no mourning in the streets.

Yet, because of her blatant arrogance and debauchery, her plagues will come upon her suddenly and rapidly.

She will experience death, mourning, and famine. She will be burned up with fire.

Rome, drunk with the blood of martyrs, (17:6; 18:24) will suddenly meet her doom and destruction.

The Lord God will in His limitless might bring about judgment by fire.

- God has not forsaken His people.
- His ears are not deaf to the cry of the martyrs.
- God still rules the nations.
- His sovereign plan cannot be overthrown by the wanton iniquitous Babylon.
- His kingdom will prevail!

The arrogant cruelty and depraved values of pagan Rome will not go unpunished.

God is a God of love. But, He is also a God of justice, holiness, and righteousness.

A day is coming when His righteous wrath will be poured out on the arrogant, depraved, godless, rebellious, woefully immoral. No one is getting away with anything. He is just. He is true. He is right.

Do you know Christ as your Savior? Listen, Jesus is your only hope of eternal salvation. Turn to Him.

34

"A SINGLE HOUR"

Revelation 18:9–24, ESV

- 60 seconds compose a minute.
- 60 minutes compose a single hour.
- A single hour is composed of 3,600 seconds.

Have you ever considered what can happen in your life, in a nation, on a flight, in a football game, in a doctor's office, in a classroom, in a worship service in the course of 60 minutes…a single hour?

As a Christian you must keep your eye, at least somewhat, on the finish line. As important is your START, more important is how you FINISH.

I know at my age that I have more of my life behind me than is in front of me. In fact, I am 52 years old. I will be 53 in January. By my calculations, I've lived somewhere in the neighborhood of 463,550 hours!

It is frightening to me that I could do something in one hour that could completely unravel, or cast a dark cloud over my life, that could disqualify me from ministry.

The same is true for you, too. All of us could wreck our lives in an hour or less—think about it—driving while intoxicated, doing drugs, gambling, having an affair, an accident of some sort, one or a series of poor financial decisions—fill in the blank, in one hour, 60 minutes, 3,600 seconds you could completely experience a dramatically changed, different life. It is very sobering.

Three times in this text (v. 10, 17, and verse 19) John employs the expression, "For in a single hour..." And the subsequent stated consequence is enormous for Babylon, be it eschatological Babylon or historical or future Rome, or even what we might identify as the "last great secular society."[218]

It is striking, arresting even what can happen to us individually or collectively as a nation or society in the span of one hour.

Let's examine this text closely.

> *Rev 18:9 And the kings of the earth, who committed sexual immorality and lived in luxury with her, will weep and wail over her when they see the smoke of her burning.*

> *Rev 18:10 They will stand far off, in fear of her torment, and say, "Alas! Alas! You great city, you mighty city, Babylon! For in a single hour your judgment has come."*

> *Rev 18:11 And the merchants of the earth weep and mourn for her, since no one buys their cargo anymore,*

> *Rev 18:12 cargo of gold, silver, jewels, pearls, fine linen, purple cloth, silk, scarlet cloth, all kinds of scented wood, all kinds of articles of ivory, all kinds of articles of costly wood, bronze, iron and marble,*

> *Rev 18:13 cinnamon, spice, incense, myrrh, frankincense, wine, oil, fine flour, wheat, cattle and sheep, horses and chariots, and slaves, that is, human souls.*

---

218 Robert H. Mounce. *NICNT: Revelation*, p. 340.

*Rev 18:14 "The fruit for which your soul longed
has gone from you, and all your delicacies and your
splendors are lost to you, never to be found again!"*

*Rev 18:15 The merchants of these wares, who gained
wealth from her, will stand far off, in fear of her
torment, weeping and mourning aloud,*

*Rev 18:16 "Alas, alas, for the great city that was
clothed in fine linen, in purple and scarlet, adorned with
gold, with jewels, and with pearls!*

*Rev 18:17 For in a single hour all this wealth has been
laid waste." And all shipmasters and seafaring men,
sailors and all whose trade is on the sea, stood far off*

*Rev 18:18 and cried out as they saw the smoke of her
burning, "What city was like the great city?"*

*Rev 18:19 And they threw dust on their heads as they
wept and mourned, crying out, "Alas, alas, for the great
city where all who had ships at sea grew rich by her
wealth! For in a single hour she has been laid waste.*

*Rev 18:20 Rejoice over her, O heaven, and you saints
and apostles and prophets, for God has given judgment
for you against her!"*

*Rev 18:21 Then a mighty angel took up a stone like
a great millstone and threw it into the sea, saying,
"So will Babylon the great city be thrown down with
violence, and will be found no more;*

*Rev 18:22 and the sound of harpists and musicians, of
flute players and trumpeters, will be heard in you no more,
and a craftsman of any craft will be found in you no more,
and the sound of the mill will be heard in you no more,*

*Rev 18:23 and the light of a lamp will shine in you
no more, and the voice of bridegroom and bride will
be heard in you no more, for your merchants were the
great ones of the earth, and all nations were deceived
by your sorcery.*

*Rev 18:24 And in her was found the blood of prophets
and of saints, and of all who have been slain on earth."*

As we unpack this text, notice first...

THE ANGUISH CAUSED BY GOD'S JUDGMENT ON BABYLON (v. 9-19).

1. The First Lament is by the Earthly Kings (v. 9-10).

*Rev 18:9 And the kings of the earth, who committed
sexual immorality and lived in luxury with her, will
weep and wail over her when they see the smoke of her
burning.*

*Rev 18:10 They will stand far off, in fear of her
torment, and say, "Alas! Alas! You great city, you
mighty city, Babylon! For in a single hour your
judgment has come."*

They weep and wail as they observe the smoldering smoke of her burning and destruction.

And, they stand at a distance fearful that her doom may visit them. Make no mistake judgment is coming to their doorstep as well. It's inevitable. The text makes clear that they were "bedfellows" of Babylon, participating in her sexual immorality and opulent living.

The judgment of God is just, righteous, sudden, swift, and rapid as underscored by the expression "For in a single hour your judgment has come..." (v. 2).

Their lament is stated in this fashion: "Woe, woe, the great city, Babylon, the strong city! For in one hour your judgment has come." (v. 2, NASB).

2. The Second Lament is Voiced by the Merchants of the Earth (v. 11-17).

The merchants of the earth weep and wail, their money train is gone. Their cash cow has been destroyed.

They could care less about Babylon; they're worried about their lucrative businesses. No one will buy their cargo anymore, their imports (v. 11).

Verses 12-13 provide us with a delineation, a cataloging of their inventory:

> *Rev 18:12 cargo of gold, silver, jewels, pearls, fine linen, purple cloth, silk, scarlet cloth, all kinds of scented wood, all kinds of articles of ivory, all kinds of articles of costly wood, bronze, iron and marble,*

> *Rev 18:13 cinnamon, spice, incense, myrrh, frankincense, wine, oil, fine flour, wheat, cattle and sheep, horses and chariots, and slaves, that is, human souls.*

By the way, it may interest you to know that this inventory is very similar to what you would find in Ezekiel 27, where Tyre is the chief maritime capital in a former period of splendor.

There are 29 items in these verses, falling into six groups:

1. Precious metals
2. Fabrics of expensive clothing
3. Ornamental pieces
4. Aromatic substances
5. Foodstuffs
6. Animals and people

Two features should be identified about this list: first, most of these items are luxury items, and second, apparently, these merchants were trafficking in PEOPLE as well as things and animals. The depth of their sin is significant covered by the façade of their lavish living.[219]

1. The Third Lament is Voiced by the Sea Merchants (v. 17b-19).

> *Rev 18:17 For in a single hour all this wealth has been laid waste." And all shipmasters and seafaring men, sailors and all whose trade is on the sea, stood far off*
>
> *Rev 18:18 and cried out as they saw the smoke of her burning, "What city was like the great city?"*
>
> *Rev 18:19 And they threw dust on their heads as they wept and mourned, crying out, "Alas, alas, for the great city where all who had ships at sea grew rich by her wealth! For in a single hour she has been laid waste.*

All those connected with commerce on the seas also lament over the destruction of Babylon.

This includes shipmasters, seafaring men, sailors, and all whose trade is on the sea…they, too, stood far away!   (v. 17).

The weep. They wail. They throw dust on their heads and lament. They had grown rich by Babylon's wealth. But, not anymore. Their business is destroyed.

Transition: By now, surely, you have picked up on the reality that all three groups—kings, merchants, and sailors speak of Babylon's sudden destruction: in one hour!

Incredibly, Babylon is undone in ONE HOUR! This once economically and politically powerful, robust, proud city is brought to her demise and destruction in a matter of 3,600 seconds. This

219 Charles C. Ryrie. *Revelation: Everyman's Bible Commentary*, p. 124.

clearly creates a despairing moment of anguish among those who lived off her abundance and prosperity.

Yet, Notice That Not All Are in Mourning and Anguish, The Saints Are Told to Rejoice (v. 20-24).

> *Rev 18:20 Rejoice over her, O heaven, and you saints and apostles and prophets, for God has given judgment for you against her!"*
>
> *Rev 18:21 Then a mighty angel took up a stone like a great millstone and threw it into the sea, saying, "So will Babylon the great city be thrown down with violence, and will be found no more;*
>
> *Rev 18:22 and the sound of harpists and musicians, of flute players and trumpeters, will be heard in you no more, and a craftsman of any craft will be found in you no more, and the sound of the mill will be heard in you no more,*
>
> *Rev 18:23 and the light of a lamp will shine in you no more, and the voice of bridegroom and bride will be heard in you no more, for your merchants were the great ones of the earth, and all nations were deceived by your sorcery.*
>
> *Rev 18:24 And in her was found the blood of prophets and of saints, and of all who have been slain on earth."*

In verse 20, it is clear that the world mourns. This is a sad commentary on life at this point. All people seem to have of any real value is material things. The world bemoans the passing of Babylon—a godless, heartless, selfish, profit-driven culture.

On the other hand, the saints are told to rejoice. Why? Because God has judged her for the way she treated the saints. Babylon had slain the saints; now God has slain Babylon.

Subsequently, in verses 21-24, we view the collapse of Babylon from within. Six times in verses 21-23, the phrase "no more" (ESV) occurs. In effect, this phrase tolls the meltdown of the city.[220]

A mighty angel hurls a great millstone into the sea, declaring that the great city will be thrown down with violence...and will be found no more (v. 21).

Three times we encounter this expression "a mighty angel"—once in 5:2 he was the guardian of the great scroll; another time in 10:1 a strong angel arrived from heaven with the little scroll. And, here a mighty angel throws this millstone into the depths of the sea... with violence, the text says.

This is indicative of how suddenly and spectacularly the judgment of God will be exacted on not only the city, but also upon the entire antichristian world in its vehement opposition to God.

The effects of this judgment are outlined in verses 22-23. First, no more music will be heard in the streets. Only silence. Second, no more will the sounds of craftsmen applying their trades be heard in the city. The economy has crashed. Third, there is no more food. The sound of the millstone is heard no more. Fourth, the lights of lamps are no more. Fifth, no more will the voice of the bride and bridegroom be heard in the city. Weddings are a reality of the past.

Then, we have what appears to be a summary of the rationale for judgment that has befallen Babylon.

FIRST, Rome's merchants had become filthy rich, they had an insatiable appetite for wealth with no regard for righteousness and morality.

SECOND, the deception of the nations by this city, which led others away from the proper and solitary worship of God.

---

220 Mounce, p. 337.

THIRD, the blood of the Christian martyrs which filled her streets. This eschatological judgment will bring history to a close.

This portrayal of the fall of Babylon describes the final judgment that will usher in the eternal state.

One day eschatological Babylon will collapse in defeat, and the Lamb will return to claim those who have been faithful to the end.

Since March 10, dear church, we have been moving steadily through Revelation. My intent is not only to instruct your mind in this portion of God's Holy Word. But, how sad if all you come away with from this series of messages is simply a notebook fat with copious notes.

My intent is not only to inflame your affections for the Conquering King, the Lord Jesus Christ. How sad just to sit back and admire Jesus, just to think highly of Christ.

My intent is to call for the question. My intent is to be used of God to move you to action.

You know when I was dating the woman who became my wife, there came a point where I had to say more than, "You are beautiful. You are smart. I admire you. I love you. I can't see myself living without you."

I finally had to call for the question: "Will you marry me?" "Will you be my wife?" My question called for a response!

I'm asking YOU… "Will you now deny yourself, take up your cross, and follow Jesus?" Will you repent and believe in the Lord? What this world offers you is ultimately temporal and material. What Jesus offers you is eternal and not rust or moths can erode. Come to Christ today!

35

"THE LONG AWAITED DAY"

Revelation 19:1–10, ESV

It may interest you to know that I asked Beth to marry me in April of 1990.

Eight months later, on December 22, we exchanged wedding vows at the altar of the First Baptist Church of Beeville, Texas.

Probably for me (as I cannot speak for Beth) the most anticipated, long awaited moment of our wedding ceremony was her entrance into the sanctuary. [Oh, thank God, she showed up...what a relief!]

My radiant, prepared, beautiful bride perfectly adorned in white, escorted down the aisle, and given in marriage by her father, Mr. Barris.

There we joined hands, and before God and a room full of family, friends, and invited guests, we committed our lives to one another, pledging faithfulness and love.

It was a time of great joy and celebration. For me, it was one of the happiest moments of my life. I even wept as Beth made her way down the center aisle. I assure you they were tears of joy and not tears of "oh no, what have I done?"

God, in his grace, had prepared for me a helpmate, a bride, a partner, a friend--God had given me more than I had asked.

It was a time of worship—prayers were prayed, the Scripture was read, songs were sung, rings were given, responses were rendered, and God's presence was felt.

I'm pretty sure my heart was singing the "Hallelujah Chorus!"

The text before us this morning describes the day for which we have all been waiting. It is the long awaited day! Picture this moment in your mind...

- God is seated on His throne (19:4).
- God has judged the notorious prostitute, Babylon (19:1-5).
- God has prepared the bride (the church) [19:6-8].
- God has prepared the marriage supper of the Lamb (19:6-8).
- God has directed all of heaven and earth to rivet their attention on Jesus Christ (19:9-10).
- Heaven's "Hallelujah Chorus" is a response to the command of 18:20, and it anticipates the second coming of Christ (19:11-21), His millennial reign (20:1-6), Satan's final judgment (20:7-10), the great white throne judgment (20:11-15), and the establishment of the new heaven, new earth, and new Jerusalem (Rev 21-22).[221]

Admittedly, much of the Revelation has been very difficult to hear. But, praise God, you have persevered and you are now about to hear unbelievably great news!

> *Rev 19:1 After this I heard what seemed to be the loud voice of a great multitude in heaven, crying out, "Hallelujah! Salvation and glory and power belong to our God,*
>
> *Rev 19:2 for his judgments are true and just; for he has judged the great prostitute who corrupted the earth with her immorality, and has avenged on her the blood of his servants."*

---

221 Daniel Akin. *Exalting Jesus in Revelation: Christ-Centered Exposition*, Kindle Edition, 5823.

Rev 19:3 Once more they cried out, "Hallelujah! The smoke from her goes up forever and ever."

Rev 19:4 And the twenty-four elders and the four living creatures fell down and worshiped God who was seated on the throne, saying, "Amen. Hallelujah!"

Rev 19:5 And from the throne came a voice saying, "Praise our God, all you his servants, you who fear him, small and great."

Rev 19:6 Then I heard what seemed to be the voice of a great multitude, like the roar of many waters and like the sound of mighty peals of thunder, crying out, "Hallelujah! For the Lord our God the Almighty reigns.

Rev 19:7 Let us rejoice and exult and give him the glory, for the marriage of the Lamb has come, and his Bride has made herself ready;

Rev 19:8 it was granted her to clothe herself with fine linen, bright and pure"—for the fine linen is the righteous deeds of the saints.

Rev 19:9 And the angel said to me, "Write this: Blessed are those who are invited to the marriage supper of the Lamb." And he said to me, "These are the true words of God."

Rev 19:10 Then I fell down at his feet to worship him, but he said to me, "You must not do that! I am a fellow servant with you and your brothers who hold to the testimony of Jesus. Worship God." For the testimony of Jesus is the spirit of prophecy.

Right away you have likely noticed that the word "hallelujah" is used four times—in verses 1,3,4, and 6.

What you may not know is that the word "hallelujah" appears nowhere else in the entire New Testament.

The word means, "Praise the Lord!" And, in this text there are several reasons to express a hearty "Hallelujah!"

First, We Praise the Lord for His Salvation (v. 1-5).

> *Rev 19:1 After this I heard what seemed to be the loud voice of a great multitude in heaven, crying out, "Hallelujah! Salvation and glory and power belong to our God,*
>
> *Rev 19:2 for his judgments are true and just; for he has judged the great prostitute who corrupted the earth with her immorality, and has avenged on her the blood of his servants."*
>
> *Rev 19:3 Once more they cried out, "Hallelujah! The smoke from her goes up forever and ever."*
>
> *Rev 19:4 And the twenty-four elders and the four living creatures fell down and worshiped God who was seated on the throne, saying, "Amen. Hallelujah!"*
>
> *Rev 19:5 And from the throne came a voice saying, "Praise our God, all you his servants, you who fear him, small and great."*

The text begins with the statement, "After this…," which is a reference to the events of chapter 18. The Great Tribulation has come to an end and the focus is now on heaven and the second coming of Christ.

This is a time of rejoicing, praise, celebration, and worship. It is a much anticipated, long-awaited day!

This great multitude cries out, "Hallelujah!" God has judged Babylon-the great enemy of God and God's people. Their worship and rejoicing is anything but reserved. They cut loose with a loud voice.

They praise the Lord for (v. 1-2):

1. His salvation
2. His glory
3. His power

4. His true and just judgments
5. His judgment of the great prostitute
6. His avenging the blood of His faithful servants

Listen to me--if you are a follower of Christ, if you have tasted of the sweet salvation of the Lord, then it makes perfect sense to praise Him for His salvation. David prayed that God would "restore to him the joy of thy salvation" (Ps. 51:12). Frankly, my salvation is my greatest treasure. It is greater than any earthly treasure, any earthly achievement, or any earthly honor or title.

- To be right with God
- To be reconciled with God
- To be justified before God
- To be a friend of God
- To have my sins covered by His grace
- To have Christ's righteousness imputed to my account
- To have my sins forgiven
- To have the victorious Christ as my personal Savior
- To know that I'm a child of God
- To know my enemies are defeated

No wonder the heavenly throng shouted, "Hallelujah!"

Yet, they are not the only ones singing the "Hallelujah Chorus!" The 24 elders and the four living creatures fall down and worship God who is seated on His throne.

They say, "Amen. Hallelujah!"

The final praise is stated by a singular voice from the throne (v. 5). It is likely not the voice of Christ, nor that of God, because of the wording. What is noteworthy is that all socio-economic categories are transcended by this call to the united worship of the church! The call to worship is to all God's servants, those who fear Him, small and great.

Transition: All superficial labels and categories disappear. All are compelled to praise God for His salvation.

Second, We Praise the Lord for His Bride (v. 6-8).

Rev 19:6 Then I heard what seemed to be the voice of a great multitude, like the roar of many waters and like the sound of mighty peals of thunder, crying out, "Hallelujah! For the Lord our God the Almighty reigns.

Rev 19:7 Let us rejoice and exult and give him the glory, for the marriage of the Lamb has come, and his Bride has made herself ready;

Rev 19:8 it was granted her to clothe herself with fine linen, bright and pure"— for the fine linen is the righteous deeds of the saints.

Here we have another great multitude lifting their voices, and notice the descriptive statement, "like the roar of many waters and like the sound of mighty peals of thunder…"

"Praise the Lord! For the Lord our God the Almighty reigns…" Oh, church, what a moment of celebrative worship! This is the fourth and final "Hallelujah!"

God reigns. God rules. God is sovereign.

This "Hallelujah" points forward to the long awaited day of the coming of the wedding Lamb. In other words, with the arrival of the reign of God comes also the long-awaited day of the marriage of the Lamb, the Lord Jesus, and His bride, the church![222]

This is an occasion for rejoicing, for celebrating, for giving glory to God.

By the way, the image of marriage symbolizing the relationship between God and His people appears multiple times in the Bible (Isa.54:5-7; Hos. 2:19; 2 Cor. 11:2; Eph. 5:21-33).

222 Aiken, Kindle Edition, location, 5875.

Robert Mounce provides some very helpful, insightful historical context:

> *"In biblical times a marriage involved two major events, the betrothal and the wedding. These were normally separated by a period of time during which the two individuals were considered husband and wife and as such were under the obligations of faithfulness. The wedding began with a processional to the bride's house, which was followed by a return to the house of the groom for the marriage feast.*
>
> *By analogy, the church, espoused to Christ by faith, now awaits the Parousia when the heavenly groom will come for his bride and return to heaven for the marriage feast that lasts through eternity."*[223]

Verse 7 speaks of the Bride preparing for her wedding day. According to the Scripture, the Bride is made ready through sanctification by the Word and Spirit (Eph. 2:10).

This is the only time in Revelation where the saints are described as making themselves ready, preparing themselves as the bride of Christ for His coming.

The text says it was granted her to clothe herself with fine linen, bright and pure—representing the righteous deeds of the saints (v. 8). Who granted her the permission to clothe herself in this way? The implication is that it was God.

Transition: Hallelujah…for the Lord's Bride!

Finally, We Praise the Lord for His Testimony (v. 9-10).

> *Rev 19:9 And the angel said to me, "Write this: Blessed are those who are invited to the marriage supper of the Lamb." And he said to me, "These are the true words of God."*

---

223 Robert Mounce. *NICNT: The Book of Revelation*, p. 347.

Rev 19:10 Then I fell down at his feet to worship him, but he said to me, "You must not do that! I am a fellow servant with you and your brothers who hold to the testimony of Jesus. Worship God." For the testimony of Jesus is the spirit of prophecy.

John is given an imperative, a command. He is told to "write this…" This is the fourth of seven blessings in the book of Revelation (1:3; 14:13; 16:15; 19:9; 20:6; 22:7,14).

Blessed are those who are invited to the marriage supper of the Lamb! Blessed indeed.

The angels adds in this verse 9: "These are the true words of God." To be certain, this is true of all of God's words.

- No deceit.
- No falsehood.
- No lies.
- No fabrication.
- TRUTH!

What's weird is what we read in verse 10. John falls down to worship the angel. Clearly, this is sin. This is idolatry.

Immediately, John receives a pointed rebuke. "You must not do that!" The angel gives him three reasons:

1. "I'm a fellow servant with you and your brothers who hold to the testimony of Jesus."
2. "Worship God." We are to worship Him and only Him.
3. "The testimony of Jesus is the spirit of prophecy."

What does that mean? Daniel Akin's take on this is that "the true spirit of prophecy always bears witness to Jesus. The true spirit of prophecy always points to Jesus."[224]

---

224 Akin, Kindle Edition, location 5928.

Dear church…everything about the Bible points to Jesus Christ, the Victorious, Conquering King!

The Baptist Faith and Message (which is a confessional of what we teach and believe as Southern Baptists) says this:

"The Holy Bible was written by men divinely inspired and is God's revelation of Himself to man. It is a perfect treasure of divine instruction. It has God for its author, salvation for its end, and truth, without any mixture of error, for its matter. Therefore, all Scripture is totally true and trustworthy. It reveals the principles by which God judges us, and therefore is, and will remain to the end of the world, the true center of Christian union, and the supreme standard by which all human conduct, creeds, and religious opinions should be tried. ALL SCRIPTURE IS A TESTIMONY TO CHRIST, WHO IS HIMSELF THE FOCUS OF DIVINE REVELATION."

Hallelujah!

Praise the Lord for His Salvation!

Praise the Lord for His Bride, the church!

Praise the Lord for His Testimony!

I cannot easily wait for this day to come. I appreciate the unique perspective of Joni Eareckson Tada. Listen closely:

Joni Eareckson Tada, who since a diving accident as a teenager has lived from a wheelchair, wrote about the day of her wedding: "I felt awkward as my girlfriends strained to shift my paralyzed body into a cumbersome wedding gown. No amount of corseting and binding my body gave me a good shape. The dress just didn't fit. Then, as I was wheeling into the church, I glanced down and noticed that I'd accidentally run over the hem of the dress, leaving a greasy tire mark. My paralyzed hands couldn't hold the bouquet of daisies that lay off center on my lap. And my chair, though decorated for the wedding, was still a big, clunky gray machine with belts, gears, and ball bearings. I certainly didn't feel like the picture perfect bride in a bridal magazine. I inched my chair closer to the last pew to catch a glimpse of Ken in front. There he was, standing tall and stately in his formal attire. I saw him looking for me, craning his neck to look up the aisle. My face flushed, and I suddenly couldn't wait to be with him. I had seen my beloved. The love in Ken's face had washed away all my feelings of unworthiness. I was his 'radiant' bride. How easy for us to think that we're utterly unlovely- especially to someone as lovely as Christ. But he loves us with the bright eyes of a Bridegroom's love and cannot wait for the day we are united with him forever."[225]

Hallelujah! Praise the Lord! Oh, what a day!

225 https://www.sermoncentral.com/sermon-illustrations/83880/wedding-supper-by-davon-huss?ref=TextIllustrationSerps

36

"THE RETURN OF THE WARRIOR-KING"

Revelation 19:11-21, ESV

Rev 19:11 Then I saw heaven opened, and behold, a white horse! The one sitting on it is called Faithful and True, and in righteousness he judges and makes war.

Rev 19:12 His eyes are like a flame of fire, and on his head are many diadems, and he has a name written that no one knows but himself.

Rev 19:13 He is clothed in a robe dipped in blood, and the name by which he is called is The Word of God.

Rev 19:14 And the armies of heaven, arrayed in fine linen, white and pure, were following him on white horses.

Rev 19:15 From his mouth comes a sharp sword with which to strike down the nations, and he will rule them with a rod of iron. He will tread the winepress of the fury of the wrath of God the Almighty.

Rev 19:16 On his robe and on his thigh he has a name written, King of kings and Lord of lords.

Rev 19:17 Then I saw an angel standing in the sun, and with a loud voice he called to all the birds that fly directly overhead, "Come, gather for the great supper of God,

Rev 19:18 to eat the flesh of kings, the flesh of captains, the flesh of mighty men, the flesh of horses and their riders, and the flesh of all men, both free and slave, both small and great."

Rev 19:19 And I saw the beast and the kings of the earth with their armies gathered to make war against him who was sitting on the horse and against his army.

Rev 19:20 And the beast was captured, and with it the false prophet who in its presence had done the signs by which he deceived those who had received the mark of the beast and those who worshiped its image. These two were thrown alive into the lake of fire that burns with sulfur.

Rev 19:21 And the rest were slain by the sword that came from the mouth of him who was sitting on the horse, and all the birds were gorged with their flesh.

Today, as you well know is the first Sunday, the first Lord's Day of a brand new calendar year.

This is the year of 2020. How appropriate to begin the calendar year by visiting this biblical text.

Do you know what is meant when your optometrist says, "You have 20/20 vision?"

Commonly, 20/20 vision refers to "normal vision." Technically, though, According to the American Academy of Ophthalmology 20/20 vision means that a person with 20/20 vision can see what an average individual can see on a Snellen eye chart when they are standing 20 feet away.[226]

In this passage of Scripture we get a clear, astounding vision of the Returning Warrior-King, the Lord Jesus Christ.

He has returned and He is marvelously arrayed and prepared for the battle to end all battles.

I want you to see four key headings in this text of Scripture:

---

226 https://www.aao.org/eye-health/tips-prevention/what-does-20-20-vision-mean

1. The King and His Horse (v. 11-13).
2. The King and His Armies (v. 14).
3. The King and His Sword (v. 15-16).
4. The King and His Conquered Enemies (v. 17-21).

First, Look with Me at the King and His Horse (v. 11-13).

Rev 19:11 Then I saw heaven opened, and behold, a white horse! The one sitting on it is called Faithful and True, and in righteousness he judges and makes war.

Rev 19:12 His eyes are like a flame of fire, and on his head are many diadems, and he has a name written that no one knows but himself.

Rev 19:13 He is clothed in a robe dipped in blood, and the name by which he is called is The Word of God.

This text begins by recounting what John saw as heaven opened… he saw "a white horse" and One sitting on it.

This is NOT the rider of Revelation 6:2. This is the LORD JESUS CHRIST! This is the return of the Warrior-King! The white horse is symbolic of victory and most likely purity.

Furthermore, I draw your attention to five names associated with this Rider—FOUR revealed and ONE concealed.

In verse 11, He is called both "Faithful and True."

In verse 12, He "has a name written that no one knows but Himself."

In verse 13, He is called "The Word of God."

In verse 16, He is called "King of kings and Lord of lords."

Oh, dear church, what a Savior is our Lord. What He is called in this text is simply glorious and significant.

Christ is faithful, reliable, trustworthy.

Christ is true, authentic, nothing false in Him.

What He says you can believe.

What He does, no other king can do- CHRIST "in righteousness judges and makes war."

Verse 12 is interesting. Not only are we given a description of His eyes like a flame of fire (symbolic of His penetrating gaze into our very souls. He sees every act, thought, and emotion. He sees what no one else sees. He knows you as no one else. It's both a thrill and terrifying reality. Very humbling indeed.), but also we are told that His head is crowned with many diadems (crowns of royalty, absolute sovereignty), "and He has a name written that no one knows but Himself." What does that mean?

As well as you might THINK you know Christ, G.E. Ladd writes, "That He also has a secret name means that the human mind cannot grasp the depth of His being."[227] This means simply that Christ transcends any level of understanding we may have of Him from our study of the Bible.

As Paige Patterson aptly puts it: "Though He may be known, He remains the unknowable One."[228]

Notice further the description of this RIDER in verse 13. His clothes are dipped in blood, most likely the blood of His enemies. Christ is also identified as "The Word of God." I LOVE THIS NAME for Christ!

"In the beginning was the Word and the Word was with God and the Word was God!"- John 1:1

---

227 Daniel Akin (secondary source). *Exalting Jesus in Revelation: Christ-Centered Exposition Commentary*, Kindle Edition, location 6059. Primary source: G.E. Ladd, *Commentary*, 254).

228 Paige Patterson. *The New American Commentary: Revelation*, p. 347.

*"The one who existed from the beginning is the one
we have heard and seen. We saw him with our own
eyes and touched him with our own hands. He is Jesus
Christ, the Word of Life."- 1 John 1:1*

When you look at Jesus, you are looking at God. When you listen to Jesus, you are hearing the voice of God.

Transition: This is a clear vision of the Returning Warrior-King on His Horse.

Second, Observe with Me the King and His Army (v. 14).

*Rev 19:14 And the armies of heaven, arrayed in fine linen,
white and pure, were following him on white horses.*

When the Warrior-King returns, He will be accompanied by His armies! Two observations you should not miss:

1. They are dressed in fine linen, white and pure. This army is comprised of angels and the redeemed.
2. This army is loyal to their King. They follow Him on their own white horses.

Transition: This is no ordinary army; this is the army of the Returning Warrior-King. We will not be present to participate-the battle is the Lord's. He fights for us.

Third, Notice with Me the King and His Sword (v. 15-16).

*Rev 19:15 From his mouth comes a sharp sword with
which to strike down the nations, and he will rule them
with a rod of iron. He will tread the winepress of the
fury of the wrath of God the Almighty.*

Rev 19:16 On his robe and on his thigh he has a name written, King of kings and Lord of lords.

What is so striking about these verses is that Christ's weapon of choice is the unparalleled authority of His Word.

Evidently, He wins this battle with the sword of His mouth. This is a reference to the Old Testament (Isaiah 11:4).

Paul writes that at Christ's return Jesus will destroy the lawless one with the breath of his mouth, for the battle the Lord fights is not with a sword but with His Word.[229]

Listen to this: "Then the man of lawlessness will be revealed, whom the Lord Jesus will consume with the breath of His mouth and destroy by the splendor of His coming."- 2 Thessalonians 2:8, NLT

Moreover, His powerful word is the means by which He will "strike down the nations, and He will rule them with a rod of iron," drawing here from Psalm 2:8-9.

Martin Luther was right when he wrote in the classic hymn, "A Mighty Fortress is Our God"— of how our Returning Warrior-King will deal with the enemy--"one little word will fell him."

Furthermore, "He will tread the winepress of the fury of the wrath of God the Almighty," drawing from Isaiah 63:1-6 and Joel 3:13-14.

He is the Sovereign.

He is the Exalted One.

He is God, the Almighty.

Additionally, He can do all of this because on His robe along the thigh He has a name, the fifth name "King of kings and Lord of lords" (17:14; Deut. 10:17; Dan. 2:47).

He is the Sovereign King alone.

---

229 Simon Kistemaker. *New Testament Commentary: Revelation*, p. 523.

No equal and no competition.

I cannot tell you fully how powerful is the Word of God.

Scripture bears this witness: "For the Word of God is living and active, sharper than any two-edged sword, piercing to the division of soul and spirit, of joints and of marrow, and discerning the thoughts and intentions of the heart."- Hebrews 4:12, ESV

Just as God's word was powerful enough to create the cosmos initially, so it is all that is needed to strike down the nations who rise against Him.

Transition: The Returning Warrior-King comes with His weapon-His Word. One final idea…

Fourth, Notice with Me the King and His Conquered Enemies (v. 17-21).

Rev 19:17 Then I saw an angel standing in the sun, and with a loud voice he called to all the birds that fly directly overhead, "Come, gather for the great supper of God,

Rev 19:18 to eat the flesh of kings, the flesh of captains, the flesh of mighty men, the flesh of horses and their riders, and the flesh of all men, both free and slave, both small and great."

Rev 19:19 And I saw the beast and the kings of the earth with their armies gathered to make war against him who was sitting on the horse and against his army.

Rev 19:20 And the beast was captured, and with it the false prophet who in its presence had done the signs by which he deceived those who had received the mark of the beast and those who worshiped its image. These two were thrown alive into the lake of fire that burns with sulfur.

Rev 19:21 And the rest were slain by the sword that came from the mouth of him who was sitting on the horse, and all the birds were gorged with their flesh.

For a few moments, let me direct your attention initially to a few interesting details:

1. This is a battle in which evil is conquered, defeated, vanquished. The beast and the false prophet are consigned to the lake of fire and sulfur.

2. Christ fights with unconventional weapons of warfare against these agents of Satan and their followers. The saints are not engaged in this final battle against evil; evil is banished forever!

3. No mention is made of the battle itself—only the outcome, the result.[230] Frankly, that's what matters most.

Verse 17 informs us that John saw an angel standing in the sun and with a loud voice he summoned these birds of prey. Kistemaker writes this: "The birds of prey who have been created to consume carcasses and thus remove unsightly scenes and dreadful smells have been called to be present at the aftermath of Christ's battle against Antichrist and his followers."[231]

This is the explicit fulfillment of Ezekiel's prophecy against Gog in the land of Magog in Ezekiel 38-39.

At this great supper of God, these birds of prey eat God's opponents slain on the battlefield of life—kings, captains, mighty men, horses, riders, the flesh of all men, free and slave, small and great (v. 18). They are lifeless and scattered everywhere on the earth.

God's final battle (commonly called Armageddon) is against all the people who have followed the Antichrist and against all the

---

230 Kistemaker, p. 526.

231 Kistemaker, p. 525.

unrighteousness and deceit perpetrated by the evil one on all levels of society. This battle is against everyone who is evil.

All earthly power has come to an end at the victorious authoritative Word of the Victor, Jesus Christ!

In verse 19 John saw the beast and the kings of the earth with their armies gathered for battle against Christ.

In verse 20, the beast and the false prophet are captured! The beast is Antichrist. The beast coming up out of the earth is the false prophet. They are Satan's henchmen. For their crafty deception in deceiving the multitudes on the face of the earth, they are banished alive into the lake of fire which burns with sulfur—the first, by the way, of countless numbers of unregenerate people and fallen angels to arrive in such a dreadful place.

This is an image taken from the prophecy of Daniel 7:11.

Finally, in verse 21, the remaining enemies of Christ are slain by the sword of the mouth of Christ. Their ultimate, eternal destiny is the lake of fire. The birds of prey gorge themselves on their flesh.

Understand this: Jesus Christ, the Warrior-King, will one day return. If you do not have a saving relationship with Christ by faith, listen to me, your eternal destiny is one of conscious torment and eternal separation from God.

You say, "Goodness, Pastor, that's harsh." Did you know that NO ONE said more about the reality of hell in the entire Bible, than did the Lord Jesus Christ?

What a compelling picture of Christ is in this passage of Revelation.

Christ—

Seated on a white horse, faithful and true, the righteous Judge, and Messianic Warrior who sees all, knows all, crowned with diadems and shrouded in mystery. He comes to conquer God's enemies once and for all, to end the history of the world with the revelation of God's Word, to rule the nations as He brings the wrath of God upon this world dominated and deceived by sin and Satan.[232]

He is indeed the King of kings and Lord of lords. He is the Returning Warrior-King.

Jesus is coming again! ARE YOU READY?

232 Akin, Kindle Edition, location 6156, quoting David Platt.

37

"THE DEFEAT OF SATAN"

Revelation 20:1-10, ESV

Last week…in Revelation 19:11-21 we rejoiced in the return of the Warrior-King, Jesus Christ.

- Antichrist has been removed.
- The False Prophet has been removed.
- Their followers have met their judicious demise.
- Anti-Christian forces have been trounced and evil has ceased.

In Chapter 20, John now turns his attention to the defeat of Satan and the end of Death and Hades.

In the opening 10 verses of chapter 20, John presents an additional aspect of the end time. It is an aspect about which the people of God can get excited and cheer!

As Simon Kistemaker rightly identifies in his superior commentary, "In it John directs full attention to Satan's imprisonment, release, defeat, and damnation."[233]

READ THE TEXT:

---

233 Simon Kistemaker. *New Testament Commentary: Revelation*, p. 531.

Rev 20:1 Then I saw an angel coming down from heaven, holding in his hand the key to the bottomless pit and a great chain.

Rev 20:2 And he seized the dragon, that ancient serpent, who is the devil and Satan, and bound him for a thousand years,

Rev 20:3 and threw him into the pit, and shut it and sealed it over him, so that he might not deceive the nations any longer, until the thousand years were ended. After that he must be released for a little while.

Rev 20:4 Then I saw thrones, and seated on them were those to whom the authority to judge was committed. Also I saw the souls of those who had been beheaded for the testimony of Jesus and for the word of God, and those who had not worshiped the beast or its image and had not received its mark on their foreheads or their hands. They came to life and reigned with Christ for a thousand years.

Rev 20:5 The rest of the dead did not come to life until the thousand years were ended. This is the first resurrection.

Rev 20:6 Blessed and holy is the one who shares in the first resurrection! Over such the second death has no power, but they will be priests of God and of Christ, and they will reign with him for a thousand years.

Rev 20:7 And when the thousand years are ended, Satan will be released from his prison

Rev 20:8 and will come out to deceive the nations that are at the four corners of the earth, Gog and Magog, to gather them for battle; their number is like the sand of the sea.

Rev 20:9 And they marched up over the broad plain of the earth and surrounded the camp of the saints and the beloved city, but fire came down from heaven and consumed them,

> *Rev 20:10 and the devil who had deceived them was thrown into the lake of fire and sulfur where the beast and the false prophet were, and they will be tormented day and night forever and ever.*

As we examine closely these ten verses, it would be helpful to consider the following headings:

1. The SEIZING of Satan (v. 1-3).
2. The REIGNING of the Saints with Christ (v. 4-6).
3. The SENTENCING of Satan (v. 7-10).

First, Then, We Consider The SEIZING of Satan (v. 1-3).

> *Rev 20:1 Then I saw an angel coming down from heaven, holding in his hand the key to the bottomless pit and a great chain.*
>
> *Rev 20:2 And he seized the dragon, that ancient serpent, who is the devil and Satan, and bound him for a thousand years,*
>
> *Rev 20:3 and threw him into the pit, and shut it and sealed it over him, so that he might not deceive the nations any longer, until the thousand years were ended. After that he must be released for a little while.*

In verse 1 an unknown angel is dispatched by God to seize Satan—also known as—the dragon—that ancient serpent—and the devil.

In this angel's hand is the key to the bottomless pit and a great chain. The angel seizes Satan, binds him, throws him into the pit, shuts it, and seals it!

The text says, in verse 2, that Satan is bound for a "thousand years." Furthermore, verse 3 makes clear that during this time Satan will not be allowed to deceive the nations until this period ends.

Right away, we have our first interpretive challenge in chapter 20. What is meant by "thousand years"?

What is the nature of this temporal designation? Is this designation to be understood as literal or symbolical?

Not surprisingly, there is no consensus among Bible scholars, pastors, and theologians regarding this "thousand years" reference.

Many Bible commentators espouse a literal explanation of 1,000 years as the interval between Jesus' return to earth and the end of time.[234]

John MacArthur[235] argues for a literal interpretation, as does Paige Patterson[236], Warren, Wiersbe, Adrian Rogers[237], and the Dallas Theological Seminary Faculty members.[238] That's a noteworthy list, for sure!

However, Robert Mounce (whose commentary on Revelation is ranked second on bestcommentaries.com) was very helpful to me here and wise. He writes, "Some commentators understand this period as a literal one thousand years, but the majority take it to indicate a lengthy period of undetermined duration."[239]

Furthermore, Mounce rightly states that "the tendency of many interpreters at this point is to become apologists for a particular view of the millennium."[240]

---

234 Kistemaker, p. 535.

235 *John MacArthur. MacArthur New Testament Commentary*, p. 944.

236 Paige Patterson, *New American Commentary: Revelation*, p. 353.

237 Adrian Rogers. *Unveiling the End Times in Our Time: The Triumph of the Lamb in Revelation*, Kindle Edition, Location, 5349.

238 The Bible Knowledge Commentary: New Testament, Revelation, p. 979.

239 Robert Mounce. *NICNT: The Book of Revelation*, p. 362.

240 Mounce, p. 360.

And, in doing so, one can completely miss the imperial themes as the return of Christ, the final judgment and removal of all wickedness, and the splendor of the eternal state.

R. Summers should be heard at this point. He declares,

> *"If verses 4, 5, and 6 of Revelation 20 had been omitted, no one would ever have dreamed of a literal thousand years of Christ's reign upon the earth—his setting up a temporal throne in Jerusalem and inaugurating a millennial reign as an earthly monarch. Yet whole systems of eschatology, theology, and philosophy of history have been constructed on this precarious basis of highly symbolical verses."*[241] *Wow!*

With that said: What's interesting is that the word "millennium" occurs six times in this chapter of Revelation and NOWHERE else in any other New Testament eschatological teachings.[242] To be fair, this reality does not diminish the importance of the subject.

Furthermore, in the Lord's eschatological discourse (Matthew 24), Jesus says nothing about a thousand-year reign with the saints on this earth.

In addition, neither Paul nor Peter mentions a millennial interim reign of Christ on earth.

As I have previously made the case, the New Testament teaches but one return of Christ and not two.

Finally, a literal interpretation of this number in a book of symbolism and particularly in this chapter filled with symbols is a pretty big obstacle.

---

241 R. Summers. Worthy is the Lamb: Interpreting the Book of Revelation in Its Historical Background, Nashville: B&H, 1951, p. 203-primary source. Secondary source: Patterson, p. 352.

242 Kistemaker, p. 535.

Therefore, it would seem at least reasonable that the numerical designation is metaphorical as opposed to literal. Either position is legitimately plausible.

Transition: The critical truth to keep in mind here is that Satan is bound, the accuser, and the deceiver is seized. That's what's critical here and should not be lost in the fervor to argue a specific millennial position.

Second, Then, We Consider The REIGNING of the Saints with Christ (v. 4-6).

> *Rev 20:4 Then I saw thrones, and seated on them were those to whom the authority to judge was committed. Also I saw the souls of those who had been beheaded for the testimony of Jesus and for the word of God, and those who had not worshiped the beast or its image and had not received its mark on their foreheads or their hands. They came to life and reigned with Christ for a thousand years.*
>
> *Rev 20:5 The rest of the dead did not come to life until the thousand years were ended. This is the first resurrection.*
>
> *Rev 20:6 Blessed and holy is the one who shares in the first resurrection! Over such the second death has no power, but they will be priests of God and of Christ, and they will reign with him for a thousand years.*

These verses describe what John observes next. He sees thrones. Who was on the thrones? "Those to whom authority to judge was committed" (v. 4).

There are clear references to thrones and judging in the Old Testament (Dan. 7:9, 22) and the New Testament (Matt. 19:28; Luke 22:30; 1 Cor. 6:2).

This is not the final judgment. They are ruling on their thrones with Christ in heaven while Satan is bound on earth. Jesus promises the overcomers to sit with Him on His throne (3:21), and this promise of reigning with Him appears frequently in the Apocalypse (5:10; 20:4, 6; 22:5; and 2 Tim 2:12).

In addition to the thrones, John sees "the souls of those who had been beheaded for the testimony of Jesus and for the word of God, and those who had not worshiped the beast or its image and had not received its mark on their foreheads or their hands' (v. 4).

These are the souls of the martyrs under the altar mentioned in Revelation 6:9. To be certain they are representative of all who gave their lives in faithfulness to their commitment to Christ.

It should be noted that all who refused to worship the image of the beast met a martyr's death. We are reminded that in the final conflict there are none who resist the Antichrist without paying for their stand with their life.

John writes at the end of verse 4: "They came to life and reigned with Christ for a thousand years."

Look at verse 5. Rev 20:5 The rest of the dead did not come to life until the thousand years were ended. This is the first resurrection.

The last sentence in verse 5 should be viewed as the concluding thought to verse 4. Therefore, the first resurrection is a spiritual resurrection for believers. The second resurrection is a physical one.

Let me define it this way. For the unbeliever, there are two deaths: one, physical, and the other, spiritual. There is one resurrection (physical). In other words, those who reject Christ, rise once, but die twice (physically and spiritually).

For the believer, the one who is born again, there is one death (physical), and two resurrections: one, spiritual, and the other, physical. In other words, those who belong to Christ die once, but rise twice (spiritually and physically). Those who share in this resurrection are blessed and holy. The second death will have no power over them.

Instead, verse 6 says, they will be priests of God and of Christ, and they will reign with Him for a thousand years.

What is the second death mentioned in verse 6? It is defined in Revelation 20:14 and 21:8 as being cast into the lake fire. It is to share the same eternal fate as the devil, the beast, and the false prophet, which is to be tormented day and night for eternity.

Transition: These precious saints will reign with Christ. They share in the first resurrection. The second death has no power over them and they will serve God and Christ.

Finally, Then, We Consider The SENTENCING of Satan (v. 7-10).

> *Rev 20:7 And when the thousand years are ended, Satan will be released from his prison*
>
> *Rev 20:8 and will come out to deceive the nations that are at the four corners of the earth, Gog and Magog, to gather them for battle; their number is like the sand of the sea.*
>
> *Rev 20:9 And they marched up over the broad plain of the earth and surrounded the camp of the saints and the beloved city, but fire came down from heaven and consumed them,*
>
> *Rev 20:10 and the devil who had deceived them was thrown into the lake of fire and sulfur where the beast and the false prophet were, and they will be tormented day and night forever and ever.*

Verse 7 declares that after the 1,000 years are ended, Satan is loosed from his prison.

He will come out swinging—actually, the text says in verse 8, that he "will come out to deceive the nations that are at the four corners of the earth, God and Magog, to gather them for battle, their number is like the sand of the sea."

Gog and Magog are enjoined to gather for a great battle. There is too many to count. This is a reference to the prophecy of Ezekiel 38-39. Gog is the individual and Magog is the geographical and political entity he represents.

The text further states in verse 9 that "they marched up over the broad plain of the earth and surrounded the camp of the saints and the beloved city, but fire came down from heaven and consumed them…"

The beloved city is Jerusalem. There will be no battle. These armies mustered together by the deceiver are consumed by a fire which falls from heaven.

The time has come to deal with the Devil forever.

Look at verse 10: God throws Satan into the lake of fire and sulfur where the beast and the false prophet are, and they will be tormented day and night forever and ever.

The Bible says, "Then He will say to those on His left, 'Depart from me, you cursed, into the eternal fire prepared for the devil and his angels" (Matt. 25:41).

Originally, hell was prepared for the Devil and his angels.

Satan is there.

The beast is there.

The false prophet is there.

All the enemies of God who have chosen not to serve Him will be there.

For those who have never experienced the new birth, those who have never repented of their sin, and believed in Christ, will be present there as well—there is no other alternative.

The big loser here in this text is SATAN. He is soundly defeated.

He failed to destroy the male child in chapter 12.

He fought a war in heaven and lost in chapter 12.

He was bound and kept in the Abyss in chapter 20.

He has been dispatched to his final destiny by being cast into the lake of fire and sulfur in chapter 20.

Satan is beaten…DEFEATED.

What a text! We can rejoice in that Satan has been seized, the Saints reign with our King, Jesus Christ, and Satan has been defeated and banished to his eternity in the lake of fire and sulfur, where he will be tormented day and night, separated from God forever and ever.

As we inch our way closer to the end of this magnificent book, you are surely coming to a clear conclusion. That conclusion is this: there are only two sides: Christ's or the Devil's. You will spend your eternity in heaven or in hell. You will be with God in heaven or you will be separated from Him in hell.

The Bible says in verse 15 of this same chapter: "And if anyone's name was not found written in the book of life, he was thrown into the lake of fire."

You must be born again. You must repent and give your heart to Jesus. He is coming! Are you ready?

38

"THE FINAL JUDGMENT OF THE UNSAVED"

Revelation 20:11–15

No one in Scripture had more to say on the subject of judgment than the Lord, Jesus Christ.

Repeatedly, Jesus informed and warned of impending doom for the unrepentant, rebellious sinner.

Ironically, Jesus spoke of the reality of hell far more often than he spoke of heaven, and always in the most vivid and disturbing terms. In fact most of what we know about the everlasting doom of unrepentant sinners comes from the lips of Jesus.[243]

After the MILLENNIAL AGE, which is a thousand year earthly reign of Christ described in Revelation 20:1-7, the Bible speaks of a FINAL JUDGMENT of the Unsaved.

> *Rev 20:11-15: "11 And I saw a great white throne and Him who sat upon it, from whose presence earth and heaven fled away, and no place was found for them. 12 And I saw the dead, the great and the small, standing before the throne, and books were opened; and another book was opened, which is the book of life; and the*

---

243   John F. MacArthur, *The Second Coming of Christ*, p. 177.

dead were judged from the things which were written in the books, according to their deeds. 13 And the sea gave up the dead which were in it, and death and Hades gave up the dead which were in them; and they were judged, every one of them according to their deeds. 14 And death and Hades were thrown into the lake of fire. This is the second death, the lake of fire. 15 And if anyone's name was not found written in the book of life, he was thrown into the lake of fire."

These verses describe the judgment of all unbelievers, all the unsaved of all the ages.

By Way of Background & Context:

As we have already discovered together, the book of Revelation is the final book in the English New Testament canon. Revelation, while primarily prophetic, is first and foremost a revelation of Jesus Christ.

The author of Revelation is John, the same John who wrote the Gospel of John. John wrote Revelation to the churches surrounding Ephesus, which had begun to feel the effects of Domitian persecution.

Bible scholars identify the date of Revelation as being written in the last decade of the first century.

John, by this time an elderly man, is in exile on the island of Patmos. The Roman authorities had banished him there because of his faithful preaching of the Gospel of Jesus Christ. While on Patmos, John received a series of inspired visions which laid out the future history of the world.

Primarily, Revelation is a message of hope. Ladies and gentlemen: God is sovereignly in control!

Let's examine this text carefully:

FIRST, NOTICE THE JUDGE (v. 11).

> *"11 And I saw a great white throne and Him who sat upon it, from whose presence earth and heaven fled away, and no place was found for them.*

Who is this "ONE" sitting on the throne?
According to Scripture, John 5:22, 27ff:

> *22 "For not even the Father judges anyone, but He has given all judgment to the Son…27 and He gave Him authority to execute judgment, because He is the Son of Man. 28 "Do not marvel at this; for an hour is coming, in which all who are in the tombs shall hear His voice, 29 and shall come forth; those who did the good deeds to a resurrection of life, those who committed the evil deeds to a resurrection of judgment."*

JESUS CHRIST is the ONE who sits on the judgment seat.

The same Compassionate One who wept and pleaded with sinners to be reconciled to God, will one day be their sovereign Judge.[244]

Jesus, as King, will take His rightful place as King, and will execute just judgment from His throne.

SECOND, NOTICE THOSE WHO ARE JUDGED (v. 12-13).

> *12 And I saw the dead, the great and the small, standing before the throne, and books were opened; and another book was opened, which is the book of life; and the dead were judged from the things which were written in the books, according to their deeds. 13 And the sea gave up the dead which were in it, and death and Hades gave*

---

244 MacArthur, *The Second Coming*, p. 179.

up the dead which were in them; and they were judged,
every one of them according to their deeds.

Who shall be judged at this judgment?

To be perfectly honest, there is a bit of discrepancy regarding who is judged at this FINAL JUDGMENT.

Some Bible scholars propose that this is a singular judgment in which believers and unbelievers alike are judged at the GREAT WHITE THRONE JUDGMENT.

Believers…to determine degrees of reward.

Unbelievers…to determine degrees of punishment.

Yet, other Bible scholars propose two judgments, where believers are judged at the Judgment Seat of Christ ([1 Cor. 3:11-15; 2 Cor. 5:10], the Bema Seat) before the Millennium begins; and, unbelievers at the Great White Throne Judgment after the Millennium has ended.

No unbeliever will be judged at the Judgment Seat of Christ and no believer at the Great White Throne Judgment.

According to Scripture and sound exegesis of this text and other ancillary texts, it is more logical to surmise that these are the UNSAVED dead of all the ages, regardless of where their bodies were disposed…the sea, the grave, or Hades.

Those who stand in this judgment are the wicked dead…great and small, the important and the unimportant.

There is no place for them to hide. "The earth and sky fled from His presence, but they found no place to hide."- Rev. 20:11

Transition: To review, we have indentified from Scripture that at the Final Judgment, Christ is the Judge. And, that the wicked, unsaved dead are the subjects of this judgment.

THIRD, NOTICE THE BASIS |FOR JUDGMENT (v. 12, 13).

Notice at the end of both verse 12 and verse 13:

> *Verse 12: I saw the dead, the great and the small, standing before the throne, and books were opened; and another book was opened, which is the book of life; and the dead were judged from the things which were written in the books, according to their deeds. 13 And the sea gave up the dead which were in it, and death and Hades gave up the dead which were in them; and they were judged, every one of them according to their deeds.*

According to Scripture, the Basis for Judgment is one's deeds, thoughts, and words.

These books divinely record one's thoughts (Luke 8:17; Rom. 2:16), words (Matt. 12:37); and actions (Matt. 16:27), and are compared to God's perfect standard (Matt. 5:48; 1 Peter 1:15, 16), and will be found wanting (Rom. 3:23).

Make no mistake: all final judgments deal with works, whether the works of believers rewarded at the Judgment Seat of Christ, or the works of the unsaved, which are in view here.

Now, we must pause here and ask several important questions:

- Is the Bible contradicting itself here?
- Is God confusing the matter here?
- Isn't salvation by grace through faith in Jesus Christ?

Let's let the Bible answer those questions:

> *Eph 2:8-10: "8 For by grace you have been saved through faith; and that not of yourselves, it is the gift of God; 9 not as a result of works, that no one should boast. 10 For we are His workmanship, created in*

Christ Jesus for good works, which God prepared beforehand, that we should walk in them."

Elsewhere, the Scripture states:

James 2:20, 26: "20 But are you willing to recognize, you foolish fellow, that faith without works is useless?..26 For just as the body without the spirit is dead, so also faith without works is dead."

Listen, friend: What you do with your life is unmistakable evidence of the loyalty of your heart.

The Scripture boldly declares: "Don't you realize that friendship with this world makes you an enemy of God? I say it again, that if your aim is to enjoy this world, you can't be a friend of God."- James 4:4

- Your words
- Your thoughts
- Your actions…will reveal what's in your heart.

Yet, notice also in this text: As an act of grace if you will, Christ demonstrates that the unsaved, based on the evidence of their lives, deserve to be cast into the Lake of Fire.

Transition: One final idea present in this specific passage.

FINALLY, NOTICE THE RESULT OF JUDGMENT (v. 14-15).

14 And death and Hades were thrown into the lake of fire. This is the second death, the lake of fire. 15 And if anyone's name was not found written in the book of life, he was thrown into the lake of fire."

Quickly: What is the "Book of Life"? Put simply, this book is the record of those who are saved whose names are written in the book of life from the creation of the world (Rev. 17:8).

The Bible teaches that this resurrection of the unsaved dead to judgment will be a physical resurrection, whereupon receiving their judgment (John 5:28-29), they will be committed to an eternal, conscious punishment in the lake of fire (Matt. 25:41; Rev. 20:11-15).

This is the second death—an eternal separation from God.

Even death and Hades are cast into the lake of fire. Not only that, but Satan has already been cast into the lake of fire, as well (Rev. 20:10).

Listen carefully: as far as biblical revelation is concerned, there are only two destinies for human souls; one is to be with the Lord, and the other is to be forever separated from God in the lake of fire.

At the Final Judgment, there will be no opportunity for unrepentant sinners to argue their case. When the books are opened and the facts revealed, the sinner will be speechless before God.

God will pronounce every lost sinner condemned.

May I ask you this morning: where do you stand with God today, in this temporal realm? Are you ready to face judgment in eternity?

True faith in Jesus is always accompanied by repentance from sin.

Repentance is agreeing with God that you are sinful, confessing your sins to Him, and make a deliberate choice to turn from sin, and put your faith in Christ.

39

"THE NEW HEAVEN & NEW EARTH"

Revelation 21:1-8

Throughout the history of the church, God's people have had a preoccupation with heaven.

As the writer of Hebrews tells us, we are but "foreigners and nomads here on earth...because we are looking for a better place, a heavenly homeland...for God has prepared a heavenly city for us." (Hebrews 11:13, 16).

Scripture refers to heaven more than 500 times.

Revelation alone mentions heaven 50 times.

By way of Background and Context:

The book of Revelation is the final book in the English New Testament canon. Revelation, while primarily prophetic, is first and foremost a revelation of Jesus Christ. The author of Revelation is John, the same John who wrote the Gospel of John. John wrote Revelation to the churches surrounding Ephesus, which had begun to feel the effects of Domitian persecution.

Bible scholars identify the date of Revelation as being written in the last decade of the first century.

John, by this time an old man, is in exile on the island of Patmos. The Roman authorities had banished him there because of his faithful preaching of the gospel. While on Patmos, John received a series of inspired visions that laid out the future history of the world. Primarily, Revelation is a message of hope. God is sovereignly in control.

Reading of the Text--Rev. 21:1-8:

> *Then I saw a new heaven and a new earth; for the first heaven and the first earth passed away, and there is no longer any sea. 2 And I saw the holy city, new Jerusalem, coming down out of heaven from God, made ready as a bride adorned for her husband. 3 And I heard a loud voice from the throne, saying, "Behold, the tabernacle of God is among men, and He will dwell among them, and they shall be His people, and God Himself will be among them, 4 and He will wipe away every tear from their eyes; and there will no longer be any death; there will no longer be any mourning, or crying, or pain; the first things have passed away."*
>
> *5 And He who sits on the throne said, "Behold, I am making all things new." And He said, "Write, for these words are faithful and true." 6 Then He said to me, " It is done. I am the Alpha and the Omega, the beginning and the end. I will give to the one who thirsts from the spring of the water of life without cost. 7 " He who overcomes will inherit these things, and I will be his God and he will be My son. 8 " But for the cowardly and unbelieving and abominable and murderers and immoral persons and sorcerers and idolaters and all liars, their part will be in the lake that burns with fire and brimstone, which is the second death." –NASU*

For a few moments, let's break these eight verses down to several manageable, glorious ideas.

First, Note the Appearance (v. 1).

> *"Then I saw a new heaven and a new earth; for the first heaven and the first earth passed away, and there is no longer any sea."*

As chapter 21 opens, all the wicked of all the ages, as well as the Evil One and his demons, have been sentenced to the lake of fire (Rev. 20:10-15). All ungodly men and angels have been forever banished and the present universe destroyed.

The phrase "a new heaven and a new earth" is derived from two passages in Isaiah (Isa. 65:17; 66:22).

Scripture indicates that God must create a new heaven and a new earth because the first heaven and the first earth passed away.

Note John's observation also that in the new heaven and the new earth there will no longer be any sea.

Presently, near ¾ of the earth's surface is covered with water. All life at present is utterly dependent on water for its survival. Evidently, our glorified bodies will not be water dependent, unlike our present human bodies, whose blood is 90% water.[245] The new heaven and the new earth will be based on a completely different life principle.

Second, Note Its Capital (v. 2).

> *"And I saw the holy city, new Jerusalem, coming down out of heaven from God, made ready as a bride adorned for her husband."*

By evidence of the text, the new Jerusalem is an actual city. The new Jerusalem is not heaven, but simply its capital city.

245 John MacArthur, *Because the Time is Near*, p. 315.

The new Jerusalem is called the holy city because everyone in it is holy (20:6). Unlike the evil cities of the present, old earth, the people in the new Jerusalem will live together in perfect harmony.

Now, the architect and builder of this new Jerusalem is God Himself. Believers who die go to the "heavenly Jerusalem," where Jesus has gone before them to prepare a place for them (Jn. 14:1-3).

When God creates the new heaven and the new earth, the new Jerusalem will descend into the midst of that holy new universe (21:10) and serve as the eternal dwelling place of the redeemed.

The city is made ready as a bride is adorned for her groom.

Third, Note Its Supreme Reality (v. 3).

> "And I heard a loud voice from the throne, saying,
> 'Behold, the tabernacle of God is among men, and He
> will dwell among them, and they shall be His people,
> and God Himself will be among them.'"

The supreme joy and glory of heaven is the Person of God (Ps. 73:25).

The Greek word translated "tabernacle" can also mean "tent" or "dwelling place."

God will pitch His tent among His people; no longer will God be seemingly far off and distant.

No more will His presence be veiled in the human form of Jesus Christ, a cloud, or pillar of fire.

God will dwell among His people. We will experience in His presence:

- unhindered fellowship with God (1 Jn. 1:3).
- we will see God as He is (Jn. 3:2).

- we will worship God (Rev. 4:10).
- we will serve God (Rev. 7:15).

Fourth, Note Its Uniqueness (v. 4-6a)

> *"...and He will wipe away every tear from their eyes; and there will be no longer any death; there will no longer be any mourning, or crying, or pain; the first things have passed away.' And He who sits on the throne said, 'Behold, I am making all things new.' And He said, 'Write, for these words are faithful and true.' Then He said to me, 'It is done. I am the Alpha and the Omega, the beginning and the end.'"*

Praise God: life in heaven will be demonstrably different than life as we know it now on fallen earth.

In heaven, there will be no tears. These verses declare an absolute absence of anything to be sorry about—no sadness, no pain, no heartache, no discouragement, no regret, no agonizing loss.

In heaven, there will be no death. The greatest curse of human existence is physical death.

Praise be to God, that in Christ Jesus, "death is swallowed up in victory" (1 Cor. 15:54).

In heaven, there will be no more pain caused by the presence of sin. Our glorified bodies will not be ravaged by the sin stains of this temporal world. Our glorified bodies will not know pain or suffering of any kind...not the breaking down of the mind, not the aching of the joints, nor sickness to various organs of the body due to cancer or disease. Oh, dear church, life in heaven will be unique and distinct from this temporal, fallen, sin-stained world.

Our bodies will not decay, decline, or waste away.

The One Who sits on the Throne declares, "Behold, I make all things new!"

These are the faithful and true Words of our God!

The One who sits on the Throne is most qualified to declare the end of redemptive history for He is the Alpha and the Omega, the first and last letters of the Greek alphabet.

God started it all. God will end it all. God is gloriously sovereign.

Now Notice, Fourthly, Its Residents (v. 6b-7).

> *"I will give to the one who thirsts from the spring of the water of life without cost. He who overcomes will inherit these things, and I will be His God and He will be my Son."*

Who will live in heaven?

The text gives two clues:

1. "those who thirst"
2. "those who overcome"

Those who are found to be in heaven are those who hunger and thirst after God and His righteousness.

To all who thirst after God, Scripture promises their thirst will be satisfied by God.

An overcomer, according to 1 John 5:4-5, is one who exercises saving faith in Jesus Christ.

Notice the assurance of Scripture to the one who overcomes and thirsts for righteousness. God states, "I will be His God."

Equally amazing…is God's promise for the one who overcomes…"and He will be My son."

In heaven, our adoption as God's children will be fully realized (Rom. 8:23; Jn. 1:12; Rom. 8:14-17).

Finally, Notice the Outcasts (v. 8).

> *"But for the cowardly and unbelieving and abominable and murderers and immoral persons and sorcerers and idolaters and all liars, their part will be in the lake that burns with fire and brimstone, which is the second death."*

Here we have a firm warning from John. He distinguishes who will be excluded from the participation in the blessings of the new heaven and new earth—all unforgiven, unrepentant, unredeemed sinners.

Here, we have a listing of characteristics of those whose lives bear no evidence of salvation. "

Their part will be in the lake that burns with fire and brimstone, which is the second death."

Make no mistake: the unsaved wicked will suffer eternal torment in the bowels of hell.

40

"THE HOLY CITY"

Revelation 21:9–22:5, ESV

As chapter 21 begins, all sinners of all ages, both demons and men, including Satan, the beast, and the false prophet have been condemned to the eternal lake of fire.

- The whole universe has been destroyed. Earth has been thoroughly pummeled.
- God creates an eternal state to be the dwelling place of the redeemed.
- The Scripture makes clear that the universe, as we know it, will be obliterated and will be replaced by a new creation that will be eternal.

This reality is a fulfillment of both the Old and New Testament prophecy. For example, listen to 2 Peter 3:10-13:

> *2Pe 3:10 But the day of the Lord will come like a thief, and then the heavens will pass away with a roar, and the heavenly bodies will be burned up and dissolved, and the earth and the works that are done on it will be exposed. 2Pe 3:11 Since all these things are thus to be dissolved, what sort of people ought you to be in lives of holiness and godliness, 2Pe 3:12 waiting for and hastening the coming of the day of God, because of*

which the heavens will be set on fire and dissolved, and the heavenly bodies will melt as they burn! 2Pe 3:13 But according to his promise we are waiting for new heavens and a new earth in which righteousness dwells.

It is somewhat surprising that very little information is given about the new heaven and new earth. But we do receive some information about the holy city, Jerusalem.

Let's read about it in Revelation 21:9-22:5.

Rev 21:9 Then came one of the seven angels who had the seven bowls full of the seven last plagues and spoke to me, saying, "Come, I will show you the Bride, the wife of the Lamb."

Rev 21:10 And he carried me away in the Spirit to a great, high mountain, and showed me the holy city Jerusalem coming down out of heaven from God,

Rev 21:11 having the glory of God, its radiance like a most rare jewel, like a jasper, clear as crystal.

Rev 21:12 It had a great, high wall, with twelve gates, and at the gates twelve angels, and on the gates the names of the twelve tribes of the sons of Israel were inscribed—

Rev 21:13 on the east three gates, on the north three gates, on the south three gates, and on the west three gates.

Rev 21:14 And the wall of the city had twelve foundations, and on them were the twelve names of the twelve apostles of the Lamb.

Rev 21:15 And the one who spoke with me had a measuring rod of gold to measure the city and its gates and walls.

Rev 21:16 The city lies foursquare, its length the same as its width. And he measured the city with his rod, 12,000 stadia. Its length and width and height are equal.

*Rev 21:17 He also measured its wall, 144 cubits
by human measurement, which is also an angel's
measurement.*

*Rev 21:18 The wall was built of jasper, while the city
was pure gold, like clear glass.*

*Rev 21:19 The foundations of the wall of the city were
adorned with every kind of jewel. The first was jasper,
the second sapphire, the third agate, the fourth emerald,*

*Rev 21:20 the fifth onyx, the sixth carnelian, the seventh
chrysolite, the eighth beryl, the ninth topaz, the tenth
chrysoprase, the eleventh jacinth, the twelfth amethyst.*

*Rev 21:21 And the twelve gates were twelve pearls,
each of the gates made of a single pearl, and the street
of the city was pure gold, like transparent glass.*

*Rev 21:22 And I saw no temple in the city, for its temple
is the Lord God the Almighty and the Lamb.*

*Rev 21:23 And the city has no need of sun or moon to
shine on it, for the glory of God gives it light, and its
lamp is the Lamb.*

*Rev 21:24 By its light will the nations walk, and the
kings of the earth will bring their glory into it,*

*Rev 21:25 and its gates will never be shut by day—and
there will be no night there.*

*Rev 21:26 They will bring into it the glory and the
honor of the nations.*

*Rev 21:27 But nothing unclean will ever enter it, nor
anyone who does what is detestable or false, but only
those who are written in the Lamb's book of life.*

*Rev 22:1 Then the angel showed me the river of the
water of life, bright as crystal, flowing from the throne
of God and of the Lamb*

*Rev 22:2 through the middle of the street of the city;
also, on either side of the river, the tree of life with its*

*twelve kinds of fruit, yielding its fruit each month. The
leaves of the tree were for the healing of the nations.*

*Rev 22:3 No longer will there be anything accursed, but
the throne of God and of the Lamb will be in it, and his
servants will worship him.*

*Rev 22:4 They will see his face, and his name will be on
their foreheads.*

*Rev 22:5 And night will be no more. They will need no
light of lamp or sun, for the Lord God will be their light,
and they will reign forever and ever.*

There is so much in these verses to consider, so let's organize
our approach to this text by examining three items of the Holy City:

1. It's Size
2. It's Source of light
3. It's Sovereign

Verse 9 opens in a familiar fashion. One of the angels who had
the seven bowls full of the seven last plagues speaks to John. This
angel invites John to come and see the Bride, the wife of the Lamb.

In verse 10 John is carried away by the Spirit to a high mountain
and given the opportunity to view the Holy City Jerusalem coming
down out of heaven from God.

What we have then is a description of the New Jerusalem in
the eternal state.

The impression you get as a reader is that the Holy City is gigantic in SIZE.

Look at verse 16: "The city lies foursquare, its length the same
as its width. And he measured the city with his rod, 12,000 stadia.
Its length and width and height are equal."

To put the size of the Holy City into some kind of perspective, this would be approximately 1400 miles cubed or about two million square miles, obviously providing plenty of room for all the glorified saints to live.[246]

Verse 17 informs the reader that the human measurement of the wall is 144 cubits, (generally, a cubit was the distance between your elbow and the tip of your third finger) or 72 yards, or 216 feet, this is likely the width of the wall.

Now, in verses 12-14, John writes: "It had a great, high wall, with twelve gates, and at the gates twelve angels, and on the gates the names of the twelve tribes of the sons of Israel were inscribed—Rev 21:13 on the east three gates, on the north three gates, on the south three gates, and on the west three gates. Rev 21:14 And the wall of the city had twelve foundations, and on them were the twelve names of the twelve apostles of the Lamb."

The Holy City has a great, high wall, with twelve gates, twelve angels and the names of the twelve tribes of the sons of Israel inscribed. The gates are strategically placed like the four points of a compass—north, south, east, and west—three gates at each point.

The wall of the city had twelve foundations, and on them were the twelve names of the twelve apostles of Jesus. This wall was built of jasper, while the city was pure, like clear glass.

The key here is that all the inhabitants of heaven will be the people of God from whatever era. You remember that Paul wrote in Ephesians that the church is "built on the foundation of the apostles and prophets, with Christ Jesus Himself as the cornerstone" (Eph. 2:20).

Furthermore, the foundations of the city wall were adorned

---

246 John MacArthur. *MacArthur New Testament Commentary*, p. 948.

with every kind of precious stone—detailed in verses 19-20—some twelve stones in all—jasper, sapphire, agate, emerald, onyx, carnelian, chrysolite, beryl, topaz, chrysoprase, jacinth, and amethyst. Some Bible scholars note that these precious stones "correspond roughly to the gems on the breastplate of the high priest."[247]

Transition: The Holy City is of an incredible size where the people of God, the redeemed of all ages, will dwell eternally.

Not Only is the Holy City Impressive in its Size, but also Note the City's Source of Light.

Look at Revelation 21:23-25- Rev 21:23 And the city has no need of sun or moon to shine on it, for the glory of God gives it light, and its lamp is the Lamb. Rev 21:24 By its light will the nations walk, and the kings of the earth will bring their glory into it, Rev 21:25 and its gates will never be shut by day—and there will be no night there.

According to John, there will be no need for light from the sun or moon because the glory of God will provide the light.

Furthermore, the lamp is the Lamb. Now, it seems to me that verse 22 is connected in its thought to verses 23-25.

Verse 22 reads: Rev 21:22 And I saw no temple in the city, for its temple is the Lord God the Almighty and the Lamb.

This is intriguing. On the one hand, there are several passages which affirm that there is a temple in heaven (3:12; 7:15; 11:19; 15:5). However, as John MacArthur distinguishes, "Here, it is clear that there is none in eternity."[248]

---

247 Daniel Akin. *Exalting Jesus in Revelation: Christ-Centered Exposition: Exalting Jesus in Revelation*, Kindle Edition, location 6959 (Primary Source: Duvall, Revelation, 289).

248 MacArthur, p. 948.

On the other hand, John surveys the city, and does not see a temple in it. Now, as you likely know the most prominent aspect of the city of Jerusalem was the temple of Solomon.[249]

How can this be? Why is there no temple? The temple is not a building. The text makes clear that the temple of the eternal state is "the Lord God Almighty and the Lamb."

There is no need for a temple in the eternal state since God Himself will be the temple in which everything exists.

The presence of God fills the entire new heaven and the new earth. We will be in the limitless presence of the Lord.

The sun and the moon have been eclipsed by the very glory of God and the Lamb. The radiance of the Lamb is sufficient to light the city.

Please look at chapter 22, verse 5: Rev 22:5 And night will be no more. They will need no light of lamp or sun, for the Lord God will be their light, and they will reign forever and ever.

Here we are told that there will be no more night. And, there will be no need for the light of a lamp or for the sun. The Lord God will be the residents' of this city's light.

Now, back again to verse 25. and its gates will never be shut by day—and there will be no night there.

The elaborate gates to the Holy City will never be shut. These gates will never close. That's interesting because the typical purpose of a gate is to have the capacity, the option to close that gate if necessary.

In the eternal state, it will not be necessary. Why? There will no longer be any threat posed by the coming of darkness. Nothing can approach the city under the cover of darkness. There is no darkness.

Furthermore, all evil has been confined already to the lake of fire. Thus, there is no reason whatsoever for closing the gates.

249 Paige Patterson. *The New American Commentary: Revelation*, p. 373.

Transition: The Holy City is of impressive size. The Holy City has as its source of light the glory of God and the lamp of the Lamb. One final thought.

The Holy City is Best Identified by Its Key Resident: The Sovereign.

Look again with me at Rev. 22:1-5: Rev 22:1 Then the angel showed me the river of the water of life, bright as crystal, flowing from the throne of God and of the Lamb Rev 22:2 through the middle of the street of the city; also, on either side of the river, the tree of life with its twelve kinds of fruit, yielding its fruit each month. The leaves of the tree were for the healing of the nations. Rev 22:3 No longer will there be anything accursed, but the throne of God and of the Lamb will be in it, and his servants will worship him. Rev 22:4 They will see his face, and his name will be on their foreheads. Rev 22:5 And night will be no more. They will need no light of lamp or sun, for the Lord God will be their light, and they will reign forever and ever.

John mentions in verse 1 the throne of God and of the Lamb. We will be with God and Christ in the eternal state, in the Holy City! Oh, praise God!

Fascinating, too, is this mention of "the river of the water of life…" This river is unlike any on earth. It may be a literal river (based on verse 2), but it is clearly symbolical of the perpetual flow of eternal life which comes from God to heaven's inhabitants.

In the Holy City, there is the tree of life. The tree bears forth twelve fruits, one for each month. These fruits are therapeutic in giving health.

Verse 3 informs the reader that there will not be anything present in the Holy City that is accursed.

No longer will we be under the curse of Adam's sin. Adam's sin ushered into humanity the curse of guilt, shame, condemnation, alienation from God, and all kinds of hardship, difficulty, pain, and suffering. This curse will be vanquished forever.

God will never have to judge sin again, since it will never exist in the new heaven and the new earth.

The curse is replaced by the throne of God and of the Lamb.

As mentioned earlier, God and the Lamb are in the new city (21:22-23; 22:1)

The New Jerusalem will be the temple of God and the throne of God will also be in it.

God's servants will also be present and will worship and serve Him. While we reign with Him, we will also have the joy of serving Him.

I love the thought behind verse 4: Rev 22:4 They will see his face, and his name will be on their foreheads.

Do you wonder what it will be like to see the face of God? We know that the Scripture tells us plainly that no unglorified person could see God and live (Ex. 33:20-23).

But now, the residents of heaven can look on God's face and survive without harm because they are now holy (Jn. 1:18; 1 Tim. 6:16; 1 Jn. 3:20).

In other words, we will have perfect fellowship with the Sovereign. His name will be on our foreheads as we are God's personal possessions—we belong to Him!

MacArthur summarizes well:

> *"The eternal capital city of heaven, the New Jerusalem,*
> *will be a place of indescribable, unimaginable beauty.*
> *From the center of it the brilliant glory of God will shine*
> *forth through the gold and precious stones to illuminate*

*the new heaven and the new earth. But the most glorious
reality of all will be that sinful rebels will be made
righteous, enjoy intimate fellowship with God and the
Lamb, serve Them, and reign with Them forever in sheer
joy and incessant praise (Revelation 12-22, 288).* "[250]

How may you secure your place in heaven? By repenting of
your sin and placing your faith and trust completely and only in Jesus
Christ as Savior and Lord!

---

250 Akin, Kindle location 7023. Secondary source.

41

"UNTIL HE RETURNS"

Revelation 22:6-21, ESV

The text before us articulates the final words from the Apocalypse. Verses 6-21 are commonly identified as the "Epilogue," or the closing section.

What's interesting in these verses is that there are several speakers, yet only one whose identity is clear—the Lord Jesus Christ!

This portion of Scripture consists of a number of rather loosely related utterances.[251]

It is critical to remember that this book is a genuine prophecy. Put simply, Revelation is a book of prophecy. The Greek title of this book is Apokalypsis, which means "revelation, unveiling, a disclosure" of unseen, future realities or events. You might recall that it's where we get our English word, apocalypse.

Whatever we have set forth about Revelation and however we may have come to understand this unique letter, it is first and foremost a book which EXALTS the Lord Jesus Christ!

Again, it must be clearly stated that the overarching purpose of Revelation is simply to encourage and comfort believers in their struggle against Satan and his cohorts. The book is a reminder that

---

251 Robert H. Mounce. *NICNT: The Book of Revelation*, p. 402.

Christ is the Victor and Satan will be vanquished. Therefore this book of consolation points our attention to the judgment of the world and the ultimate victory for the people of God. Revelation is a message of hope, for Christ will vindicate His saints!

Revelation has taught us so much about which we can rejoice and celebrate. Such as...

- Revelation, first and foremost, is about Jesus Christ. One of the greatest depictions of the Lord Jesus is found in Revelation 1:8-18. What a vision we have in Revelation of the transcendent, triumphant Christ!
- John gives us a vibrant picture of worship in heaven which stirs our hearts and motivates us to faithful obedience.
- Revelation gives us vivid clues and truths as to the unveiling of end times or last things. Revelation's contribution is primarily to eschatology, the doctrine of last things.
- Revelation points us to the second coming of Jesus Christ. He will defeat Satan, settle accounts with those who reject Him, and bring His faithful people into eternal blessedness.
- Revelation declares the sovereignty of God declaring the providential rule over the kingdoms of men and will accomplish His sovereign purposes regardless of whatever is the opposition.
- Revelation teaches about the final judgment. We need to be certain of our commitment to Christ. No one who rejects Jesus will escape God's punishment.
- Revelation is a book about HOPE—oh, the hope we have in Jesus Christ. One day God will create a new heaven and a new earth. All believers will live with Christ forever in perfect peace and security.

And, now...we explore the final text in this extraordinary book.

Rev 22:6 And he said to me, "These words are trustworthy and true. And the Lord, the God of the spirits of the prophets, has sent his angel to show his servants what must soon take place."

Rev 22:7 "And behold, I am coming soon. Blessed is the one who keeps the words of the prophecy of this book."Rev 22:8 I, John, am the one who heard and saw these things. And when I heard and saw them, I fell down to worship at the feet of the angel who showed them to me, Rev 22:9 but he said to me, "You must not do that! I am a fellow servant with you and your brothers the prophets, and with those who keep the words of this book. Worship God."

Rev 22:10 And he said to me, "Do not seal up the words of the prophecy of this book, for the time is near. Rev 22:11 Let the evildoer still do evil, and the filthy still be filthy, and the righteous still do right, and the holy still be holy." Rev 22:12 "Behold, I am coming soon, bringing my recompense with me, to repay each one for what he has done. Rev 22:13 I am the Alpha and the Omega, the first and the last, the beginning and the end." Rev 22:14 Blessed are those who wash their robes, so that they may have the right to the tree of life and that they may enter the city by the gates. Rev 22:15 Outside are the dogs and sorcerers and the sexually immoral and murderers and idolaters, and everyone who loves and practices falsehood. Rev 22:16 "I, Jesus, have sent my angel to testify to you about these things for the churches. I am the root and the descendant of David, the bright morning star."Rev 22:17 The Spirit and the Bride say, "Come." And let the one who hears say, "Come." And let the one who is thirsty come; let the one who desires take the water of life without price. Rev 22:18 I warn everyone who hears the words of the prophecy of this book: if anyone adds to them, God will add to him the plagues described in this book, Rev 22:19 and if anyone takes away from the words of the book of this prophecy, God will take away his share in the tree of life and in the holy city, which are described in this book. Rev 22:20 He who testifies to these things says, "Surely I am coming soon." Amen. Come, Lord Jesus! Rev 22:21 The grace of the Lord Jesus be with all. Amen.

This text sets forth at least four actions we are to take UNTIL HE RETURNS...Until He returns:

1. Keep the Scriptures (v. 7, 18-19)
2. Worship God (v. 9)
3. Be Holy (v. 11)
4. Long for His Return (v. 7, 12, 20)

1). Until He Returns Keep the Scriptures (v. 7, 18-19).

Rev 22:7 "And behold, I am coming soon. Blessed is the one who keeps the words of the prophecy of this book."

Rev 22:18 I warn everyone who hears the words of the prophecy of this book: if anyone adds to them, God will add to him the plagues described in this book, Rev 22:19 and if anyone takes away from the words of the book of this prophecy, God will take away his share in the tree of life and in the holy city, which are described in this book.

Jesus reminds us that He is coming soon. The Lord Jesus Christ, the Conquering, Warrior King is coming again. It is certain. It is not up for debate! From the very moment Satan was defeated by the atoning death of Jesus on an old rugged cross and by His triumphal resurrection, we have been and are moving in the direction of the Lord's return. He is coming soon.

Again, we find ourselves reading the sixth beatitude within the book of Revelation. The blessing is for those who keep the words of this book. The Holy Spirit has superintended the recording of what God has revealed concerning the end of all things. Stand fast, church! Stand fast and faithful in the face of the great persecution about to visit you! Keep these words. These words are true and trustworthy.

This is divine revelation. These words are from God. Be encouraged by them. Obey them. Be informed by them. Let these words raise your affections for Christ and turn your attention to His true and just words. Let these words guide your life.

Remember Revelation 1:3? It states, "Blessed is he who reads and those who hear the words of the prophecy, and heed the things which are written in it; for the time is near" (NASB). Jesus says, "If you keep my words you will be blessed!"

In verses 18-19 we have a warning. We are warned against adding to or taking away from this prophetic message. We are not knowingly to alter or distort the message of this prophecy.

It's a very serious issue to tamper with the Word of God. This warning not only applies to Revelation, but by implication to all 66 books of the Bible. To do so, is to invite God's severe judgment into your life.

If you do, God will add the plagues of Revelation, indicating a harsh and severe judgment. Additionally, God will take away his share in the tree of life and in the holy city.

What does this mean? Scary, huh?

John MacArthur is helpful in understanding these words. He writes: "No true believer would ever deliberately tamper with Scripture. Those who know and love God will treat His Word with the utmost respect. They will say with the Psalmist, "Oh how I love Your law!" (Ps. 119:97; cf. Pss. 119:113; 163, 167, John 14:23); and I delight in Your law" (Ps. 119:70; cf. Pss. 1:2; 119:77, 92, 174). That does not, of course, mean that believers will never make errors in judgment or mistakenly interpret Scripture incorrectly or inadequately. The Lord's warning here is addressed to those who engage in deliberate falsification or misinterpretation of Scripture, those who Paul denounces as Peddlers of the Word of God" (2 Cor. 2:17). (Revelation 12-22, 310)[252]

Transition: Until He returns, keep the Scriptures.

2). Until He Returns Worship God (v. 9).

> *Rev 22:8 I, John, am the one who heard and saw these things. And when I heard and saw them, I fell down to worship at the feet of the angel who showed them to me, Rev 22:9 but he said to me, "You must not do that! I am a fellow servant with you and your brothers the prophets, and with those who keep the words of this book. Worship God."*

Curiously, John is corrected by an angel for an ill-advised act of angel worship. We read of something similar in Revelation 19:10. John seems to be caught up in the moment and he falls before the angel to worship him.

John is prevented from doing this by the angel. The angel states that he, too, is a fellow servant with John and the prophets, and those who keep God's Word.

The worship of angels, although expressly prohibited, did exist in pockets of the Christian community, for example in the church in Colosse (Colossians 2:18).

The honor of worship is reserved for God alone. The angel urges, "Worship God!" Succinct. Precise. The point of our lives as followers of Christ is to worship. The supreme affection of our hearts is to be reserved for God. The matchless attention of our minds is to be kept for God.

---

252 Daniel Akin. *Christ-Centered Exposition: Exalting Jesus in Revelation*, Kindle Edition, Location 7310 secondary source; primary source- John MacArthur, *Revelation, 12-22*, p. 310).

Transition: Until Christ returns, we worship. We worship the King of kings, Lord of lords. We worship the Great I Am. We worship the Alpha and the Omega. We worship the God of Abraham, Isaac, and Jacob. We worship the Sovereign and Ruler over all things.

3). Until He Returns Be Holy (v. 11).

> *Rev 22:11 Let the evildoer still do evil, and the filthy still be filthy, and the righteous still do right, and the holy still be holy."*

For John and his audience, and for us, the Bible makes clear that the end is near. One truth is abundantly clear, we are closer to the Lord's return today than we were yesterday!

Two primary categories of people are identified in this verse-- Those who are evil and do evil and those who are righteous and do right.

John elaborates a bit in verse 15. 22:15 Outside are the dogs and sorcerers and the sexually immoral and murderers and idolaters, and everyone who loves and practices falsehood.

From John's perspective the end is so close that there is scant little time for people to amend their character and habits.

- The evildoer will do evil.
- The righteous will do right.
- The holy will still be holy.

The central thrust of the Christian life is to walk as Jesus walked. The Bible says, "The one who says he abides in Him ought himself to walk in the same manner as He walked" (1 John 2:6, NASB).

How did Jesus walk? Jesus Himself said, "but so that the world may know that I love the Father, I do exactly as the Father commanded me" (John 14:31, NASB).

Scripture says, "But as He who called you is holy, you also be holy in all your conduct, since it is written, 'You shall be holy as I am holy'" (1 Ptr. 1:15-16).

The call of the Christian life is one to obedience and holiness in the pattern of Jesus Christ. Jesus lived a perfect life as an obedient son. Paul wrote, "Being found in appearance as a man, He humbled Himself by becoming obedient to the point of death, even death on a cross" (Philippians 2:8, NASB).

Transition: Until He returns we are to live holy, obedient lives in the example of Christ.

4). Until He Returns Long For His Coming Again (v. 7, 12, 20).

> *Rev 22:7 "And behold, I am coming soon. Blessed is the one who keeps the words of the prophecy of this book."*
>
> *Rev 22:12 "Behold, I am coming soon, bringing my recompense with me, to repay each one for what he has done.*
>
> *Rev 22:20 He who testifies to these things says, "Surely I am coming soon." Amen. Come, Lord Jesus!*

I call your attention to the third time the Lord Jesus speaks. He says plainly that He is coming soon.

John responds by saying, "Amen. Come, Lord Jesus!"

The answer to man's greatest problem and need is JESUS CHRIST. Man's life is incomplete without Christ. And, so is history incomplete until Christ returns. It is for His return that we as the people of God eagerly await.

Let us remain faithful.

Let us remain loyal.

Let us wait and long for His coming again.

The end of all things has been set before us in the Revelation. We do not have to wander around in uncertainty. We know how the story ends! Jesus is the Conquering King, the Victorious Christ!

One day, when He gloriously returns, He will put away all evil and usher in a new eternal state.

Rev 22:17 The Spirit and the Bride say, "Come." And let the one who hears say, "Come." And let the one who is thirsty come; let the one who desires take the water of life without price.

And, to this we say along with John, "Come, Lord Jesus!"

Trust Publishers House,
the trusted name in quality Christian books.

Trust House Publishers
PO Box 3181
Taos, NM 87571

TrustHousePublishers.com

CPSIA information can be obtained
at www.ICGtesting.com
Printed in the USA
BVHW041023290320
576275BV00018B/1110

9 781945 774423